# WARLORDS

# WARLORDS

## The Struggle for Power in Post-Roman Britain

Stuart Laycock

*To Clare, Freddie and Lizzy*

*Thanks to John Conyard and Comitatus for permission to use their photographs of late Roman re-enactment. Thanks to Robert Vermaat and Raymond's Quiet Press for cover photographs.*

First published 2009

The History Press
The Mill, Brimscombe Port
Stroud, Gloucestershire, GL5 2QG
www.thehistorypress.co.uk

Reprinted 2010



British Library Cataloguing in Publication Data.
A catalogue record for this book is available from the British Library.

ISBN 978 0 7524 4796 4

Printed in Great Britain

# CONTENTS

# INTRODUCTION

> Britain has kings but they are tyrants, and it has judges but they are corrupt. They spend their time terrorizing and robbing the innocent while protecting and promoting bandits and criminals. They have plenty of wives but also mistresses and lovers. They readily take oaths but perjure themselves. They make vows but they lie. They make war but the wars they make are unjust wars, wars against their own countrymen. They pursue crime in their lands but they also have criminals to dinner, cosying up to them, rewarding them. They give generously to worthy causes but in the meantime their crimes pile up, a towering mountain of guilt. They sit in judgement but rarely look for a just verdict. They despise the harmless and the humble but value above all the blood-soaked, the arrogant, the murderous, the adulterous – enemies of God who ought to be destroyed and erased from people's memories.
>
> (Gildas, *On the Ruin of Britain*, 27)

This is how the sixth-century writer Gildas describes the British warlords of his day, in an extraordinary passage (to be explored in more depth later) that gives the most graphic description of warlords in post-Roman Britain.

The picture Gildas paints of warlord character and behaviour is instantly recognisable to anyone who knows anything about warlords anywhere in the world, at any time from the dawn of history right up to today. And the fact that these characters were the celebrities of their day, their deeds relatively well known among their contemporaries, suggests that there is much truth in Gildas' comments (if there wasn't, then his readers would know). Having said that, Gildas is, of course, not even pretending to provide a totally balanced picture of these warlords, and it is possible to imagine that some of them might have been regarded with some affection by at least a proportion of their subjects – as 'lovable rogues' perhaps. Moreover, for all their failings in other areas, they were at least a source of basic protection in uncertain and violent times.

*1* Late Roman cavalryman showing what a warlord at the end of the Roman period might have looked like. *(Courtesy of John Conyard and www.comitatus.net)*

Gildas offers us no description of the appearance of post-Roman warlords. At the end of the Roman period and shortly afterwards they would presumably have looked much like any other late Roman commander. The late fourth-century ivory diptych shown in Figure 2 is thought to depict the late Roman general Stilicho, and his appearance is probably about as close as we can get to knowing what a British warlord of the late fourth or early fifth century would have looked like. He wears leggings with a richly patterned, long-armed tunic and a cloak secured by a large crossbow brooch. Around his waist is a belt from which hangs his *spatha* sword. In his left hand he supports a large round shield, with a spiked central boss. In his right hand he holds a spear. He wears no armour. (Interestingly, armour seems to have been worn less in the late Roman period than earlier, but the lack of armour in this carving may simply be because the subject is not shown in combat; he would certainly have worn a helmet in the field.) The fantastic gold buckle (*3*) from the late fourth-century Thetford Treasure, with a classical figure on the buckle plate and two horseheads forming the buckle loop, could well have belonged to a British equivalent of just such a figure.

However, Roman cultural influence faded markedly in the centuries after the end of Roman rule, particularly across large swathes of southern and eastern

*2* Ivory carving probably showing the late Roman commander Stilicho.

*3* The Thetford buckle is a fine example of the buckles worn by rich and powerful figures in Britain at the end of the Roman period.

England, where new Anglo-Saxon styles came into fashion. The Sutton Hoo burial, thought to be that of Rædwald, king of East Anglia, gives us the richest example of what a post-Roman Anglo-Saxon warlord could have looked like. There are elements in this burial that link back to the Roman style (such as the basic form of the helmet, the standard, the golden shoulder clasps, plus of course, the Mediterranean silverware buried with him), but there are also whole new cultural references, such as the extensive use of inlaid garnets and glass in the Frankish fashion, the intertwined designs on the great gold buckle, and the Scandinavian mythological scenes on the helmet decoration. Of course, Rædwald (or whoever else it was buried under the mound all those centuries ago) was at the top end of the scale but many other warlords must have adorned themselves in a basically similar manner.

In regions beyond the reach of Anglo-Saxon culture at that time Roman habits persisted (particularly under the influence of the local church) but even here warlords were beginning to adopt some elements of non-Roman style. In these areas, though, the styles in question link not so much to continental Germanic kingdoms as to Ireland and pre-Roman British traditions. The period saw a resurgence of metalwork with swirling designs similar to those found in Britain in the pre-Roman period (the enamelled disks on hanging bowls of the period are among the finest examples), and the description of warriors in 'Y Gododdin', a poem describing events some time probably in the sixth century but written later, suggests that in some ways they resembled their pre-Roman ancestors (even if the word for chain mail, *llurig*, is derived from the Latin word *lorica*):[1]

Men headed for Catraeth with a battle-cry,
Fast horses and dark armour and shields,
Holding spears high, their points deadly sharp,
With shining chain mail and flashing swords.

('Y Gododdin')

Helmets were probably not generally worn among pre-Roman Britons and it is interesting to note that helmets are never mentioned in 'Y Gododdin'. By contrast helmets are regularly mentioned in the early Anglo-Saxon poem 'Beowulf'.

Whether among Britons or Anglo-Saxons, the experience of combat in the fifth and sixth centuries would doubtless have been in many ways familiar to anyone time-travelling there from early first-century Britain.

The spears thrown by the noble commander,
As he charged forward, carved a broad path,
He was raised for battle with mother's help,
While he aided others his sword slashed,
Spears of ash scattered by his strong hand...

('Y Gododdin')

And if the post-Roman warlords' appearance hadn't changed much, neither had their pattern of warfare. Almost always their wars were waged against neighbouring warlords in Britain, but very occasionally they formed brief alliances to counter threats from overseas. In fact, recent research suggests that a re-emergence of patterns of tribal fighting in the power vacuum left by the collapse of Roman control in Britain at the end of the fourth century and in the early fifth century (as opposed to the situation in mainland Europe where new large-scale Germanic kingdoms immediately took over and in many ways maintained existing Roman administration) may well have largely been responsible for the ending of the complex Roman British economy and the disappearance of the Roman British lifestyle.[2]

As Tacitus put it, shortly after the Roman invasion:

> In fact, nothing has assisted us more when fighting this mighty nation than their inability to work together with each other. It is only rarely that two or three states unite to repel a common enemy, and in this way, fighting separately, they are all conquered.
>
> (Tacitus, *Agricola*, 12)

And Gildas made exactly the same point after the end of the Roman occupation:

> For it has always been the way with our nation, as now, to be powerless in repelling foreign enemies, but powerful and bold in making civil war.
>
> (Gildas, *On the Ruin of Britain*, 21)

The earliest British warlord, and indeed about the earliest named Briton of whom we have any record, is Cassivellaunus, who is primarily known for leading a British alliance against Caesar's second invasion of Britain in 54 BC. However, it is clear from a reading of Caesar's text that this alliance among the British tribes was very much the exception; in many ways it seems that Cassivellaunus was a sort of prototype of the British warlords described by Gildas some 500 or 600 years later. Caesar states that prior to the arrival of the Roman army Cassivellaunus had been at permanent war with his neighbours. He had also killed the king of a neighbouring tribe, the Trinovantes, after which the son of that king, Mandubracius, had fled to Caesar for support. The alliance that Cassivellaunus briefly led was quickly abandoned by the Trinovantes (perhaps not surprisingly under the circumstances) and also by a number of other tribes, including a tribe that Caesar describes as the Cenimagni, possibly a misinterpretation of the phrase *Iceni magni*, 'the great Iceni'.

The Romans, of course, regarded Britons collectively, lumping together all the people living on the island of Britannia, regardless of tribal differences, and Gildas had something of a similar view, either inherited from Roman sources or perhaps developed independently as a counter-weight to the developing Anglo-Saxon presence in Britain during his lifetime. However, the majority of Britons, both in the time of Cassivellaunus and in the time of Gildas, would probably not have regarded themselves as 'British'. As far as nationality went, they would have thought only in terms of their tribe, or in the days of Gildas in terms of the kingdoms that developed on the basis of the tribal territories in the post-Roman period. Mandubracius would have seen himself as Trinovantian, not British, and he would not have thought of Cassivellaunus as a fellow-countryman in any real sense. It is in some ways rather similar to the situation in Europe today. Europeans today accept that they are European, a part of the wider European Union, but very

*4* Coin referring to Commius, a warlord probably from Gaul.

few would define their nationality as European. They see themselves as British, or French, or Italian. British warlords in post-Roman Britain would have felt no loyalty to other British warlords from other tribal territories, and would have had no qualms about forming an alliance with an overseas power against other British tribal territories if they saw any advantage in such a move. It should be no more surprising for us to see the Trinovantes allying themselves with Rome against Cassivellaunus, than it is for us to see the Scots allying with France against England in the medieval period.

It was not, however, just Romans who came across the English Channel in the first century BC. In an early demonstration of how power could translate across the Channel, a warlord from Gaul seems to have decided to set up shop in Britain

5 Coins of Tasciovanus showing warlike motifs.

as well. Commius is an interesting character. Caesar describes at some length his assorted military adventures as a leader of the Atrebates in northern Gaul. The last that is heard of him in Gaul, though, is that he had fled across the Channel to Britain. Shortly after this, the name Commius starts appearing on British coins in the area of a tribe that came to be known as the Atrebates. It is therefore assumed that this is the same Commius[3] and (since there is no archaeological evidence for an extensive influx of foreigners and foreign culture into the area in question at this stage) that somehow Commius established a new political entity with a new name on the basis of an existing British political entity. Subsequent rulers of the area repeatedly describe themselves as COMF, short for '*Commii Filius*' or 'son of Commius', pointing to the central role of this character in the creation of the area's new identity. The Atrebates became one of the key tribal powers in pre-Roman Britain (probably even taking over the territory of the Cantii briefly), and, as we shall discuss later, probably in post-Roman Britain too.

However, there was another tribal superpower in central and southern Britain that was to outshine even the Atrebates in the struggle for power in pre-Roman Britain – the Catuvellauni. Cassivellaunus may well have been an early ruler of this tribe. According to Caesar, Cassivellaunus came from an area just north of the Thames and adjoining Trinovantian territory, which puts him pretty much in the same area as the Catuvellauni. Furthermore, the two names are sufficiently similar to wonder if Caesar might not have mangled the name of Cassivellaunus in the same way that he probably did with the name of the Iceni.

Tasciovanus and Cunobelin are two warlords who certainly do seem to have been instrumental in the rise of the Catuvellauni. The coins of Tasciovanus appear across a large swathe of central and eastern England, while those of Cunobelin spread even further, as Catuvellaunian influence seems to have expanded to

*6* Coin bearing the legend 'CARA' and probably linked to Caratacus.

include the entire territory of the Trinovantes and the Cantii, plus parts of the territory of the Iceni, Dobunni and Atrebates.[4] Some scholars have argued that the adoption of Catuvellaunian/Trinovantian coinage across this large territory might simply represent some form of peaceful extension of influence. However, in the light of Caesar's comments about the possible early Catuvellaunian ruler Cassivellaunus being constantly at war with his neighbours, and bearing in mind the warlike motifs on a number of the coins of Tasciovanus and Cunobelin (5), it seems more reasonable to see this as some form of conquest.

This interpretation seems to be confirmed by events in northern Atrebatic territory in the period before the Roman invasion under Claudius. Around AD 35 coins issued in the name of Epatticus appear in northern Atrebatic territory around Silchester. The coins reflect some elements of Atrebatic design but they also incorporate elements of Catuvellaunian design, and Epatticus describes himself, as Cunobelin also does on his coins, as a son of Tasciovanus. Subsequently Epatticus' coins are replaced by coins of the same style but bearing the inscription 'CARA' (*6*).[5] This legend may well refer to Caratacus, identified by the Roman historian Cassius Dio as Cunobelin's son and a Catuvellaunian warlord. Then, shortly before the Roman invasion of AD 43, Cassius Dio describes a British king named Berikos fleeing to the court of Claudius to seek help in getting his kingdom back. Berikos is assumed to be Verica, an Atrebatic king who was issuing coins in the area to the south of that controlled by Epatticus and CARA. It seems reasonable to assume, therefore, that just before the invasion Caratacus and the Catuvellauni had expanded forcibly into wider Atrebatic territory, and perhaps even that Verica helped to bring about the Roman invasion by securing the Romans as allies and bringing them into Britain to fight the Catuvellauni.

And indeed, when the Romans did invade, it is clear that they were specifically targeting the Catuvellauni rather than Britons in general. They made directly for the capital of the Catuvellaunian/Trinovantian confederation at Camulodunum, with Caratacus' brother Togodumnus dying in the process. As with Caesar's second invasion back in 54 BC, there seems to have been no real question of British solidarity here. Many of the tribes probably instead hastened to ally themselves with the new power in British politics. Cassius Dio, for example, records some 'Bodunni' (a name widely assumed to be a mangling of Dobunni) who had previously been ruled by the Catuvellauni, quickly joining up with the Romans. We know that the Romans left British kings in power in Icenian and Atrebatic territory, and there is no reason to suggest they behaved much differently in other areas. Again, we should not be surprised by this. Other British tribes would have regarded the quarrel between the Catuvellauni/Trinovantes on one side and the Atrebates/Romans on the other as nothing to do with them. Out of sheer self-interest they would come to political terms with whichever side won. Both sides were foreigners to them, even if the Romans were foreigners from slightly further away.

Much more surprising, in fact, is that in a highly unusual development by British tribal standards, Caratacus, having managed to escape the Roman invaders, was able to persuade two tribes from what is now Wales, the Silures and Ordovices, to fight the Romans alongside him. It is hard to know how a Catuvellaunian warlord from central England managed to persuade tribes from so far away to take an interest in his war. However, personal charisma (Caratacus seems to have charmed the Senate too when he was finally taken to Rome as a prisoner), plus large amounts of valuables, may have had something to do with it. It seems, too, that after the Roman rampage through the territory of the Durotriges in Dorset, it had begun to dawn on some Britons that Roman rule might not be entirely such a good thing.

Even at this stage, however, there were still plenty of Britons for whom the idea of ganging up against the Romans, just because they came from across the Channel, seemed bizarre. When resistance among the Silures and Ordovices collapsed, Caratacus fled north to the territory of the Brigantes but their queen, Cartimandua, promptly handed him over to the Romans.

Most British warlords were, of course, men. Cartimandua, however, demonstrates that British women could be equally powerful. This, of course, was confirmed just a few years after the capture of Caratacus by the explosion into British and Roman history of Boudica, queen and war leader of the Iceni. Boudica has usually been portrayed as attempting to throw the Romans out of Britain but there is very little evidence to suggest that this is actually what she was trying to do. If one ignores the inevitably Romano-centric nature of accounts by Roman historians, Boudica's actions look much more like those of a traditional British warlord. There was no concerted attempt to raise other tribes to rebellion, no concerted attempt to attack the Romans across the breadth of Britain. Instead, there was a great deal of looting and destruction in the territory of the Iceni's main tribal rivals, the Catuvellaunian/Trinovantian confederation.[6] It is true that Tacitus portrays the Trinovantes as the allies of Boudica, rather than her victims, but there are reasons to suppose that he may have got it wrong. After Boudica's rebellion, for example, the Trinovantian royal compound at Gosbecks outside Colchester continued to be occupied presumably by some form of Trinovantian leadership, while the Romans seem to have allowed the Trinovantes to dig new defensive earthworks after the rebellion.[7] Tacitus knew that the Roman *colonia* at Camulodunum, in Trinovantian territory, had been attacked and burnt, and perhaps simply assumed that the Trinovantes were in some way involved.

All in all, the history of Britain up to the end of the first century AD produces significant evidence of a large crop of British warlords in pursuit of power in Britain. And as we shall shortly see, in that respect (and quite a few others, as it turns out) the fifth and sixth centuries AD in Britain were much the same. In this book we shall see how ambitious men used a variety of strategies to achieve their goals. Some chose to seize power by working within the traditional Roman power structure. Others chose a new route, working within an independent British context, and still others chose to work within the newly developing Anglo-Saxon power structures. In all cases, though, their goal was power.

Of course, exploring the history of the fifth and sixth centuries in Britain is always going to be a controversial process. Fifty years ago it was widely accepted that the surviving historical accounts of the period, including Gildas and Bede and the Anglo-Saxon Chronicle, could give a broadly reliable outline of what happened in Britain in the period around and after the collapse of Roman control. However, more recently that position has been almost totally reversed, with scholars becoming reluctant to accept the historical sources at face value; indeed, some dismiss them all as pseudo-history and demand evidence solely from archaeological sources instead, treating the period almost like prehistory.

Sadly, though, archaeology has not yet been able to replace the more traditional historical sources with a coherent and comprehensive narrative of what was actually happening in Britain in the crucial years. Instead the process of relying almost entirely on archaeology has to a certain extent stripped the English and Welsh nations of their birth stories, because interpreting the archaeological evidence for the period is proving just about as difficult and controversial as interpreting the historical evidence. So if the archaeology cannot supply all the answers on its own, then it seems sensible to look again at the traditional historical accounts in the light of new archaeological research, and see if it is possible to create from the two combined sources of information an understandable and broadly convincing new account of post-Roman Britain and of the men who dictated the course of its early history.

# CHAPTER 1

# GERONTIUS

Gerontius must be one of the most influential Britons of whom nobody has ever heard. No, he's not Elgar's Gerontius and his dream, such as it was, was probably just one of power. He was a warlord who conquered Spain and Portugal with the help of British militiamen over a thousand years before Drake 'singed the King of Spain's beard'. He played a key part in the end of Roman rule in Britain and even, arguably, in the end of the Western Roman Empire, before dying with his wife in a blazing building surrounded by mutinous troops.

During the roughly three-and-a-half centuries that Britons were part of the Roman Empire, they played a distinctly low-key role in Roman political life. Other parts of the Empire such as Africa, Pannonia and Gaul produced a string of political figures who played a significant role in central Roman government, up to and including emperors. Britain, however, despite being the springboard for a number of attempts on the imperial throne (including those by the ill-fated Clodius Albinus at the end of the second century and the much more successful Constantine at the beginning of the fourth), produced throughout most of the Roman period few, if any, native sons or daughters who made a significant political impact in Rome. Two usurpers, the obscure Bonosus (*c.* 281) and the rather more successful and long-lasting Magnentius (ruled 350–353), both seem to have had British fathers – but equally both were born on the continent to non-British mothers.

The apparent reluctance of the British aristocracy to become involved in imperial politics, compared to their continental counterparts, may have much to do with the unusual nature of Rome's occupation of Britain, when compared with the manner in which it controlled other parts of the Empire. Britain was the last major western territory added to the Empire. Parts of Africa, for instance, had already been occupied by Rome for almost 200 years by the time Claudius' legions scrambled ashore on British soil. There had been a Roman province in the south of Gaul for almost as long, and it had been almost 90 years since Vercingetorix and his Gallic alliance had finally succumbed to Caesar. Britain, by comparison with most of the rest of the Empire, became Roman late and even then it was, in reality, only partially Romanised. We talk of the centuries of Roman occupation of (most of) Britain as 'Roman Britain', yet there was, in truth, nothing very Roman about much of Britain during this period. Southern, central and eastern areas do indeed show ample archaeological evidence of a widespread adoption of Roman lifestyles, but evidence of cultural Romanisation in Cornwall, Wales and north-west England is mainly restricted to ceramics, glass and a few trinkets. And the number of such artefacts becomes even smaller if we look further north. Scotland, of course, remained largely beyond Roman reach, both politically and commercially, which explains the scanty evidence there, but in Cornwall, Wales and north-west England the absence of evidence of Roman lifestyles must be seen, to some extent, as indicating a specific rejection of Romanisation. The inhabitants could have had access to a Roman lifestyle if they chose to. They did not.

Large parts of Britain, even where it was under Roman control, never adopted Roman culture. What's more, even in the ostensibly Romanised centre, south and east of the island, it would be wrong to assume that the use of Roman items indicates that the locals had necessarily adopted a specifically Roman identity in addition to the trappings of the Roman lifestyle. In the same way, Britons

7 Dragonesque brooches were made and worn in Britain well into the second century, showing a strong survival of British tastes and style under Rome.

today may wear American clothes, eat American food and listen to American music but none of this indicates that they see themselves as Americans.

As already touched upon, when the Romans took control of Britain in AD 43, they found an island occupied by a large number of different tribes, with different cultures, different backgrounds and maybe even, for all we know, different languages (or certainly very different dialects). Fighting between tribes and cross-border raiding were probably common phenomena. There was no such thing as a united British identity. The inhabitants of the island would have seen themselves as Catuvellauni, or Brigantes, or Dobunni, or Iceni, or Atrebates or any of a large number of other tribal identities. And the Romans did little to change this in the period after the invasion. Like all experienced imperialists, they wanted to control their new country with as little fuss and trouble as possible, and that meant, among other things, working with the existing traditional political structures rather than imposing a whole raft of new and different ones. In the Mediterranean regions where city-states had long been the building blocks of political life, the Romans gave them local political control, with each becoming on some level a smaller version of Rome itself. In Britain, where there were no city-states for the Romans to build on, they instead used the tribes as the basis for local government. The tribes became self-administering *civitates* (the Roman name for their key unit of local government) and the traditional British tribal aristocracies almost certainly largely remained in place as the leaders of these new *civitates*. A common feature of British archaeology in the early Roman period is the appearance of Roman-style villas near, or even on top of, significant pre-Roman dwellings, suggesting the widespread continuity of estates and land tenure from pre-Roman into Roman times. Even more significantly, there is plenty of evidence to suggest that Britons continued to see their national identity in terms of their former tribes, rather than gradually over the centuries coming to see themselves as 'Britons' or as Romans.

On a number of inscriptions from the Roman period we can see Britons clearly identifying themselves by their tribal nationality. A sandstone base at Colchester, for instance, carries an inscription referring to '*Similis Ci(vis) Cant(iacus)*', a citizen of the *civitas* of the Cantii. A tombstone from South Shields records the nationality of Regina, wife of Barates the Palmyrene, as '*natione Catvallauna*', 'of the Catuvellaunian nation' (*8*). A certain Aemilius, who had served with the Classis Germanica, is recorded on a tombstone from Cologne as '*civis Dumnonius*', 'a citizen of the Dumnonii'.[1] References to individuals being British do appear on inscriptions, but these tend to be found not in Britain but on mainland Europe, where British tribal identities might, among a population largely ignorant of them, be expected to take a lower profile. Even at the end of the Roman period, just across the Channel one Sidonius Apollinaris identifies himself as 'Arvernius', one of the Arvernii, and his friend Aper as 'Aeduus', one of the Aedui. Similarly, many *civitas* capitals in Gaul abandoned their Roman names during this period and in

D M · REGINA · LIBERTA · ET · CONIVGE ·
BARATES · PALMYRENVS · NATIONE ·
CATVALLAVNA · AN · XXX

*8* Inscription identifying a British woman as of Catuvellaunian nationality.

common usage reverted simply to the name of the local tribe. Thus, for example, we have Paris (Roman Lutetia) from the Parisi, Avranches (Roman Ingena) from the Abrincati, Trier (Roman Augusta Trevorum) from the Treveri, and Vannes (Roman Darioritum) from the Veneti. In Gaul, however, any potential renewal of the expression of independent tribal identities was prevented by the introduction there of large Germanic kingdoms that directly took over from Roman control, and perhaps also by the more developed state of the Roman Catholic Church in Gaul at the end of the Roman period (as compared to the situation in Britain at the same time). If tribal identity could be so long-lived in Gaul, it would surely have been much stronger in a Britain that was Romanised later than Gaul and much less completely.

There is a sense also in literary references from the fourth and early fifth centuries that even after being part of the Roman Empire for hundreds of years, Britons were still seen as being somehow different and separate from the rest of the Empire. The poet Ausonius, for instance, composed a number of epigrams based on the assumption that being good and being British were mutually exclusive. Gildas also, writing perhaps 100 years after the end of Roman rule, shows no inclination to identify the British with people from the rest of the Empire. In his account of the arrival of the Romans in Britain and their departure he draws a consistently clear distinction between Britons and Romans. Perhaps it has something to do with Britain being an island. The rest of Western Europe seems to have adapted to inclusion in the Roman Empire with more enthusiasm. Perhaps we can see something similar today in the European Union. While countries like France and Germany, despite occasional gripes, seem happy enough to be integral members of the EU, Britain seems instinctively to want to keep itself separate. It remains a member of the EU, for the moment, because of the clear economic advantages from doing so, but one suspects that general British public sentiment remains deeply suspicious of the EU, even after decades of membership, and should the advantages of membership ever become less clear, there would doubtless be a serious push for the UK to leave, just as Britain was eventually to leave the Roman Empire in 409.

The pre-Roman tradition of conducting intermittent hostilities with neighbours seems to have continued into the Roman period. As mentioned in the Introduction, Boudica and her Iceni did not just attack Romans. They also targeted the Catuvellauni, a tribe with whom they may well have had long-standing border disputes (judging by the spread of Catuvellaunian coinage into formerly Icenian territory under Cunobelin, and by the digging of a probably pre-Roman defensive ditch, Mile Ditch, across the Icknield Way corridor near Cambridge).[2] Equally, towards the end of the second century (in a move which has no contemporary parallel in other parts of the Empire) towns close to the borders around a number of British *civitates* (again including the Catuvellauni) were fortified, creating a defensive ring around these tribal territories. These defences are again suggestive of cross-border tribal raiding and should probably be linked to the appearance of two groups of villa and town fires identified within the territory of the Catuvellauni and Trinovantes. One of these groups of fires lies in the north-west of Catuvellaunian territory and, judging by the road layout in the area, could be linked to Brigantes raiding south from the Peak District. The second group lies in the Essex area and may be linked to Iceni raiding southwards from their tribal territory, just as they had under Boudica.[3]

There are also hints of internal trouble as well, in addition to raiding from outside Rome's area of control, in the mysterious event of 367–369 that has come to be known as the 'Barbarian Conspiracy'. Certainly the response to the events of those years seems to have involved a major tribal element. Military buckles and belt fittings appear across civilian areas and sites in the archaeologically Romanised areas of Britain, suggesting an arming of the civilian population (*9*), probably with official permission, judging by the appearance of a range of triangular plate buckles identical to those in use in military areas in mainland Europe. Different regional styles of buckle and belt fittings suggest the appearance of specific tribal militias in a number of different tribal regions (*colour plate 10*). This is consistent with the increasing establishment of private armies, known as *bucellarii*, in the Roman world in the late fourth and fifth centuries, and with the evidence of Roman use of tribal and *civitas* militias in a number of emergency situations at various other times across the Empire. For instance, an Athenian militia led by the historian Dexippus was used to repel marauding Goths in Greece in the late third century, and in 406 Honorius issued two edicts encouraging locals to volunteer for emergency defence.[4] It is also consistent with Gildas' description of the Romans arming the Britons before they finally left Britain, and with a number of inscriptions from Hadrian's Wall which seem to indicate tribal units from the Dumnonii and Durotriges (and possibly the Catuvellauni) engaged in construction work on the wall and probably defending it too.[5]

At the end of the fourth century and the beginning of the fifth there is more evidence of tribal border clashes. Late or post-Roman linear earthwork defences, in conjunction with concentrations of buckles/belt fittings and unretrieved

*9* British buckles from the end of the Roman period of the type probably worn by, and manufactured specifically for, British militiamen.

hoards, suggest the possibility of conflict in a number of areas. The clearest case is perhaps in the Wiltshire/Avon area, where a line of burnt villas lies along the same axis as Wansdyke, a huge linear defensive earthwork probably separating the territory of the Belgae from that of the Dobunni. A rash of unretrieved hoards across the territory of the *civitas* of the Belgae also strongly suggests major trouble in this same area.[6]

It is in the context of all of this that we need to set the reluctance of the British aristocracy to become involved in Roman imperial politics. Certainly for almost the entire period of the occupation their political ambitions and aspirations remained at a tribal rather than an imperial level. Despite this persistent insularity, the beginning of the fifth century saw the arrival of two Britons who were to play a significant role in Roman political affairs. One would have been surprising enough, but the appearance of two such men is remarkable and is likely to indicate something very important about events in Britain as Roman power here died.

Traditionally the end of Roman Britain is regarded as taking place either in 409, when the historian Zosimus indicates that Britain rebelled against Rome, or in 410, when the Emperor Honorius officially accepted the independence of the Britons (if Zosimus is, in fact, referring to Britain, rather than Bruttium in southern Italy, as some have suggested). He was, having said that, in no position to do otherwise, being rather preoccupied with Alaric's rampaging Visigothic army at the time, and wrote to the cities of Britain telling them that from thereon they should be responsible for their own defence.

However, in one sense Britain had escaped Roman control a few years earlier, in 406. In that year the historian Zosimus records that soldiers in Britain rebelled and appointed as their emperor a man known only as Marcus. After a short time, though, Marcus lost favour with his backers and was replaced by one Gratianus (not the same Gratianus/Gratian, son of Valentinian I, who was emperor of the Eastern Roman Empire from 375 to 383). Another historian, Orosius, records that this Gratianus was '*municeps eiusdem insulae*', '*municeps* of the same island', i.e. Britain.[7] There has been some confusion over the word *municeps*. The word derives ultimately from the word *municipium* (from which we get modern words like 'municipal'), which originally meant a specific category of Roman town with particular privileges. Some have suggested on the basis of this that Gratianus must have been some kind of town official. In fact, the word *municeps* seems to have had a much more general meaning and should simply be translated as something like townsman. The really significant element, though, is that Gratianus was British. For the first time in almost 400 years of occupation, a Briton was proclaimed Roman emperor in Britain. It is even possible that we can be more precise about his origins. In its original sense a *municeps* was, not surprisingly, specifically a citizen of a *municipium*, and in Britain only one town, Verulamium, is known to have enjoyed that status. Having said that, Orosius came from Spain where *municipia* were much more widespread, so he could well have been using the word in a rather less precise sense.

Gratianus' hold on power was, however, also brief. After a few months, as with Marcus, Gratianus' backers tired of him in turn and replaced him with a man called Constantine, known to history as Constantine III (*10*). Duly following in the footsteps of previous commanders in Britain (including Magnus Maximus just over 20 years before), Constantine crossed to the continent with an army in an attempt to take control of the Western Empire as a whole.

Unfortunately we don't know much about Constantine's background. He may have been British too. One interesting point, which may link Constantine to both his predecessor Gratianus and to Verulamium, is that the few coins of Constantine III that have been found in Britain have almost all turned up in, or on the edge of, the territory of the Catuvellauni and Trinovantes. The capital of the Catuvellauni was at Verulamium, and, as already mentioned, their neighbours the Trinovantes had formed a confederation with the Catuvellauni in pre-Roman times. As we shall see later, these two tribes were probably also politically united in post-Roman times as well. Constantine's coins were all minted in mainland Europe and the fact that they turn up here, in Catuvellaunian/Trinovantian territory, rather than in a location closer to the

*10* Constantine III.

*11* The Argeliers buckle. A British buckle of Catuvellaunian style, found in southern France and possibly linked to the activities there of Gerontius and Constantine III. *(After Aurrecoechea Fernandez, 1999)*

continent, like Kent for instance, may indicate that Constantine's administration had particularly strong links with this area. A late fourth- or early fifth-century buckle of a specifically Catuvellaunian style, decorated with dots, was also found at Argeliers in southern France (*11*). Since Constantine III made Arles (*colour plate 7*) his capital for most of his short reign, this is another potential link between his expedition and Catuvellaunian territory.[8]

Whether or not Constantine III was British, however, we do know for certain that his general Gerontius was. The two original generals of Constantine's expeditionary force, Justinianus and Nebiogastes, were killed by Sarus, a commander representing the emperor in Rome, shortly after Constantine crossed the Channel. Their places were then taken by Edobichus, described as a Frank, and Gerontius, described as a Briton.

It has been generally assumed, since Constantine is shown in the sources as emperor and Gerontius as merely one of his generals, that Gerontius was a relatively minor figure. However, it would be unwise to rely too much on assumptions based on simplistic and in some ways anachronistic views of the comparative status of emperors and generals. At the time of Gerontius and Constantine III, imperial regalia did not always indicate where the real seat of power lay. It was, for instance, not Honorius who dispatched Sarus to confront Constantine III's generals but Stilicho, a general who ostensibly served Honorius but was in many ways the real power in the Western Roman Empire of the time. This phenomenon of weak puppet emperors controlled by powerful generals and other, often non-Roman, leaders was one that was to recur throughout the last century of the Roman Empire in the west.

Thus the Frankish general Arbogastes was the effective power behind Valentinian II in the late fourth century and was responsible for promoting Eugenius to a short-lived spell on the imperial throne in the years 392–394. Similarly Gundahar, king of the Burgundians, and Goar, king of the Alans, set up Jovinus as emperor for a couple of years (411–413) in Gaul, after the fall of Constantine III. Priscus Attalus gained the dubious distinction of being the puppet emperor of two Germanic leaders, first of Alaric in 409 and then later of Ataulf. The Germanic general Ricimer (son of a Suebi prince and the daughter of Wallia, king of the Visigoths) by contrast set up a string of emperors. The first of them was Majorian, who became emperor of the west in 457, but when he started having ideas of his own, Ricimer forced him to abdicate and put Libius Severus on the throne instead. After the death of Libius Severus in 465, possibly on Ricimer's orders, Ricimer for a time accepted Anthemius, the candidate of the Eastern Emperor Leo, as Western emperor. Eventually, however, Ricimer decided he needed his own man on the imperial throne again, and so besieged and killed Anthemius, replacing him with Olybrius.

The selection and rapid demise of both Constantine's immediate predecessors, Marcus and Gratianus, potentially looks like a similar process of powerful backers looking for an appropriate puppet emperor and rejecting two candidates as unsuitable before finally settling on Constantine. Could it be, therefore, that it was the generals who chose Constantine rather than Constantine who chose the generals? Constantine is described by Orosius as a lowly soldier at the time of his elevation to the position of candidate for the imperial throne, and Orosius further claims that he was chosen purely because of his name, which would presumably evoke happy memories of the earlier, successful attempt on the imperial throne launched from Britain by Constantine I. In contrast, Zosimus describes Edobichus and Gerontius, at the point when they took control of Constantine's armies, as being respected by Sarus, their opponent, for their ability and bravery. In other words, they were major figures already. Sozomen also points out that Gerontius was Constantine's most important general, so he clearly remained a major figure after Constantine's elevation to imperial status.

One reason why so many of the generals mentioned above chose to rule through puppet emperors is that they themselves were of Germanic origin and the idea of a 'barbarian' German on the imperial throne was seen as inappropriate, even though Germans controlled many of the Empire's armies, as well as forming a large part of them. It is worth noting, therefore, when considering whether Constantine III was originally a puppet ruler, that at least two of Constantine's generals, Nebiogastes and Edobichus, were of Germanic origin. Gerontius, of course, was not, but he still might have thought of himself as not sufficiently Romanised to be emperor. Perhaps he came from one of the less Romanised parts of Britain. Certainly, when he eventually split with Constantine, Gerontius eschewed the imperial throne for himself and seems to have followed the puppet emperor route, making an otherwise almost unknown figure called Maximus emperor under his control.

If Constantine III had indeed started life as a puppet emperor, however, he rapidly seems to have decided to become something more than that, in the same way that Anthemius broke free from Ricimer's control. This has always been an occupational hazard for kingmakers. The year 406 had been a busy one in Rome's north-western provinces. As well as the rebellion in Britain, that year also witnessed the event which still seems to mark not the end but certainly the beginning of the end of the Empire in the west. On the last day of the year an army of Vandals, Sueves and Alans crossed the frozen River Rhine near Mainz and entered the Empire, never to be evicted. Constantine seems to have understood something of the danger and is recorded by Zosimus as restoring the Rhine frontier defences to an extent not seen since the time of Julian about 50 years before.

Despite this sudden interest in frontier defences, however, there can be little doubt that the main preoccupation of Constantine and his backers at this point was not to deal with the invaders from outside the Empire in any particularly resolute fashion, but instead to pursue his bid for power within the Empire. After

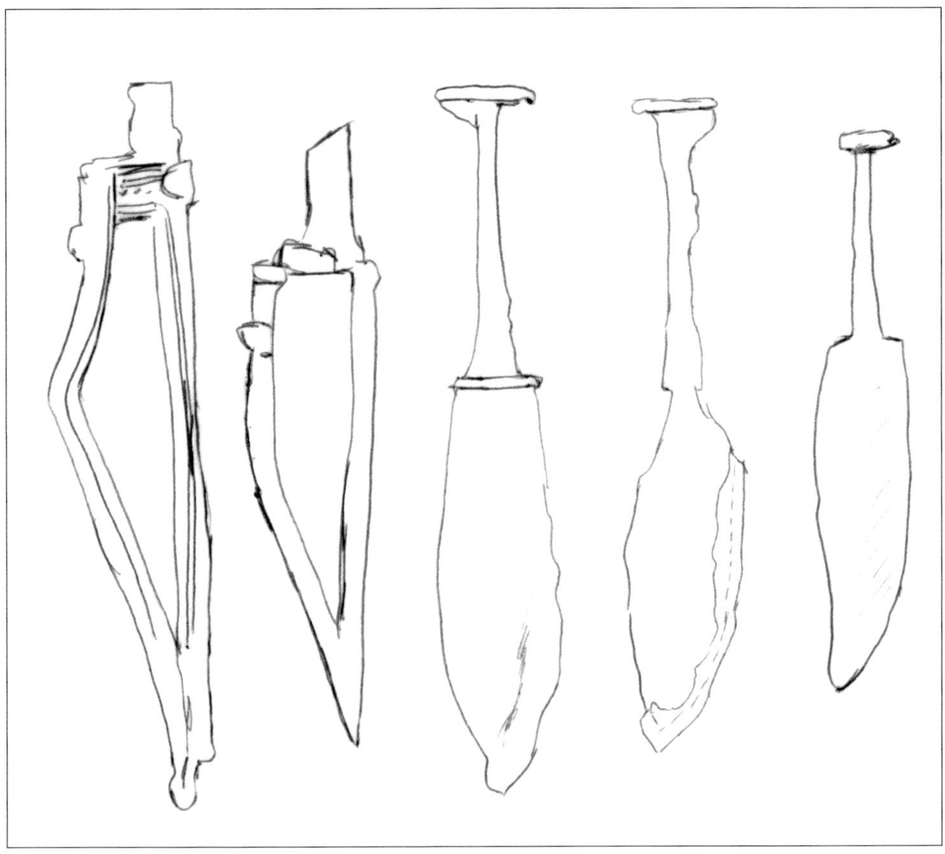

*12* Knives of the sort found in association with belt sets in Spain (left two) and Britain (right three). *(After Aurrecoechea Fernandez, 1999 and Clarke, 1979. Not to scale)*

a victory over the Emperor Honorius' general Sarus, Gerontius, instead of turning north to march against the Vandals, Sueves and Alans, turned south with Constans, son of Constantine, to fight against forces in Spain that were still loyal to Honorius.

The exact nature of these forces offers an interesting commentary on events in the far west of the Roman Empire as the last century of its existence dawned. More importantly, it is linked both to events in Britain at the time and quite probably to Gerontius as well. Two of Honorius' relatives in Spain, Didymus and Verinian, are said to have been in command of a force of 'armed peasants and slaves',[9] which nevertheless managed to kill a substantial proportion of Gerontius' forces before Didymus and Verinian were themselves finally captured and executed. As members of the imperial family, the pair may well have had extensive estates on the Iberian peninsula and thus could be expected to have had large numbers of peasants and slaves under their control. However, the ability of this ragtag army to inflict real losses on Gerontius' forces perhaps seems to imply that Didymus and Verinian were commanding something rather more militarily important than a bunch of reluctant retainers with scythes thrust into their hands.

Just as the distribution and design of buckles and belt fittings in Britain in the last decades of the fourth century seem to indicate the rise of tribal militias there, so something rather similar appears to have been happening in Spain at around the same time. Buckles and belt fittings had previously been restricted to military areas, but towards the end of the fourth century they start appearing in civilian contexts as well. Interestingly, unlike in Britain where burial with grave goods was rare by this time, here the buckles and belt fittings are regularly found in burial contexts (as well as loose examples being found elsewhere), and the evidence from these burials indicates they were being worn to support military-type daggers (*12*). Even more interestingly, the different distribution patterns of different designs of buckle and belt fittings seem to indicate that two of the most powerful of the pre-Roman Spanish tribes, the Vaccaei and the Carpetani, had raised and equipped tribal militias. What is more, the capital of the Vaccaei, at Palencia, lies at the centre of a cluster of Vaccaean buckles/belt fittings, and it appears, judging by the fact that Gerontius' ultimately victorious troops were allowed to ravage the area, to have been at least a base for the forces of Didymus and Verinian. Thus it seems reasonable to conclude that the 'armed peasants' who held Gerontius and Constans at bay for a while may not have been just retainers on an unwilling outing to the battlefield organised by their masters, but something more significant altogether.[10]

Which brings us to the composition of Gerontius' own army. It is normally assumed that rebel would-be emperors making a bid for power from Britain relied on units from the Roman forces stationed here to support their attempt. Certainly the unusual concentration of Roman military units in Britain (compared to many other parts of the Empire) must have been one major reason why Britain was the starting point for a number of coups over the centuries. However, as discussed above, by the late fourth century the conventional Roman army was almost certainly not the only armed force present in Britain. A number of tribes had probably raised and equipped tribal militias in the period after the events of 367–369, and it is even probable that, when not eyeing up potential tribal adversaries, some of these militiamen cooperated with the conventional Roman army in the defence of Britain. As mentioned above, Gildas states that the Romans armed the Britons prior to their final departure; he also adds that they built a defensive wall and the Saxon Shore forts along the southern and eastern coast to be manned by the Britons. While Gildas is clearly wrong in thinking that Hadrian's Wall and the Saxon Shore forts were built right at the end of the Roman occupation, he may well be right in thinking that they were (at least partially) manned by Britons by that time. The inscriptions recording tribal units working on Hadrian's Wall suggest as much, while the excavator of Portchester Castle recorded 'ordered

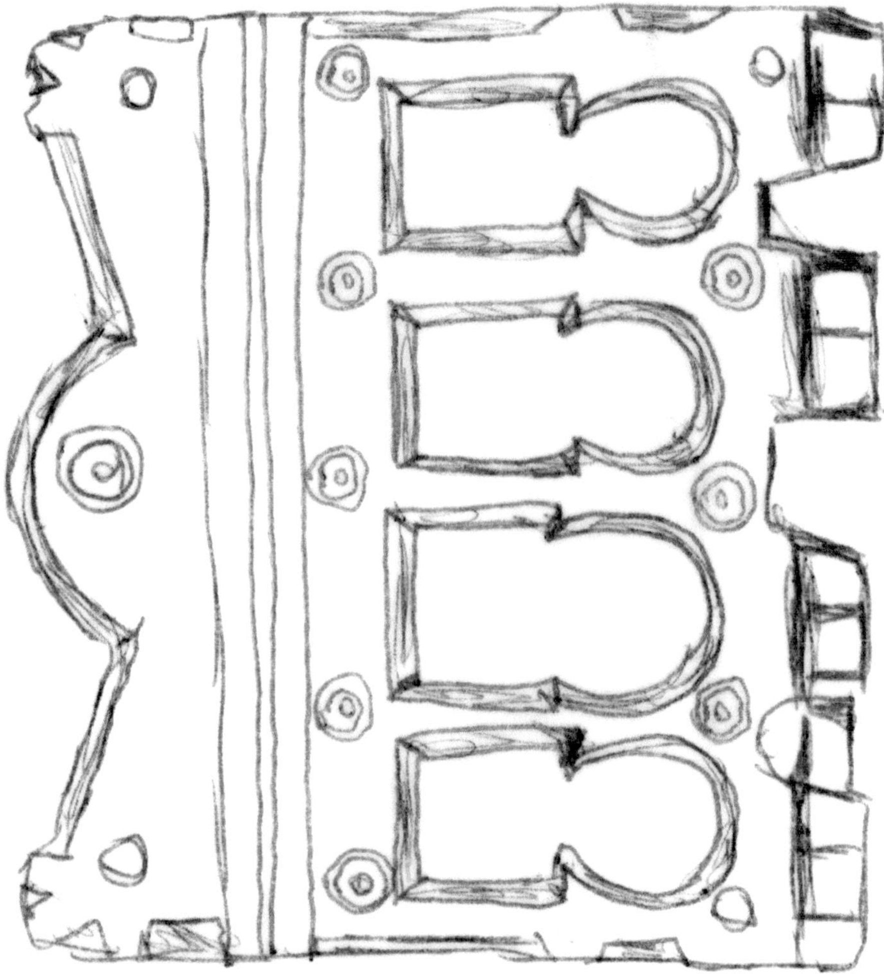

*13* Buckle plate with integral half propeller belt stiffener, of British type but found in Aquileia. *(After Sommer, 1984)*

occupation' there in the period 354–364 followed by 'disordered occupation' from 364 onwards.[11] Such a change in occupation patterns could well mark a shift from a regular Roman army unit to less well-disciplined tribal militiamen.

If militiamen were cooperating with conventional Roman army units in Britain, then there is no reason why some of them should not have extended that cooperation into overseas ventures, and there is evidence which suggests that this is exactly what they did. We have already mentioned the Catuvellaunian buckle found in the south of France, a major area of activity for Constantine III and his forces, and other pieces of British militia equipment have also been found abroad. A distinctively British buckle plate, featuring half a propeller belt stiffener integrated into the buckle plate, has, for instance, been found at Aquileia

*14* Buckle plates from Britain with integral half propeller belt stiffeners.

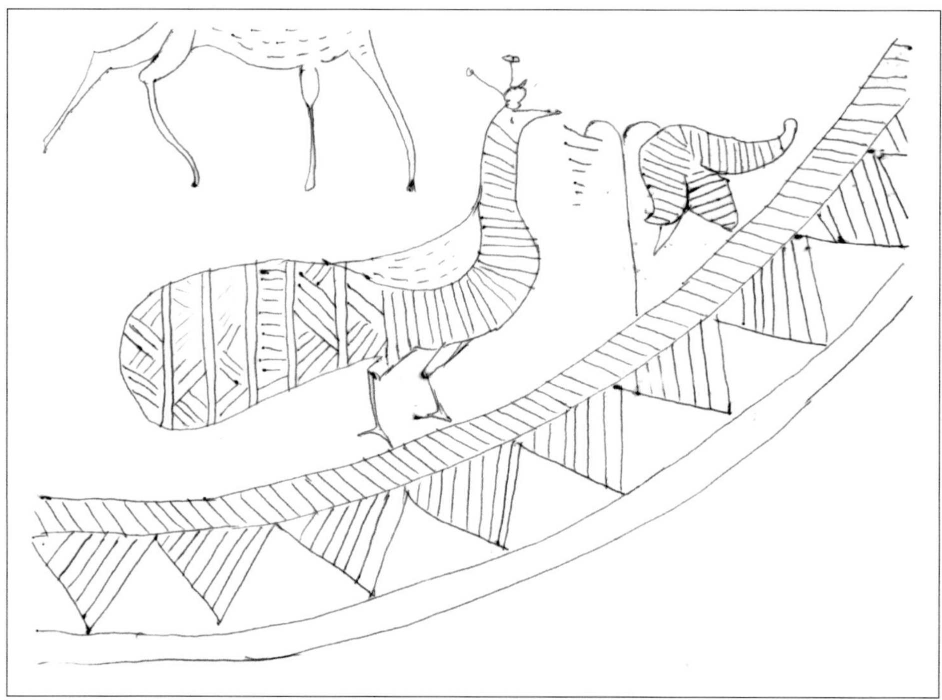

*15* Peacock on the Cervianus disc.

in Italy (*13, 14*). This was not one of Constantine III's areas of interest and thus this buckle plate is more likely to be linked to the activities of Magnus Maximus, who rebelled in Britain in 383 and met his death at Aquileia in 388. The use of British militiamen by Magnus Maximus seems to be confirmed by the statement made by the historian Sozomen that, for his invasion of Italy, Magnus raised 'a large army from Britons, neighbouring Gauls, Celts, and other nations'.[12] In Spain, the Roman period site of Iruña/Veleia, in an area of the north where Gerontius would certainly have operated, has produced two distinctively British buckles, including a horsehead type.[13] An openwork buckle plate from Tirig, while fitted to a Spanish buckle, appears itself to be of a distinctive British type.[14] What is more, some British buckles found in Britain suggest elements of Spanish design. A certain type of buckle found in Icenian territory, while retaining the human head on top of the loop which seems to be a distinguishing feature of Icenian buckles, otherwise has more in common with designs from Spain and southern France than with other British designs.[15]

Precisely where the unique Cervianus disc came from is unknown but it was published in France as long ago as 1698 and is now located in Paris. This incised metal disc shows two groups of soldiers clustered around two standards. The groups are identified in an inscription on the disc as being from the *Legio II Augusta* and the *Legio XX Valeria Victrix*. The disc is marked with the name Aurelius Cervianus and also bears a good luck message, '*utere felix*'. People have suggested a third-century date for the disc based on the depiction of the soldiers' uniform, but this overlooks the fact that on formal items such as coins, troops with standards and emperors were shown with 'classic' early equipment like this well into the fourth century and beyond. Such a practice stresses the military heritage and distinctive nature of key personnel and is akin to the habit of modern-day American colour parties dressing in the uniforms of a much earlier period. Equally, others have suggested that the disc should be linked to Constantine III, on the basis that only at that date are the two legions in question likely to have been found together in the same place. What is particularly interesting in this context, though, is that if this disc does indeed commemorate the expedition of Constantine III to the mainland of Europe, then there are elements on it which also seem to record militia contingents as part of the force. For a start, the style of incised work that characterises the disc is also one that is typical of some categories of British horsehead buckle plates of the late fourth century. More specifically, though, there are symbols on it which may represent particular British militia units. At the top of the disc are the animal symbols of the two legions, the boar of *Legio XX* and the capricorn of *Legio II*. Beneath the soldiers, though, are more animals. In the centre is a scene of a stag holding hounds at bay and a lion. The stag takes centre stage and is likely to be a pun on the owner's name Cervianus, *cervus* being the Latin word for a stag. At the bottom of the disc, though, there are two peacocks and a tree, which seem to have nothing at all to do with the hunting scene (*15*). Two peacocks and a tree represent a Christian symbol that is found, for instance, among the mosaics at Ravenna. It is also, however, a design that is repeatedly found on one category of British horsehead buckle plates (and associated fittings) and seems, in terms of distribution, to be linked to the region around Water Newton. It has been argued, on the basis of a Roman milestone measuring distance from Water Newton, that by the late fourth century this area may already have been a semi-independent or even independent element of the Catuvellaunian tribal territory.[16]

The decorative element around the edges of the Cervianus disc is also interesting. On one level it can be seen as a simple row of triangles with hatching. However, geometric shapes (mainly diamonds and triangles) with cross-hatching seem to be the defining decorative element of buckles and belt-fittings linked to Dobunnic areas. With so many stylistic links between the Cervianus disc and British militia buckles of the late fourth century, it is hard to dismiss them as mere coincidence.

If British tribal militiamen did, in fact, form a significant element within the forces of Gerontius and Constantine III, then we must ask more questions about the precise position and role of the Britons Gratianus the *municeps* and Gerontius himself. As already noted, the British aristocracy seem to have rejected Roman politics throughout the more than three-and-a-half centuries of Roman occupation, until suddenly, right at the end of that occupation, two major British figures appear at almost exactly the same time, both linked to the same rebellion. Could this new-found British self-confidence and assertiveness be linked to the rise of the tribal militias in Britain? It seems feasible. With tribal armed forces at their disposal, the British aristocracy would suddenly have new authority and influence within the Roman power structure in Britain, perhaps to the extent that for the first time they could see their way clear to make bids for power within the Roman system. It is entirely conceivable that at the very same time when Germanic war leaders dominated so much of the senior Roman military hierarchy, partly because of their very ability to raise Germanic troops swiftly and easily, the British war leader Gerontius likewise may have owed his position at least partly to his ability to raise British militiamen swiftly and easily.

With Gerontius in control of Spain, the time might have seemed right for Constantine to turn his efforts towards dealing with the Vandals, Sueves and Alans, who by this time were making themselves unpopular with the locals in Gaul. Jerome, in a letter written from Bethlehem, goes into some detail about the towns destroyed by the invaders. He says that Worms, Reims, Mainz, Amiens, Arras, Therouanne, Tournai, Strasbourg and Speyer had all been destroyed and that there had been damage to Aquitaine, Narbonensis and Novempopulana. Instead of dealing with the invaders, however, Constantine's search for power again took precedence, and he launched an attempted invasion of Italy. He, however, abandoned this and ran back to Arles when a local collaborator in

*16* Late Roman mosaic from Tarragona showing one Optimus, inhabitant at around the time of Gerontius' activities there.

Italy was discovered and executed. The whole shambles does not reflect well on Constantine's military capabilities and seems to confirm the judgement of Orosius that Constantine had not been initially chosen for his courage; it again also suggests that the absent (in this instance) Edobichus and Gerontius may have been the true driving force behind his original grab for the imperial throne.

Constantine, though, still seems to have been attempting to seize real control for himself. After the disaster in Italy, Zosimus and Sozomen record that he sent his son Constans back to Spain accompanied by a new general, Justus.

*17* Funerary inscription of Marturia from Tarragona, dated to 393 by its reference to the consulship of the emperor Eugenius.

*18* Maximus, acclaimed as emperor by Gerontius.

If Constantine III did start life as some kind of puppet emperor, this seems to be the final example of the puppet cutting the strings. Certainly that seems to be how Gerontius saw it, because at this stage he rejected Constantine entirely and went in search of another puppet ruler who wouldn't prove so troublesome. He chose a certain Maximus. One writer records that Maximus was Gerontius' son, but unless his wife Nunechia was of particularly high rank there seems no particular reason why Gerontius would elevate his son rather than himself, and generally it seems preferable to accept the alternative account which makes Maximus a senior member of his personal staff. Maximus was duly acclaimed emperor and installed by Gerontius at Tarragona (*16–18*).

Gerontius' rejection of Constantine may, however, have had effects well beyond Spain, because at the same time Zosimus records that Britain (and copying Britain, Armorica) rose in rebellion against Constantine's administration. This was the decisive moment when Britain finally passed out of Roman control, never to return to it. No explicit link is made in the texts between the actions of Gerontius in Spain and Britain's declaration of independence, but it is hard not to see at least the possibility, even probability, of such a link. At the most fundamental level both events seem to represent the new-found sense of British self-confidence and assertiveness. Zosimus describes the Britons deliberately ejecting Roman officials, organising their own administration and militarily confronting – and beating – foreign raiders on their own account. This is not a pitiful remnant, tearfully waving goodbye to departing Roman soldiers in the manner seen in some Victorian depictions of the end of Roman Britain. These are powerful, self-confident people deciding that they don't need Rome any more and that their tribal militias will do a better job of defending them. Of course, the link may be even more significant than that. If it is right to see Gerontius as a warlord with close connections to the British militias, then it seems perfectly reasonable to suggest that the rebellion in Britain and the rebellion in Spain may have been coordinated at least on some level. With Armorica in rebellion too, in fact, almost the entire Celtic far west of the Roman Empire had broken away from the rest.

At this point, it's worth pausing for a moment to consider what was happening in Armorica as the rebellion against Constantine III unfolded. Zosimus specifically links events in Britain and Armorica in 409, stating that the Armoricans copied the approach of the Britons at this point. Bearing in mind the close links between Armorica and Britain in pre-Roman and Roman times (it has, for instance, been suggested that in the pre-Roman period the Dumnonii of Devon and Cornwall had more in common with the Armoricans of the time than with other Britons), links which continued with the development of the Breton identity there in post-Roman times, this would hardly be surprising. What is interesting, though, is that we know a little more about events in Armorica after 409 than we do about events in Britain after 409, and this is where we meet a mysterious group called the *bagaudae* or *bacaudae*.

These armed groups operating in Gaul and Spain are briefly mentioned by sources in the third century and then receive increasing attention in the fifth. At this time there is a mention of them being active in Armorica. The evidence of what the *bagaudae* really were is sparse and sometimes contradictory, but the most convincing explanation is that they were basically armed peasant militias which came to prominence at times of crisis. In the light of previous discussions concerning the development of tribal militias in Britain and Spain, it seems perfectly feasible to see them as another example of the same phenomenon, essentially a revival, perhaps in the instance of the *bagaudae* in a slightly less organised form, of the pre-Roman tribal war band. Certainly the location of their operations seems to be in remote areas where the survival of tribal loyalties might be expected to be at its strongest. Thus they are found in mountain regions, like the *bagaudae* who ambushed Sarus retreating from his clash with Gerontius, and in the far west of the Roman Empire. Alongside Armorica, they are also found in the north of Spain, in an area not too far distant from where the tribal militias of the Vaccaei and Carpetani were presumably operating, and not far from the Basque regions, which retained their pre-Roman identity through Roman times, into post-Roman times and up to the modern day. In time, no doubt, some of these *bagaudae* became more regular and more like proper tribal armies, much like the British militias. A unit of Armoricans is, for instance, recorded along with contingents from various Germanic peoples in the forces commanded by Aëtius at his famous victory over Attila's Huns in 451 on the Catalaunian Plains. In Spain, the mysterious 'Senate of Cantabria' (originally the tribal area of the Cantabri) mentioned by sixth-century sources may also be an indication of tribal political power in the post-Roman period.[17]

If Gerontius did raise Britain against Constantine III, he did not stop there. Rather than confronting the Vandals, Sueves and Alans, he again seems to have put the battle for imperial power first and decided to use them against Constantine, stirring them up to attack him. Gerontius then followed this up with a full-scale invasion of the south of France, killing Constans at Vienne and subsequently laying siege to Constantine in Arles. Yet again Constantine appears to show a distinct lack of military talent. However, it was not to be Gerontius' day either. As he was besieging Arles, an army loyal to Honorius arrived on the scene. Gerontius and his troops may, in addition, have been aware that his former comrade Edobichus, still working with Constantine III, was also in the process of raising an army to relieve the siege of Arles.

Whatever the situation, a large section of Gerontius' army, including the Spanish element, seems to have decided that it had backed the loser in this particular confrontation and that it was time to make a hasty switch of allegiance. The result was the amazing last stand of Gerontius, as told by Sozomen, with an ending that could have come straight out of a Hollywood epic:

> Due to his retreat, the Spanish soldiers turned completely against Gerontius and planned how to kill him. They formed up in a tight group and attacked his house in the night. He, though, with Alanus, his companion, and a few servants went to the top of the house and killed no less than three hundred of the attackers. When they ran out of arrows the servants escaped by secretly letting themselves down from the building. Gerontius too could have escaped in that way but chose not to because love for his wife Nunechia held him back. At dawn the next day the attacking soldiers set fire to the house and when he saw that there was no hope of safety left, Gerontius cut off Alanus' head, in compliance with his wishes. After this his wife was crying and pressed herself to the blade, begging, as a last gift from him, to die at her husband's hand rather than be left to the soldiers. This woman, through her bravery, showed herself worthy of her religion as a Christian, and in this way she died a merciful death. She left for future generations an unforgettable memory. Gerontius then stabbed himself three times with his sword and, realising that he was not fatally wounded, he drew his dagger which he wore at his side and thrust it into his heart.
>
> (Sozomen, *Ecclesiastical History*, 9, 13)

With this dramatic episode, the life and eventful career of the British warlord Gerontius came to an end, but his influence on events continued. Constantine III was subsequently finished off by the same army that so scared Gerontius' troops, and Edobichus, in yet another treacherous twist to the tale, ended up being murdered by a former friend. The Vandals, Sueves and Alans took the opportunity offered them by the fighting between Gerontius and Constantine III, and by the resulting chaos in Gaul and Spain, to cross the Pyrenees and occupy much of Spain. Eventually, the Vandals were driven out of the Iberian peninsula, but only across the straits of Gibraltar to Africa, where they created a new kingdom in what had been Roman Africa. They would be replaced in Spain and south-western France by the power that had driven them out: not Romans but Visigoths, with their own semi-independent kingdoms. The Sueves, by contrast, stayed settled in their kingdom in western Spain and Portugal, and shortly after the time of Gerontius a Burgundian kingdom based at Worms was added to the increasing numbers of Germanic kingdoms within the old imperial frontiers.

Lots of people may never have heard of the British warlord Gerontius, the man who sank the Roman Empire, but they should have done. His efforts to seize power in Europe may have ultimately failed, but they did assist in the planting of separate Germanic entities deep within the Empire, thus helping to change the course of British and European history forever.

But if his deeds are forgotten, his name at least survives. The name Gerontius, or Geraint, is derived from the Greek word for old, and was a relatively common name in the Eastern Roman Empire, but much less common in the fifth-century Western Empire. It was, however, the name of a number of figures in post-Roman British history and literature, most notably Geraint ap Erbin, Geraint of the South mentioned in the 'Y Gododdin', Geraint the hero of the poem the 'Battle of Llongborth' (see Chapter 7), and Geraint king of Dumnonia in the eighth century. The story of Magnus Maximus' expedition from Britain to take over the Roman Empire lived on in Welsh memory and in poems like 'The Dream of Macsen Wledig'. It is likely that Gerontius' deeds were immortalised in similar poems, now lost, and perhaps in some sense through the Arthurian character Geraint. Still today Geraint is a very well-known Welsh name.

# CHAPTER 2

# VORTIGERN

In contrast to Gerontius, most people have at least heard of Vortigern, yet he remains an elusive figure floating in the fog of fifth-century British history, hard to tie down to specific locations and specific strategies.

Faced with the array of difficult, questionable and sometimes apparently contradictory evidence that we have for Vortigern, a recent trend has been to dismiss him entirely as either totally fictional or, if factual, as a character who has passed beyond the point where we can say anything certain about him. However, an investigation of the state of British tribal politics at the end of the Roman period casts new light on Vortigern, and the process produces a picture of the time that not only leaves space for a Vortigern character, actually fitting what we are told about him rather well, but also seems to explain some of the apparent contradictions in the evidence.

As touched on previously, traditional tribal identities remained strong in Britain throughout the occupation, and after the Romans' departure there is clear evidence to suggest that Britain fragmented into separate political units largely based on the old tribes, in contrast to mainland western Europe where new, large-scale Germanic kingdoms took over (and often maintained) the Roman political and administrative structures largely intact. Some of the names in Britain changed, reflecting the new circumstances, and one or two new entities, Brycheiniog, for instance, appeared, squeezed into border territory between older political units, but largely the geographical and political entities seem to have remained the same.[1]

Thus, the territory of the Dumnonii became the kingdom of Dumnonia, and Durotrigan and Dobunnic entities seem to have reasserted themselves, judging by post-Roman cultural differences on either side of Wansdyke (*19*). To the south of this late Roman or post-Roman linear defensive earthwork lies an area in which there was refortification and re-use of hillforts, and imported fifth- and sixth-century Mediterranean pottery can be found. To the north is an area where hillforts were not taken up again and grass-tempered pottery is found (which, by contrast, is largely absent in the south). In Wales, it has been suggested that the tribal area of the Demetae became Dyfed, while that of the Ordovices was renamed eventually as Gwynedd, and the Cornovii were reborn as Powys; the territory of the Silures seems to have split in two to become in the west the entity known as Glywysing and in the east Gwent (taking its name from Venta Silurum, the capital of the *civitas* of the Silures).[2]

However, this continuation of political entities seems to have occurred not only in the British west, where one might reasonably expect more continuity, but also, crucially, in the Anglo-Saxon east as well. It used to be thought that the Anglo-Saxon kingdoms of the sixth century had emerged by a process of small, even family-sized units slowly conglomerating into ever larger units until finally the main Anglo-Saxon kingdoms were created. However, as we will explore further in later chapters, it is now increasingly being suggested that just as the British kingdoms of the west were the direct successors to the British tribal *civitates* in that area, so the Anglo-Saxon kingdoms of the east were also the direct successors to the British tribal *civitates* there.[3] The geography of the *civitates* and of the Anglo-Saxon kingdoms, and the way in which they divide up the available territory, are just too similar. These geographic similarities and the increasing archaeological evidence of Britons living alongside Anglo-Saxons in

*19* Wansdyke.

*20* Kingdoms of post-Roman Britain located in present-day Wales and England.

the new Anglo-Saxon territories instead suggest very firmly that the arrival of the Anglo-Saxons did not fundamentally transform the political geography of eastern Britain, but instead maintained and continued it. In this context then, the key to understanding Vortigern must be to see how and where he might fit into the geography of British and Anglo-Saxon tribal politics of the time.

The alleged act, of course, for which Vortigern is best known is inviting the Anglo-Saxon leaders Hengest and Horsa, plus their followers, to settle in Britain. The earliest detailed reference to the settlement of Anglo-Saxons in Britain appears in the works of the British cleric Gildas, writing probably some time in the early sixth century. Gildas writes about a *superbus tyrannus* who, he says, invited Anglo-Saxons to settle in Britain, only to see them later rebel after a dispute about rations turned nasty. Two of a number of surviving early texts of Gildas include a specific identification of the *superbus tyrannus* as Vortigern, and Bede in his later paraphrasing of Gildas again explicitly identifies him as Vortigern. As has also frequently been pointed out, *superbus tyrannus* is a possible Latin translation or even pun on the original meaning of the British name Vortigern, and even if Gildas did not in his original text specifically identify the *superbus tyrannus* as Vortigern by name, then it is likely that he knew his readers would understand from the phrase *superbus tyrannus* that he was indeed discussing Vortigern. He is very careful, by contrast, to give names to all the other British leaders he mentions.

The only indication Gildas gives about the location of the Anglo-Saxons of his *superbus tyrannus* is a vague one:

> Invited by the luckless king, they first sank their claws into the eastern side of the island, pretending that they had come to defend the country, when really they were going to attack it.
>
> (Gildas, *On the Ruin of Britain*, 23)

Understanding what Gildas might have meant by the phrase 'the eastern side of the island' is more difficult than analysing the issue of the *superbus tyrannus*/Vortigern.

Archaeology suggests that the earliest Anglo-Saxon settlement in Britian took place some time between around 425 and 450 in the territory of the Catuvellauni and the Trinovantes.[4] This process of settlement included the establishment of an extensive Anglo-Saxon presence in the Upper Thames region, in the area around Dorchester-on-Thames. However, it is difficult to see how Gildas, probably writing somewhere in the West Country, perhaps Dorset, could make a statement that the Anglo-Saxons sank their claws into the 'eastern side of the island' about a settlement at Dorchester-on-Thames, which by any standards is right in the middle of Britain and, if anything, perhaps slightly towards the west. Equally, there is evidence that, though there was early Anglo-Saxon settlement at a number of strategic locations all along the borders of the territory of the Catuvellaunian/ Trinovantian confederation, the confederation itself remained under some form of British control until after the time that Gildas was writing. The Anglo-Saxon Chronicle entry for 571, from a time probably only a few decades before monks started making written records and therefore probably reasonably reliable, states that: 'This year Cuthwulf fought against the Britons at Bedcanford and captured four towns, Limbury, Aylesbury, Benson and Eynsham.'

The four towns captured are all in Catuvellaunian territory, as would be Bedcanford, if, as has often been suggested, this can be identified as Bedford. If the Catuvellauni continued to hold these towns until 571, it seems highly unlikely that an Anglo-Saxon takeover of the scale suggested by Gildas could have taken place here at the time he suggests, given that two of the towns, Benson and Eynsham, are situated right in the Upper Thames area of early Anglo-Saxon settlement.

Archaeology, however, does indicate Anglo-Saxon settlement in the period 440–500 across much wider parts of the 'eastern side of the island', including Lincolnshire, East Anglia and, of course, Kent. Bede in his account of the Anglo-Saxon arrival, though mainly paraphrasing Gildas, does briefly add a mention of Hengest and Horsa by name and indicates that they were said to have been the first commanders of the Anglo-Saxons. Further, he links them to Kent. But for fuller details of the basic Hengest and Horsa and Vortigern story, we have to turn to the Anglo-Saxon Chronicle. Here, Vortigern is recorded as inviting in Hengest and Horsa. There is no mention of the squabble over rations, but the link to Gildas is made clear by the subsequent description of Hengest and Horsa fighting against Vortigern, and the link to Kent is made clear by the Chronicle locating there (at Crayford and probably Aylesford) the only two of the four of Hengest's alleged battles where sites can reasonably be identified.

Fifty years ago the narratives of Gildas and the Anglo-Saxon Chronicle were largely seen as two different versions of the same event and were widely accepted as being essentially true. By contrast the trend in recent years has been to think that, although Gildas' account may still contain much truth, the Anglo-Saxon Chronicle version of fifth- and early sixth-century events should not be relied on. Certainly the Chronicle account of those years was not based on careful, contemporary, chronological record-taking: there is too much evidence within the account of repetition, artificial chronological structures and occasional, fairly apparent fictitious 'fleshing out' for that.[5]

However, the Anglo-Saxon Chronicle, unlike many other early medieval documents, contains hardly any material that is obviously fictitious or mythical. It does not weave in dramatic accounts of evil villains, glamorous heroes and dramatic plot-twists. Its approach is dry and curt, and its account of history prior to the fifth century is, as demonstrated by other sources, broadly accurate, as is its account of history after the sixth century. There still seems to be no compelling reason to reject the idea that the Chronicle account of the fifth and sixth centuries is at least based on real memories of the period (even if, no doubt, re-interpreted in the light of later priorities), probably preserved in the form of an oral epic poem which contained core factual elements like the names of people and battles, just as later sagas often did. Supporting this idea is the fact that Gildas himself, writing probably less than a century after the events in question, seems to be relying largely on such a poem. In his account he mentions that the Anglo-Saxons arrived in three *cyuls*, giving an Anglo-Saxon word for ships, and states that one of the Saxons had forecast they would hold the island for 300 years. Both elements look likely to have come from a widely known saga account of the landings (very widely known, bearing in mind Gildas was probably writing somewhere in the west of the island) composed within some 60 to 90 years or so of the events themselves. This is a timespan across which it is perfectly reasonable to expect the transmission of broadly accurate historical information. It is equally then reasonable to assume that such information could have been subsequently retained for another hundred years or so until Anglo-Saxon kingdoms started converting to Christianity and monks, presumably, started making written records.

Think of your own family. I could not, without doing research, say anything much about the lives of my great-grandparents, but I can give an account of the main events of my own grandparents' lives from stories they told me and stories my parents told me. This means that, assuming I am still alive in 30 years' time, I will be able to give a fairly accurate and substantial account based purely on oral tradition of what my family were doing more than 120 years before, including how, for instance, my mother's father fought the Germans in the First World War and was gassed and how his brother was decorated for bravery. I could even work out a relatively accurate chronology for the First World War events in question, without referring to recorded dates, because I know without looking anything up that my grandfather died when I was about 6, and before he reached 70, and I've been told that he joined the army young, when he was about 16 or even 15. Obviously life expectancy in the fifth and sixth centuries would have been less than it is now, and the length of a generation shorter, but in a period before television and all the myriad forms of entertainment we have now, it is also safe to assume that people spent a lot more time telling each other stories about their families and even people in pre-modern times often lived to reasonably old ages, though proportionately the number who did so was obviously smaller. It is therefore reasonable to think that they might know a lot about the lives not just of their grandparents, but even of their great-grandparents and maybe even their great-great-grandparents, and that they might also know a lot about the history of the families and communities around them as well. In addition it is worth bearing in mind that while we assume early Anglo-Saxon society was essentially illiterate, we don't actually know that. There are suspicions that some Roman churches may have stayed in use in early Anglo-Saxon kingdoms, and in any event, the early Anglo-Saxons were in close contact with literate societies in the west of Britain and just across the Channel in northern France. All of this does not, of course, prove beyond doubt that the Anglo-Saxon Chronicle's account of Hengest and Horsa's landing in Kent is true, but it certainly suggests that it may be based on the facts.

While there is some evidence linking Vortigern with Kent, there is also apparently contradictory evidence that appears to link him to an entirely different part of Britain. The *Historia Brittonum*, a rather strange, often fragmented account of Britain's history, was probably written somewhere in northern Wales in the ninth century and has, in recent decades, suffered a much worse decline in its reputation than even the Anglo-Saxon Chronicle, with many current historians lambasting previous generations for placing much reliance on it. Certainly large sections of the *Historia Brittonum* are clearly mythical (very much more obviously so than anything found in the Anglo-Saxon Chronicle). There is, for instance, the attempt to derive the name Britannia from Brutus, and the strange mythical tale of Vortigern building a fortress only to be thwarted by the fighting of two serpents. There is also a list of so-called 'wonders'. Some of these clearly refer to genuine phenomena, such as the River Avon's tidal bore. Others clearly don't. One such example is:

> There is another wonder in the area called Buelt. There is a pile of stones there with one stone above the rest which carries the imprint of a dog's paw. When Cabal, the dog of the warrior Arthur, was hunting the boar Troynt, he made this imprint in the stone and later Arthur built a mound of other stones under it, and this mound is called Carn Cabal. Men may take away the stone in their hands for a day and a night but on the next day it is there on top of the mound.
>
> (*Historia Brittonum*, 73)

This doesn't exactly inspire confidence in the *Historia Brittonum* as a straightforward, reliable historical source. However, in addition to the obviously mythical material, there are substantial chunks of factual history, as confirmed by other sources. One of the more factual elements may relate to Vortigern's descendants. The *Historia Brittonum* records that Pascent, son of Vortigern, was ruler of Builth and Gwrtheyrnion, an area in central/eastern Wales. Gwrtheyrnion is a real place and it does seem, on the evidence of the name if nothing else, to be named after someone called Gwrtheyrn, which is a Welsh variant of the name Vortigern. It is, of course, possible that the author of the *Historia Brittonum* deduced a link to Vortigern simply from the name of the territory. However, the reference in the *Historia Brittonum* does seem to have some independent contemporary corroboration. The famous Pillar of Eliseg, which stands outside Llangollen, bears a probably early ninth-century inscription. This is now illegible, but a copy recorded in the seventeenth century gives a list of the ancestors of Eliseg, king of Powys. Among them is found Pascent, described as a descendant of 'Guarthi–', the end of the name being illegible. In the *Historia Brittonum* Pascent is listed as the son of Vortigern, so it seems likely that 'Guarthi–' would originally have read 'Guarthigirn', another Welsh version of Vortigern. Ninth-century dynasties were not, of course, averse to making up illustrious ancestors to boost their real origins. However, considering that about the only thing anyone seems to have known for certain about Vortigern by the ninth century was that he was responsible for the arrival in Britain of the Anglo-Saxons, who were by then already starting to overrun Wales, he would seem a particularly odd choice for an imaginary ancestor of a Welsh dynasty.

It seems more likely that there was indeed thought to be some genuine connection between Vortigern and the west of Britain, and there is a certain amount of supporting evidence for such a view. The *Historia Brittonum* records Vortigern's ancestors as Guortheneu of Guitaul, Guitaul of Guitolin, and Guitolin of Gloui. Nothing is known of any of these characters and not much is mentioned about

*21* Late Roman officer with infantry. The battle of Wallop might have looked something like this. *(Courtesy of John Conyard and www.comitatus.net)*

them in the *Historia Brittonum*. Thus there seems no particularly good reason for them to be dragged into the genealogy merely to add colour. They may therefore represent real characters genuinely linked to Vortigern or (if the names are there just to make up the numbers) they may at the very least represent names derived from real aspects of his history.

In this context Guitaul, Guitolin (in Latin *Vitalis* and *Vitalianus*) and Gloui are all of potential interest. Gloui, as the writer of the *Historia* explicitly points out, links Vortigern to Gloucester, referred to as *Caer Gloui*, or 'Gloui's fort' in Welsh. The name Gloucester is, of course, ultimately derived from the Roman-period name Glevum. So either Gloui was a real personal name based on this, or the word could denote a geographic link between Vortigern and Gloucester, perhaps as we might call a Londoner 'a son of London'. Either way, this appears to be a connection between Vortigern and Gloucester. Gloucester had never been part of Powys or Builth and Gwrtheyrnion, so the link to it appears to add to the story, rather than just replicate existing detail.

Equally, Guitaul and Guitolin may link Vortigern to another mysterious reference in the *Historia*. This records an early fifth-century battle between Ambrosius and one Guitolinus at Guoloph or Wallop. The reference is very short and lacks detail, which may suggest that rather than being a poetic/mythological elaboration (like

*22* The great hillfort at Danebury, perhaps once called Wallop.

the battling serpent story told at some length), it might be a genuine survival from some early chronological annals, like the Gallic Chronicles, for instance. There are very few other recorded instances of the name Vitalinus and it is therefore reasonable to suggest that the two references to Vitalinus in the *Historia Brittonum* may well refer to the same person.[6] Elsewhere in the *Historia* there is another reference, again very brief and without explanation, which records that Vortigern was in fear of Ambrosius. Taken altogether, this could mean that the reference to Guoloph may be a genuine memory of a battle involving Vortigern and/or Vortigern's family at Wallop. Obviously, many place names have disappeared or altered beyond recognition since the ninth century, but the most likely known candidate for the site of this ancient battle is the group of villages in Hampshire (Nether Wallop, Middle Wallop and Over Wallop) bearing a name which has no obvious Anglo-Saxon roots and is likely to be British. The great hillfort of Danebury, with its evidence of late, probably post-Roman, refortification,[7] overlooks these three Wallop villages and the valley of the Wallop brook, just over a mile away (*22*). Bearing in mind that Danebury is a later Saxon name, it is perfectly possible that Wallop was the hillfort's original name.

A connection between Vortigern and this part of Britain may also be confirmed by an entry in William of Malmesbury's history. Born a few years after the Norman Conquest, the son of a Norman father and an English mother, William spent most of his life as a monk at Malmesbury in Wiltshire and had particular local knowledge of the surrounding area. For instance, he discusses inscriptions in the churchyard at Glastonbury in a way which indicates he has studied them at first hand. Though not above the occasional error of judgement, he is generally reckoned by the standards of the age to be a highly reliable and careful historian. For a man of his time, he sometimes takes exceptional care with his sources. In one passage, for example, he points out for the reader a discrepancy between the Anglo-Saxon Chronicle and Bede's history, remarking that the Chronicle has Ethelbert ruling for 53 years, while Bede makes it 56.

In his history William described how Cenwalh, king of Wessex won two victories over the Britons, one at a place he calls 'Wirtgernesburg', or 'Vortigern's fort', and a second at a mountain called 'Pene–'. The Anglo-Saxon Chronicle also mentions Cenwalh fighting two battles, one in 652 at Bradford-on-Avon and another in 658 at Peonnum. The names of the second battle given in the two sources are so similar that they presumably to the same battle, and this assumption has led many historians to conclude that Wirtgernesburg should therefore be identified as Bradford-on-Avon. Certainly it seems likely that any battle Cenwalh fought would have been located within marching distance of his kingdom. It could, of course, be argued that the name Wirtgernesburg was simply applied by the Anglo-Saxons to some defensive structure, perhaps a hillfort, that they associated with the Britons and therefore wanted to name after a British character. However, as this is perhaps the only Anglo-Saxon place name incorporating Vortigern's name, it is more likely that there was genuinely thought to be some specific connection between Wirtgernesburg and Vortigern.[8]

Powys, Gwrtheyrnion, Gloucester, Wallop and Bradford-on-Avon are all in the western part of Britain, but they are spread over a wide area (and that's even before we get to the question of Kent). So, if we are hoping to build any remotely credible picture of Vortigern, we must try to locate him within some kind of power structure that might link all these different areas.

Some historians, in their search to understand the post-Roman power structures of Britain, have seen Vortigern as a figure controlling most or all of the territory of Roman-period Britain, or at least controlling one of the provinces that made up Roman Britain. The most popular candidate for such a province controlled by Vortigern is Britannia Prima, which covered much of western Britain. In this context, the statement in Gildas that the *superbus tyrannus* consulted his council before inviting in the Saxons is sometimes seen as significant. However, there is no reason why this council need be anything more than a body made up of councillors from a single tribe or *civitas*. *Tyrannus* in the fifth and sixth centuries did not have quite the accusatory tone of the modern-day word 'tyrant'. It denoted a person who had illegitimately seized power, rather than indicating that his rule was necessarily dictatorial or tyrannical in the modern sense. Such figures might well rely on, and consult with, a tribal or *civitas* council, if only to gain themselves support.

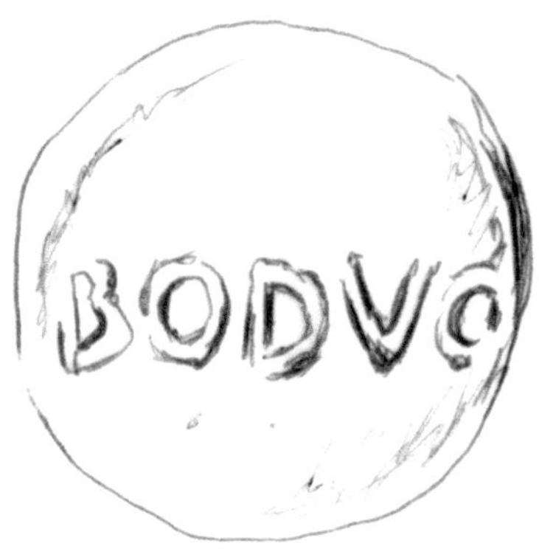

*23* Dobunnic coin.

Generally, though, there seems to be little evidence for the survival of provincial administrative structures, or anything on a larger scale, after the end of Roman rule. The provincial structure of Britain had changed several times during the period of Roman rule. Around the beginning of the third century AD the unified province of Britain was split into two separate provinces, Britannia Inferior and Britannia Superior, and around the beginning of the fourth century it was further subdivided into four provinces known as Britannia Prima, Britannia Secunda, Flavia Caesariensis and Maxima Caesariensis. Finally, in the late fourth century a fifth province, Valentia, was added to the jigsaw. The unsettled nature of the provincial structure in Britain suggests that it is unlikely to have developed deep roots within the British mentality before the end of Roman rule. Many of the provinces bundled together tribes and *civitates* which had very little in common (Britannia Prima, for example, included the heavily Romanised east and parts of the almost completely unromanised west), and it seems highly likely that the process of fragmentation, which eventually led to the re-emergence of the tribes as independent kingdoms, started as soon as Roman rule ended, or indeed, as touched on in the last chapter, possibly even before that.

Vortigern would, therefore, have lived in a Britain that was fragmented into tribal *civitates*, and if we are to make any sense of the available evidence about him, we must look for some kind of tribal power structure that explains the apparent geographic contradictions of his story. Interestingly enough, just such a possible tribal context for Vortigern does exist, and there is archaeological and historical evidence to support it. At its heart lies the tribe and *civitas* of the Dobunni.

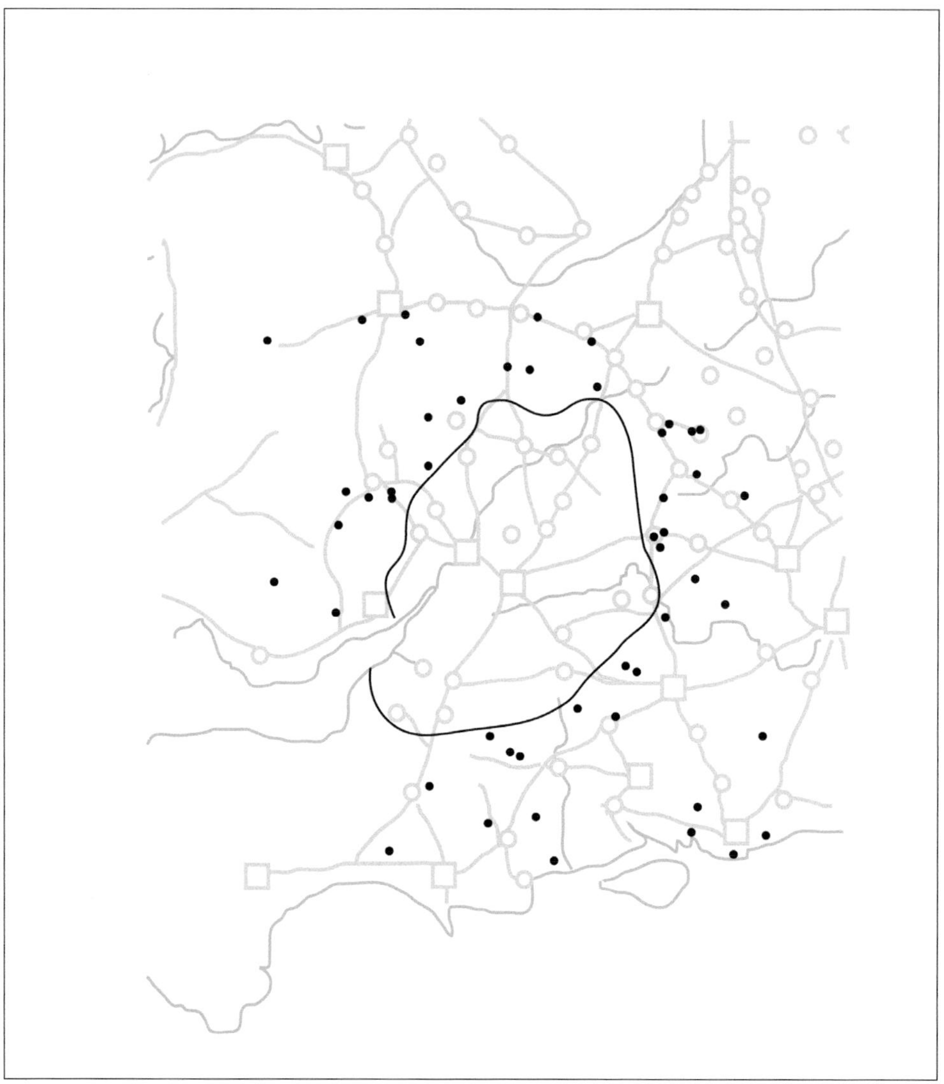

*24* Distribution of Dobunnic coins set against towns and roads of Roman Britain. Black dots show finds of individual coins. Area enclosed by black line shows main area of distribution of Dobunnic coins. *(After Cunliffe, 2005)*

Determining tribal boundaries in Britain is far from an exact science, depending as it does on the distribution of pre-Roman coinage, backed up by evidence from inscriptions and the accounts of writers in the Roman period. However, a combination of these various approaches does produce a picture of tribal territories that has a certain coherence and plausibility, and from it we can deduce that in pre-Roman times the Dobunni occupied an area of western Britain comprising basically the historic counties of Gloucestershire, Worcestershire and Herefordshire, plus the western part of Oxfordshire, the northern part of Somerset and the north-western part of Wiltshire. Two features of the geography are particularly worth noting at this point. South of the River Avon lay a Dobunnic area which seems in some sense to have been separate from the rest of the tribal territory north of the river. There are differences in some of the pre-Roman coins that circulated north and south of the river, and differing styles of pottery.[9] What's more, in the Roman period this southern part of Dobunnic territory seems to have been detached by the Romans (in one of the extremely few instances where Roman *civitas* boundaries appear to have been markedly at odds with the pre-Roman tribal boundaries) and lumped together with a section of Atrebatic territory to create the *civitas* of the Belgae. A second point worth noting is the spread of Dobunnic coinage beyond the probable core tribal boundaries into territory associated with other tribes. In the south-east Dobunnic coinage distribution stretches down almost as far as the Hampshire border. In the north-east there is a spread of coins expanding north of the Thames from Abingdon into what would have been Catuvellaunian and Corieltauvian territory. In the west there is a spread of coins into the border areas of Silurian territory, while in the north the coins spread up the valley of the River Severn towards the Cornovian capital of Wroxeter (*24*).

In pre-Roman times the Dobunni seem to have been a powerful tribe, with a possible capital in the form of the *oppidum*, a sort of large hillfort without a hill, at Bagendon, not far from the later Roman period capital of Cirencester. However, they appear to have fallen prey to Catuvellaunian expansionism. In the last decades before Claudius invaded, coin evidence suggests that the Catuvellauni, under their leaders Cunobelinus and Tasciovanus, developed a mini-empire in the centre and east of England. At its core lay the tribal territories of the Catuvellauni and Trinovantes (consisting essentially of Northamptonshire, Bedfordshire, Buckinghamshire, Cambridgeshire, Hertfordshire, Middlesex, Essex and the eastern part of Oxfordshire) joined in some form of confederation. However, Catuvellaunian power also subsequently extended to include the tribal territory of the Cantii, and probably slices of Icenian, Corieltauvian, Atrebatic and Dobunnic territory as well.[10] Coins of Cunobelin expand into what was probably previously Dobunnic territory north of the Thames, and in his description of the Claudian invasion Cassius Dio describes part of a tribe he calls the Bodunni as being under the control of the Catuvellauni. No other reference to a tribe called the Bodunni is known and it is widely assumed here that Dio had misheard or simply confused the name of the Dobunni.

During the Roman period the Dobunni seem to have flourished, apart from suffering the initial blow of losing their southern region to the neighbouring *civitas* of the Belgae. They may even have attempted to take revenge on the Catuvellauni at one point, with some suspicious-looking fires appearing in the archaeology on the Catuvellaunian side of the border around the late second century AD. Certainly, from the second century onwards the Dobunni, like the Catuvellauni, seem to have organised a defensive system for their *civitas*, based on fortifying towns along the *civitas* borders, while leaving towns well inside the borders undefended (unless they were prestige locations such as the *civitas* capital).[11] In the fourth century a number of large and hugely expensive villas were built in Dobunnic territory and two mosaic schools emerged within the tribe's *civitas*. Interestingly, the distribution of these Dobunnic mosaics, where it extends beyond Dobunnic borders, is similar in a number of respects to the distribution of pre-Roman Dobunnic coinage where it extends beyond the tribal borders. The distribution of Dobunnic mosaics again extends into Silurian territory in the west, into Cornovian territory in the north and into Atrebatic territory in the east.[12] This suggests a continuation of contacts and influence from pre-Roman times in these areas. In the late fourth century, as discussed in the last chapter, the Dobunni were one of the tribes that seem to have raised and armed their own tribal militia at this time. On the evidence of the Cervianus disc this militia may be connected to Constantine III's expedition overseas, but it may also have seen action against a neighbouring tribe even before the end of Roman rule. As touched upon in the last chapter, a rash of unretrieved hoards in the same area, plus a line of burnt villas and the construction of Wansdyke to defend against a perceived threat from the direction of Dobunnic territory all suggest conflict along the Dobunni border with the *civitas* of the Belgae. Perhaps it was an attempt to reclaim the section of Dobunnic territory removed by the Romans early on in the occupation. If so, judging by the presence of Wansdyke, built along the northern border of this lost territory, plus the differences in post-Roman cultures north and south of it, any such attempt does not seem to have been successful. It appears to have been the Durotriges from the south, not the Dobunni from the north, who ultimately absorbed this territory.[13]

All of which brings us to Vortigern. Gloucester, linked to Vortigern genealogically by the *Historia Brittonum*, was one of the major cities of the Dobunni. Bordering on the territory of the Dobunni in the west and north is the area that would later form Builth and Gwytheirnion and Powys (the probable post-Roman form of the tribal territory of the Cornovii). As already discussed, this is a region that shows signs of Dobunnic influence. Bradford-on-Avon, on the north bank of the Avon, is either just inside the southern border of Dobunnic territory, if it was marked by the Avon here in Vortigern's time, or is just beyond it, if it was marked by Wansdyke. The likely location of the battle of Wallop lies a little to the south and east of Dobunnic territory, but a cluster of Dobunnic buckles found not far from Wallop suggests Dobunnic militiamen operating in this region at the end of the Roman period.[14]

Vortigern's apparently close association with Powys suggests that his power base could not have been Dobunnic alone. So perhaps we should think in terms of a Cornovian dynasty taking over its richer, more powerful neighbour to the south, a neighbour it had long had close contacts with. Something similar was probably the origin of the Catuvellaunian/Trinovantian confederation discussed previously, with the Trinovantes being mentioned by Caesar as almost the most powerful tribe in Britain, shortly before their neighbours the Catuvellauni emerged on to the scene and took them over.

There is some evidence of close connections between Dobunni and Cornovii during the Roman occupation. The earliest 'Roman' civilian settlement at Wroxeter, the Roman-period capital of the Cornovii, appears in fact to have had a heavily Dobunnic flavour, with the presence of Dobunnic coins and Malvernian pottery. This sense of shared fashions and styles of artefacts persists through the occupation. A type of so-called Polden Hill brooch, dating from the late first and early second century, has a distribution that seems to consist of Dobunnic territory with the addition of a large chunk of Cornovian territory, suggesting a certain sharing of fashions. The distribution of a number of types of pottery also spreads across Dobunnic and Cornovian territory, including again Malvernian Coarse Wares, Severn Valley Wares and Soft Pink Grog-Tempered Wares. As mentioned previously, Dobunnic style mosaics from the late Roman period are also found in Cornovian territory. Shared culture could indicate that some kind of confederation at the end of the period would have been feasible. Certainly one of the leading experts on the area in the Roman period sees evidence of strong economic and political links between Cornovii and Dobunni during the occupation. It is true that no Dobunnic buckles or belt fittings have come from Cornovian territory, but then, as with most of Wales, no late Roman (or immediately post-Roman) buckles and belt fittings at all have been found in the area, indicating that whatever warriors from this area wore in the immediate post-Roman period, it did not usually include buckles.[15]

The name of the kingdom of Powys itself may support the possibility of such a scenario. The name Powys seems to derive from the Latin word *pagenses*, which could either mean pagans or people from the countryside.[16] Since Powys was a Christian kingdom for most, or probably all of its life, it seems fairly unlikely that it would adopt the name 'Pagans', which leaves the 'Rustic' alternative. Wroxeter, capital of the Cornovii is one of the most notable examples of urban survival

25 Part of a *plumbata*, a lead-weighted projectile of a type possibly used by Dobunnic forces at the end of the Roman period.

*26* Caerwent, possibly part of Vortigern's territory.

into the fifth and sixth centuries, so again it seems rather unlikely that the less Romanised and less urbanised Welsh kingdoms to the west of the Cornovii/ Powys would be calling them rustic. By contrast the Cornovii/Powys might have seemed very rustic to the highly Romanised and urban culture of the Dobunni, and if we are thinking of a Cornovian dynasty ruling the Dobunni, then maybe 'Rustic' is an epithet they could wear with a sort of pride.

We have already mentioned fortified Dobunnic border towns and Dobunnic militia buckles and belt fittings, but there is even more direct military evidence that suggests that an aggressive, expansionist Dobunnic/Cornovian confederation, in the mould of the pre-Roman Catuvellaunian/Trinovantian confederation, would have been well placed to flex its muscles in the scramble to divide up Britain in the post-Roman power vacuum.

One of the problems of understanding patterns of military activity in late and post-Roman Britain is in distinguishing surviving examples of late and post-Roman British weapons from early Anglo-Saxon ones. However, one type of late Roman weapon is very distinctive and seems never to have been used by the Anglo-Saxons. It thus provides evidence that can be safely used to draw conclusions about the late Roman and early post-Roman period. The weapon in question is the *plumbata* or lead-weighted dart (*25*). Basically it was like a large arrow, but was thrown by hand and weighted with lead to give it added impact when it hit its target. Perhaps the reason it was never used by early Anglo-Saxons and was not adopted by post-Roman warriors generally is that it would only have been effective if used by disciplined, well-organised units experienced in its use. It is not essentially a direct-fire weapon. You can't simply aim at an enemy and throw. For best effect you have to launch the *plumbata* into the air on a trajectory that will bring it down on an enemy unit, and it would be of most use when launched in volleys. As such, it was a particularly inappropriate weapon for poorly trained militiamen.

Not surprisingly a number of examples of *plumbata* have been found at Roman-period military sites in Britain, including Burgh Castle, Caernarfon and Richborough. What is more remarkable, though, is that a number of *plumbatae* have also been found in and around the edges of the territory of the Dobunni and the Cornovii, on what were basically civilian sites. Examples have come from Kenchester, Nettleton and Cirencester, with an amazing nine *plumbatae* coming from Wroxeter alone, by far the largest number found on any site in Britain. To this list, we should also probably add the two examples from Caerwent.[17] Again Caerwent was fundamentally a civilian site, and it could be argued that it lay within the Dobunnic sphere of influence. Dobunnic coins cluster in the area in pre-Roman times and a late fourth- or early fifth-century buckle and buckle plate with geometric Dobunnic designs was found there. It has also been noted that fifth- and sixth-century Mediterranean pottery occurs in the area of Silurian territory to the west of Caerwent, although Caerwent itself, like the rest of the Dobunnic territory, lacks such pottery, suggesting a cultural border here in Post-Roman times.[18] It has been argued that the territory of the Silures was split in two in the post-Roman period, with the area bordering Dobunnic territory (including Caerwent) forming the kingdom of Gwent.[19]

A Dobunnic/Cornovian confederation would thus have been a wealthy and well-armed power in western Britain. The vital question then is to what extent would such a confederation have been likely to attempt to exercise power in areas as far away as Kent?

We have already seen in the context of the Cervianus disc and Constantine III's bid for imperial power that Dobunnic militiamen probably played a role far beyond their tribal boundaries in the period before Vortigern. But there is also evidence relating to Vortigern that may perhaps shed more light on this wider role in the late Roman period. The Pillar of Eliseg not only mentions Britu, a son of Vortigern, it also records Britu's mother, naming her as Sevira, and describing her as the daughter of Magnus Maximus, who set off from Britain in 383 to seize the imperial throne. Magnus Maximus became a major figure in early medieval Welsh storytelling (perhaps originally through the stories told by returning British militiamen) and it could be argued that his appearance in the list of ancestors of the kings of Powys is simply an instance of a ninth-century dynasty acquiring for itself an illustrious ancestor. This is certainly possible.

Magnus Maximus also makes an appearance in a medieval genealogy of the kings of Dyfed. In the case of the Dyfed genealogy, though, there seems little doubt that Magnus Maximus has simply been added in to spice up the list. His son is given as Dimet, which is presumably a reference to the Demetae, the tribe that created the kingdom of Dyfed, while Magnus Maximus himself is said to be descended from Constans, Constantine, Constantius and St Helena. The Pillar of Eliseg, however, does not go on any such extended genealogical forays into illustrious Roman families, and it is interesting that instead of simply slotting Magnus Maximus into the male line (as happens in the Dyfed genealogy and in many other instances where an illustrious fake ancestor is added), the inscription refers to his descent through the female line and through an otherwise unrecorded figure, Sevira, with a perfectly correct Roman name. It is therefore at least conceivable that Magnus Maximus was indeed Vortigern's father-in-law. We have already discussed the evidence for extensive British involvement in the coup attempts by both Magnus Maximus and Constantine III. It is not impossible that Magnus Maximus might have had family links with British aristocracy, too. Any attempted coup needs lots of cash behind it, and there was certainly plenty of that around in Dobunnic territory in the late fourth century. Perhaps a marriage between Vortigern and Sevira was part of a deal to provide financial backing for the coup.

The mechanics of any connection between Dobunnic territory and Kent, however, are a rather different matter. The Atrebates are something of an enigma in British tribal terms. In pre-Roman times there is evidence of a shared culture and shared coinage across much of Sussex, Hampshire, Berkshire and Wiltshire, and this entity is customarily termed Atrebatic. There is also, however, evidence of cultural sub-groupings within the overall territory.[20] These sub-groups are presumably reflected to some extent in the later division of the territory under Rome into the *civitas* of the Regni in Sussex, the *civitas* of the Atrebates in northern Hampshire and part of Berkshire, and the *civitas* of the Belgae, stretching across southern Hampshire and through Wiltshire as far as Bath (and probably the Bristol Channel). This last unit, as mentioned above, originally had a Dobunnic western part and an Atrebatic eastern part. Confusing the issue even further, the pre-Roman Atrebates seem to have been culturally British, but appear to have taken their tribal identity from a tribe in Gaul also called the Atrebates. This may have occurred when Commius, a leader of the continental Atrebates, fled to Britain after first siding with Julius Caesar in Gaul and then fighting against him. Subsequently, the British Atrebates struck coins in the name of a man called Commius, and it is widely assumed this is the same man as the Commius from Gaul (or possibly his son). According to Caesar, the continental Atrebates were one of the tribes collectively known as Belgae, and again this continental heritage is presumably reflected in the name of the *civitas* of the Belgae in Britain in the Roman period.

*27* The walls of Silchester.

In the immediate pre-Roman period the Atrebates appear to have competed for power with the rising might of the Catuvellauni north of the River Thames. This rivalry particularly seems to have expressed itself in a lengthy battle for control of Kent, with the Atrebates pushing into it from the west and the Catuvellauni expanding into it from the north. Thus a limited distribution of coins of the Catuvellaunian ruler Tasciovanus in Kent is followed by the appearance there of coins minted in the name of the Atrebatic ruler Eppillus, and it has been suggested that the recurrence of the figure of Victory on the coins of Eppillus indicates the commemoration of some kind of military triumph.[21] However, if so, Atrebatic joy was to be short-lived because subsequently coins of the Catuvellaunian ruler Cunobelin appear all across Kent.[22] Ultimately, in this confrontation the Catuvellauni came out on top, taking control not just of Kent but also probably of Atrebatic territory around Silchester. Having said that, the Atrebates may in a sense have had the last laugh, because it seems to have been a plea from the exiled Atrebatic king Verica that finally prompted Claudius to invade Britain, with his primary target being the capital of the Catuvellaunian/Trinovantian confederation at Camulodunum.

If, as suggested previously, the Dobunni did attempt to retake the Dobunnic half of the *civitas* of the Belgae, it seems highly likely that such a move would also have brought them into conflict with the Atrebates, bearing in mind that

*28* Distribution of Dobunnic buckles and belt fittings shown over towns and roads of Roman Britain. *(Laycock, 2008)*

the other half of the *civitas* of the Belgae was Atrebatic. Just as Wansdyke is important evidence for potential conflict along the southern border of the Dobunnic *civitas* at the end of the Roman period, so other fortifications offer hints of a clash between the Dobunni and the Atrebates on the south-eastern border of the Dobunnic *civitas* at around the same time. The small town of Mildenhall, probably an Atrebatic town on the border with the Dobunni, has uniquely strong late fourth-century fortifications which may have been used to close off every access route into the town, with the exception of the road leading away from Dobunnic territory. Equally, probably post-Roman linear earthworks defend the Atrebatic capital of Silchester from attacks from the north and from the north-west, both directions from which a Dobunnic attack would have come.[23]

However, if this was the purpose of the defences, they do not seem to have been entirely effective, because Dobunnic belt fittings are found inside Atrebatic territory, including one example from Silchester itself (*28*). A fragment of skull dating to the fifth century has also been found in the ditch by Silchester's north gate[24] and more generally there is the strange issue of Silchester's abandonment. Very unusually among major Roman sites in Britain, Silchester was not only wholly abandoned in the period after the end of Roman rule but it remained abandoned. Caistor by Norwich is another major Roman period town that was not later built over, but unlike Silchester there is evidence here of early Anglo-Saxon occupation in the area, and as the modern name of the site itself suggests, Norwich is in some sense a successor town that adopted the Roman road links originally built for Caistor. In addition to being a major Roman site, Silchester was also a major pre-Roman site, so its complete abandonment is a particular puzzle. There is some evidence for a well at Silchester being intentionally blocked in the fifth century, which has been taken to suggest deliberate evacuation of the site. This doesn't seem to be the sort of thing Anglo-Saxon raiders did, so it might suggest some kind of deliberate action by Dobunnic raiders. The battle of Wallop too, with its probable location deep in the Atrebatic heartlands, would fit into a pattern of the Dobunni invading Atrebatic territory.

In the context of the political fragmentation and power vacuum in Britain at the end of the Roman period, it is perfectly conceivable that a powerful Dobunnic/Cornovian confederation would attempt to absorb some neighbouring tribal territories. We have already seen this pattern with the Catuvellaunian/Trinovantian confederation in pre-Roman times and it was a pattern that definitely continued in post-Roman times. In the ninth and tenth centuries, for instance, the kingdom of Gwynedd expanded and absorbed first Powys then Ceredigion and subsequently Dyfed.[25] Equally, of course, in Anglo-Saxon territory the same centuries also saw a number of instances of one kingdom being absorbed into another.

*29* Dobunnic belt fittings, showing characteristic geometric decoration.

*30* Quoit Brooch Style buckle and buckle plate showing characteristic roundels. Compare the border construction with fig. 29 and the roundels with fig. 41. *(After Suzuki, 2000)*

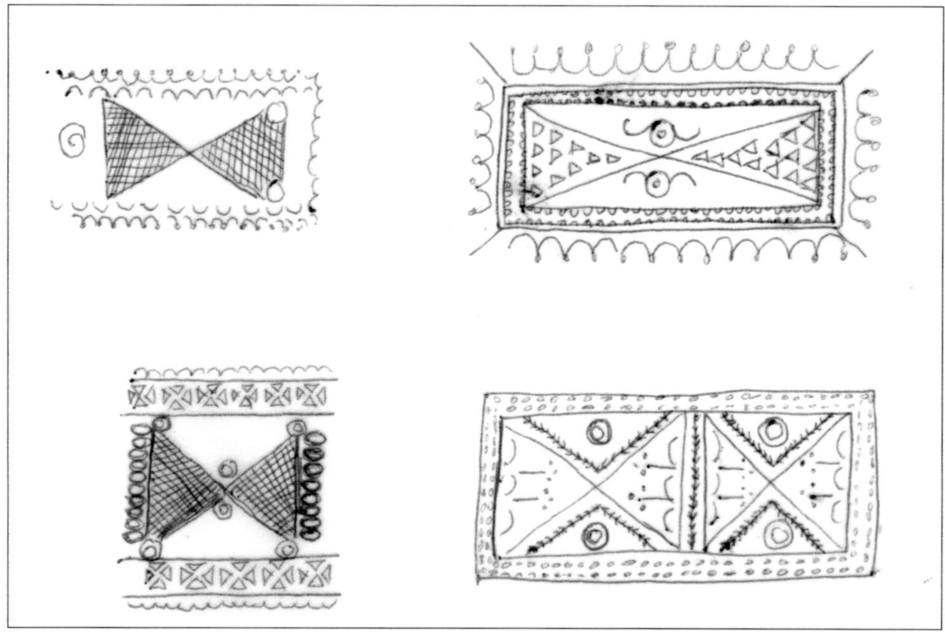

*31* Comparison of motifs on Dobunnic and Quoit Brooch Style belt fittings. Left two Dobunnic *(after Hawkes & Dunning, 1961)*; right two Quoit Brooch Style. *(After Suzuki, 2000)*

If the Dobunni/Cornovii did add the area around Silchester to their growing empire, just as the Catuvellauni/Trinovantes had almost certainly added it to theirs in pre-Roman times, then it would give us a potential Dobunnic connection to Kent, because in pre-Roman times it would most likely have been from the Silchester area that the Atrebates would have launched their take-over of Kent. Connections between the Silchester area and Kent would have been good, in both pre-Roman and post-Roman times, either along the Thames or via ancient routes along the Downs.

A Dobunnic/Cornovian 'empire' stretching all the way across England to Kent may seem a strange concept, but it has curiously precise echoes in later British history. Urien of Rheged in the sixth century seems to have expanded his empire from his base in north-western Britain as far as the North Sea coast, while in the seventh century Cadwallon of Gwynedd in north Wales also extended his authority across northern England as far as the North Sea coast. If Vortigern spread his authority as far as the coast of Kent, he would only be doing exactly what his British successors also did.

So what we need to do now to assess whether such a Dobunnic link to Kent is not just possible but credible is to see if there is any evidence of Dobunnic influence in Kent at the end of the Roman period. And as it happens, there is. A small number of Dobunnic buckles have been found in Kent. One example (plus a stylistically linked strap end) comes from the Roman fort at Richborough, probably one of the main embarkation points for a coup attempt on the continent. So this example could conceivably be connected with the grabs for imperial power by either Magnus Maximus or Constantine III. Two other examples, however, come from elsewhere in Kent and are therefore less likely to be connected with either of those two expeditions. Even more to the point is that Dobunnic buckle and belt fitting design seems to have influenced the design of local buckles and belt fittings, suggesting Dobunnic influence in Kent on a much deeper and longer-lasting level than anything represented by Dobunnic militiamen passing through on their way to the continent.[26]

The so-called Quoit Brooch Style is something we will touch on again later, but essentially it is a style of metalwork that developed in Kent some time in the late fourth and early fifth centuries.[27] It incorporates a substantial element of continental influence derived from late Roman chip-carved buckles and belt fittings of a type found mainly in mainland Europe. However, to this it adds a significant proportion of distinctively British design features and in most cases, as has been pointed out in a thorough survey of the Quoit Brooch Style, these design features derive from British buckles and belt fittings.[28] To be more precise, they derive from Dobunnic buckles, and belt fittings. For instance, one significant group of Quoit Brooch Style buckle and belt plates feature an array of geometric roundels, triangles and border arrangements that have by far their closest parallels on Dobunnic buckle plates (*29–31, 41*). The style of carving on a number of Quoit

Brooch Style buckles, with the use of exceptionally light and fine incised lines, is also most closely paralleled on Dobunnic buckle plates. A number of design features on other Quoit Brooch Style items, such as the unusual cross-hatched square on the Lyminge Quoit Brooch, are also found on Dobunnic items. There are also similarities between the Cervianus disc, with its Dobunnic connections, and Quoit Brooch Style items.

The precise implications of Quoit Brooch Style remain controversial. However, in the light of recent work on the possible connections between regional belt fitting styles and tribal militias,[29] it seems reasonable to regard at least those Quoit Brooch Style buckles and belt fittings with a more distinctively British rather than continental stylistic bias as the equipment of a tribal militia based in Kent. The fact that small numbers of Dobunnic buckles and belt fittings are found in Kent, combined with the possibility that a tribal militia in Kent was equipped with belt fittings showing derivation from Dobunnic buckles and belt fittings, does seem to indicate significant Dobunnic links with Kent in the late and/or post-Roman period, however curious it seems from a geographical point of view. One conceivable form of such links would be Dobunnic political influence over Kent. This would not necessarily have been in the form of absolute authority, but could have been exercised through a local ruler. This, incidentally, is for what it's worth what the *Historia Brittonum* indicates, suggesting that a local ruler named Gwyrangon was overruled by Vortigern on decisions about the Saxons and eventually lost power to them.

One last major question remains to be answered though. We have shown that a Vortigern character, leading an expansionist Dobunnic/Cornovian confederation, could have been in a position to have invited Hengest and Horsa to settle in Kent, but why would he have wanted to?

Gildas, as on so many other issues, is not very clear on the facts relating to this particular question. He writes that the Saxons were invited in to defend against '*aquilonales gentes*', the 'northern nations'. This has been assumed by people from Bede onwards to mean the Picts, and such an interpretation may indeed be accurate. Picts could conceivably have been a problem even as far south as Kent. In the 'Barbarian Conspiracy' of 367–369, for instance, the historical sources may suggest Picts raiding as far south as London. But it is equally possible that the enemies Vortigern wanted Hengest and Horsa and their followers to confront were located slightly closer to home.

Gildas seems to know a fair bit about the history of Britain at around the time of the end of Roman rule, but it is questionable how much he actually knew about the details of the Anglo-Saxon arrival. As already discussed, his main source seems to be an Anglo-Saxon saga and his other information seems very limited. He does not mention the earlier Anglo-Saxon settlements around Dorchester-on-Thames, and his description of Anglo-Saxons sacking towns and tumbling towers after they rebelled seems much more like something Gildas had read in the Bible or in Virgil's *Aeneid*, rather than anything that archaeology suggests actually

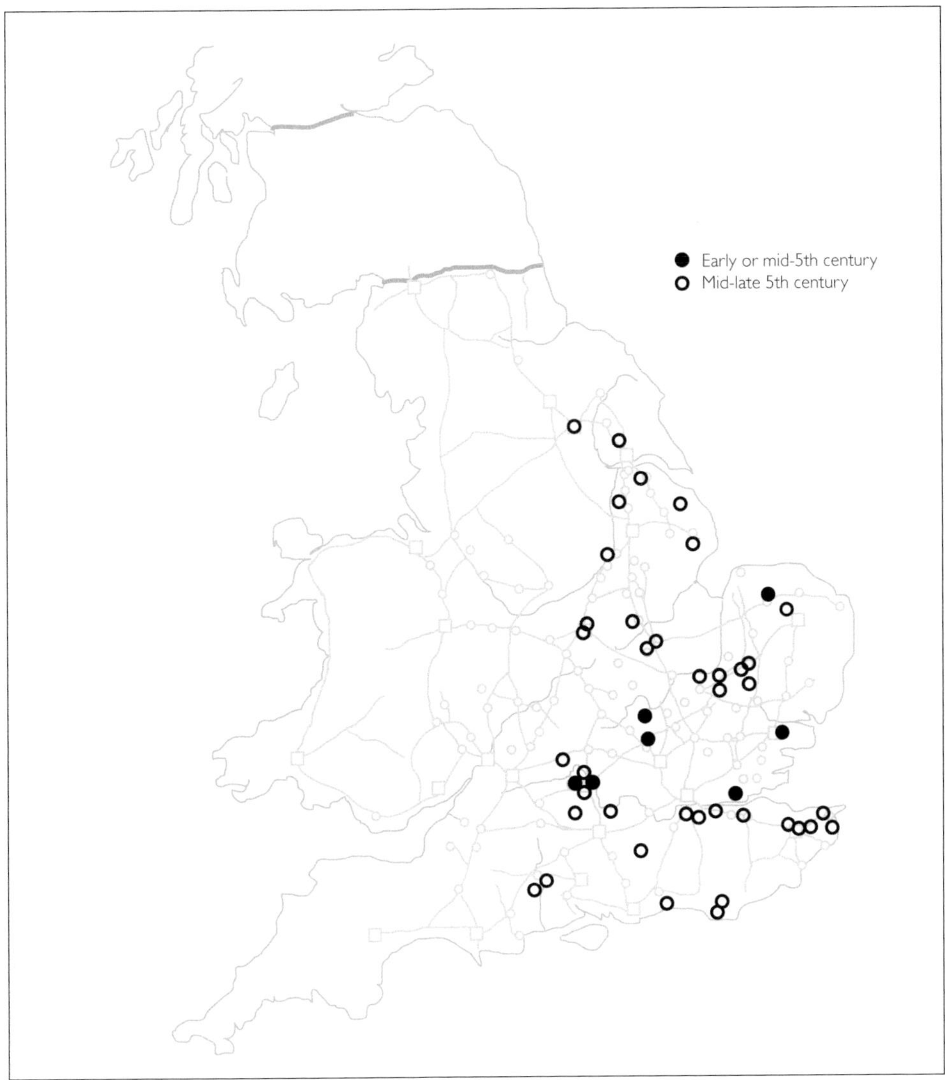


*32* Evidence of early Anglo-Saxon settlement at strategic spots around the borders of the Catuvellaunian/Trinovantian confederation. *(After Dark 2000 et al.)*

happened at the time. Therefore, it may be that rather than go in search of the real reasons for Vortigern's actions, Gildas simply latched on to the most obvious enemy (the Picts had certainly been a problem for the Roman-controlled part of Britain in the fourth century) and assumed the arrival of Hengest and Horsa was something to do with it.

If Vortigern did bring Anglo-Saxons into Kent his real motives may well have been tribal politics. One potential tribal threat has already been mentioned, in the shape of the Atrebates to the south of the Wallop battlefield. Quoit Brooch Style buckles are also found in Atrebatic territory, though most examples there come from later Anglo-Saxon graves so it is hard to be sure whether they arrived in Atrebatic territory at the time of Vortigern or long afterwards. Much closer than the Atrebates, though, just across the Thames, lay the old rivals for power in Kent, the Catuvellauni/Trinovantes.

As mentioned previously, the Dobunni probably held a grudge against the Catuvellauni anyway for seizing previously Dobunnic territory in the Upper Thames region. They may have already attempted to take revenge on the Catuvellauni in this area in the late second century and they may have tried again at the end of Roman rule. Certainly plenty of buckles and belt fittings from the period are found in the area. Even more relevant is the evidence from early Anglo-Saxon settlements around the borders of the Catuvellauni and Trinovantes, which seem to have been deliberately arranged by the Catuvellauni and Trinovantes themselves in order to defend their territory against external threats (*32*). It can't be coincidence that almost all the major land and river routes in and out of Catuvellaunian/Trinovantian territory are protected by these early Anglo-Saxon settlements, that these are historical evidence for Catuvellaunian control of some of these as late as 571, and that there is archaeological evidence in a number of these areas for cooperation between the early Anglo-Saxons and Britons.

For example, the major Anglo-Saxon settlement at West Stow in Suffolk is located directly next to the major late Roman site at Icklingham, with large quantities of Roman pottery and coinage being found at West Stow. The presence of Roman brooches, pottery, artefacts and coins in the early Anglo-Saxon cemetery at St John's College cricket field, Cambridge, has given rise to the suggestion that a mixed British and Anglo-Saxon community was burying and cremating its dead there. Similarly, excavations in the cemetery at Frilford have shown that only 13 cremations and 28 inhumations out of about 212 burials are characteristically Anglo-Saxon. Across the Thames at Barton Court Farm near Abingdon a small hut or cottage built on the site of a third-century villa seems to have been abandoned some time in the fifth century, but early fifth-century Germanic pottery is also found on the site suggesting two cultures coexisting.[30]

The zone of early Anglo-Saxon settlement in the Upper Thames region would presumably have guarded against Dobunnic incursions there. Another settlement was at Mucking, which lies just across the Thames estuary from Kent. At some stage too, a ring of Anglo-Saxon settlements appeared south of the Thames, apparently guarding the approaches to London from the south. These settlements should probably be understood as connecting with the ring around Catuvellaunian/Trinovantian territory north of the Thames. The name Surrey, for instance, is derived from '*suthre ge*', meaning 'southern region'. The term *ge* is thought to indicate a very early date for the name, and the fact that Surrey is called the southern region presumably indicates some kind of link with a northern region, this being, presumably, Catuvellaunian territory north of the Thames. Something similar is found in the names Suffolk (south folk) and

Norfolk (north folk) for the constituent parts of the kingdom of East Anglia. These Surrey settlements could be a reason why Vortigern would have invited Hengest and Horsa into Kent in the first place, or they may have developed later, after the Saxon rebellion, in response to the weakening of Vortigern's grip on the area. The two battles that can be located with any certainty, at Aylesford and Crayford, took place almost exactly on the dividing line between the Surrey Anglo-Saxon settlements and the culturally separate Anglo-Saxon and Jutish settlements in Kent.

There is one other potential tribal opponent that Vortigern might have wished Hengest and Horsa to confront: the Cantii, the tribe of Kent itself. If the Dobunni did control Kent, then it was a vulnerable territory at the end of a very long supply line from the Dobunnic heartlands. In that context, a garrison of Anglo-Saxon mercenaries personally loyal to Vortigern might have seemed a very attractive option in helping control unhappy locals.

Whatever the reasons for Vortigern's original invitation, things did not allegdly go to plan. Hengest and Horsa rebelled and fought four battles against the British. The Anglo-Saxon Chronicle tells us that the first battle, probably at Aylesford, was fought against Vortigern. The remaining three could also have been against Vortigern or his son Vortimer, as the *Historia Brittonum* suggests, or they could have been against other British enemies from different tribal backgrounds, or even against the Anglo-Saxon mercenaries of other British enemies.

There is one other element of the Vortigern story that is worth reviewing at this point, and that is the story of Hengest's daughter. According to the *Historia Brittonum*, British attempts to counter the rebellion of the Anglo-Saxon chiefs were hampered by Vortigern's infatuation with Hengest's daughter. Not only had Vortigern originally yielded Kent to Hengest in return for marriage to his daughter, but later British attacks on the Saxons were restrained because of this marriage bond. It is, of course, entirely possible that this romance is pure fiction and it should probably be treated as such. However, it is worth making one point. As we shall examine in more detail later, some early 'Anglo-Saxon' kings have British names, which suggests links between early Anglo-Saxon leaders and British aristocrats. There has been a tendency to assume any marriages would have consisted of male Anglo-Saxon leaders marrying British women. However, the presence of early fifth-century Anglo-Saxon women's brooches in many areas of early Anglo-Saxon settlement does suggest the presence of at least some early Anglo-Saxon women. In this context, therefore, the idea that Vortigern might have married Hengest's daughter is not inconceivable.

After the conflict with Hengest and Horsa, Vortigern disappears back into the obscurity from which he had briefly emerged. Two versions of his end are related in the *Historia Brittonum*. Neither particularly has the ring of truth, but either is possible. One story has Vortigern wandering the hills in despair, a broken man.

The other has him burning to death in one of his fortresses with his wives. The latter story, of course, seems rather similar to the last stand of Gerontius.

As to Vortigern's Dobunnic/Cornovian empire, if that is what it was, the Dobunnic part seems to have survived as late as 577, when the Anglo-Saxon Chronicle records a victory by Cuthwin and Ceawlin over the British kings of Cirencester, Gloucester and Bath at Deorham, assumed to be the village of Dyrham near Bath. The fact that the chronicle records separate kings for the three individual Dobunnic cities might suggest the fragmentation of Dobunnic territory, unless the three 'kings' were in fact just three commanders, but the fact that all three were fighting on the same side at the same battle suggests Dobunnic power was still a factor to be reckoned with up to that point. And even after 577 there is some suggestion of a continuing entity with borders rather similar to those of the Dobunnic core territories. The 'new' Anglo-Saxon kingdom of the Hwicce, which incorporated Cirencester, Worcester, Gloucester and probably Bath as well, looks suspiciously like the core of the old Dobunnic tribal territory/ *civitas* under a new name.[31] To the north, occupation of the *civitas* capital of the Cornovii at Wroxeter seems to have continued as late as the sixth or even seventh century and, eventually, as indicated above, the *civitas* of the Cornovii seems to have been transformed into the kingdom of Powys.[32]

# CHAPTER 3

# HENGEST

In 1949 a courageous and dedicated crew rowed a replica Viking ship (presumably at that time thought to be a close approximation to an early Anglo-Saxon ship) from Denmark to Thanet to commemorate the 1500th anniversary of the date given by the Anglo-Saxon Chronicle for the arrival of Hengest and Horsa in Britain (*33*). The ship was named *Hugin* after one of Odin's ravens, and today it can be seen sitting on the clifftop at Pegwell Bay, just a little way up the coast from the Roman fort at Richborough (*34*) and a place known as Ebbsfleet (the less well-known of the two present-day Kent Ebbsfleets). This is a commonly suggested location for the place called 'Ypwinesfleet' where the Chronicle says the brothers landed. At the time the *Hugin* set sail, it was widely taken for granted that Hengest and Horsa were real people and that the story of their being invited by Vortigern to Kent as mercenary muscle and subsequently rebelling was essentially the truth.

Of course, fashions change and in recent years there has been a tendency to write off Hengest and Horsa as myth. The main arguments for a mythical nature for the brothers can be briefly stated. For a start, there is the very fact that they are brothers. Founding pairs of brothers are known in other cultures, for instance, Romulus and Remus. Then there is the point that both their names essentially mean horse in Anglo-Saxon, Horsa being obvious and Hengest being a word for stallion. Finally, although later kings of Kent traced their lineage back to Hengest, they referred to themselves by the name Oiscingas, meaning descendants of Oisc, a character who seems to have ruled Kent after Hengest and Horsa. He is sometimes described as the son of Hengest, though that seems rather questionable.

Are these arguments convincing? The sibling issue doesn't seem too major a hurdle to the pair being real. It is true that pairs of brothers do sometimes appear in myths, but equally they also appear in history sometimes too. In the late sixth century, for instance, the brothers Ceawlin and Cutha/Cuthwulf jointly led the forces of the West Saxons for a time. Politics in post-Roman Britain was often

*33* The *Hugin* sailed from Denmark to Britain to commemorate the 1500th anniversary of the Anglo-Saxon Chronicle's date for the arrival of Hengest and Horsa in Britain.

*34* Richborough is very close to one of the two Ebbsfleets in Kent, the possible site of the landing of Hengest and Horsa.

a family game, with family members working together (or sometimes against each other).

On the other hand, it is also possible that Horsa represents some kind of poetic duplication of the character of Hengest, or perhaps an accidental one. It may be, for example, that Horsa ('the horse') was originally tacked on to Hengest's name as something like an explanation or translation, and was later mistaken for an entirely separate character. Certainly a figure called Hengest, who may be the same as the Kentish Hengest, appears on his own, without Horsa, in a story about a violent clash with the Frisians, and Horsa himself seems to disappear suspiciously rapidly from the story in Kent.

Such a poetic duplication would, of course, also explain the similar names, though there again that could also be explained by family connections. It is a well-known feature of Anglo-Saxon ruling families that they often chose alliterative names. As with Ceawlin and Cutha, 'C' seems to have been particularly popular in the early West Saxon royal family, with Cerdic, Cynric, Cadda, Coenbryht and Cædwalla also featuring in the royal list, while 'S' seems to have been favoured by the East Saxon royal family, with Sledda, Sæbert, Sexred, Sæward, Sigebert, Swithelm, Sighere, Sebbi, Sigeheard, Swæfred, Saelred, Swæfbert, Sigeric and Sigered all appearing in the list of kings.

Nor does the use of 'horse' or 'stallion' as a name seem to be automatically indicative of a mythical nature for these two characters. Most mythical characters have names that are nothing to do with animals, and equally plenty of historical characters have had names that contained animal references. Wulf or wolf, for instance, is a common element in Anglo-Saxon names (Cuthwulf, Eardwulf etc.), while the common Scandinavian name Bjorn means 'bear'. Gildas mentions two British kings of the period with the names Maglocunus and Cuneglasus, in which the 'cun–' element means 'hound'. This, of course, is even before we get on to the question of nicknames. Warriors and soldiers down the centuries have shown a particular fondness for animal *noms de guerre*. In the Balkan wars of the early 1990s, for instance, there was a positive menagerie on the battlefield. To name but a few of the units concerned, there were Cobras, Tigers, Lions and Panthers, plus separate units of Wolves fighting for the Serbs, the Croats and the Bosnians. I'm not aware of a unit of Stallions in Bosnia (although a white, winged horse was one symbol of the Bosnian 5th Corps), but in an age when horses were more associated with warfare than leisure activities, 'stallion' would be a perfect nickname for any warlord.

The confusion over the precise connection between Hengest and Oisc is interesting in terms of understanding what was happening in fifth-century Kent, but again does not seem fatal to the possibility that Hengest was probably a real historical figure. As we shall discuss later, there is archaeological evidence for at least two separate waves of Anglo-Saxon immigration into Kent in the fifth century, and it may well be that Hengest and Oisc in some sense represent these different waves.

The arguments in favour of Hengest being historical can also be stated succinctly. First, as discussed in the last chapter, the story of Hengest's rebellion as told in the Anglo-Saxon Chronicle tallies with the account of Gildas, who was writing perhaps less than a hundred years after the events, and by around the ninth century, when the Chronicle and *Historia Brittonum* were being written down (using earlier material), both Anglo-Saxons and Britons accepted as fact the basic account of Hengest and Horsa's rebellion against Vortigern and their founding of the kingdom of Kent. Secondly, as we have already seen, the account of their activities is consistent with a feasible reconstruction of Vortigern's life. Thirdly, there is nothing particularly mythical in the basic account of what Hengest and Horsa are supposed to have done: rebelling, fighting a few battles and founding a kingdom is hardly the stuff great mythology is made of (though the *Historia Brittonum* does spice things up a bit with some sex and feasting). Fourthly, and perhaps most significantly, even if there were no accounts of Vortigern inviting the brothers in as hired muscle, then the course of Roman and British history through the fourth and fifth centuries would make it extremely likely that similar figures did exist.

It is hard for those raised on a Hollywood version of history, in which firm-jawed soldiers conquered the world in the name of Rome, to understand quite how un-Roman the 'Roman' army actually was by the beginning of the fifth century. Behind the military uniformity, of course, it had been for centuries a thoroughly multi-national force, with men from across the Empire and beyond signing up for their years of service. However, by the fifth century the armed forces fighting on Rome's behalf were increasingly Germanic. The movement westwards of Germanic tribes in the fourth century not only brought new challenges for the imperial authorities, it also made available a seemingly inexhaustible supply of immigrant labour ready and willing to do the dirty and dangerous work of fighting for Rome (or for assorted factions attempting to seize power in Rome).

Germanic immigrants probably filled a significant percentage of the recruiting quotas of the remaining conventional units of the Roman army. So many figures in the upper echelons of the Roman army were Germans by this time that the rest of the army must logically have featured a high proportion of Germans as well. However, the Roman authorities also rapidly discovered that now there wasn't quite the same need to go to all the trouble of recruiting and running a conventional army. Groups of Germanic prisoners of war could be settled in local towns as garrisons (the *gentiles*) or larger groups could be settled elsewhere in the Empire and called upon to fight when needed (the *laeti* and the *foederati*). As a last resort a Roman commander facing a crisis might simply descend on the nearest available tribe and offer them cash for some 'freelance' fighting. Reliance on cohesive, self-administering Germanic groups within the Empire (as opposed to individual Germans fully integrated into Roman army units) obviously presented certain potential problems. In particular, it fostered the growth of independent German political entities within Roman borders, which would eventually lead to the collapse of the Western Roman Empire. However, in the meantime the Romans found their new supply of cheap Germanic fighters extremely useful.

Thus, for instance, the Roman general Constantius used Wallia and his Visigoths to force the Vandals and Alans out of Spain between 416 and 418. When Aëtius was faced with attacks by the *bagaudae* in Gaul in the 440s he sent Goar and his Alans against them, and when it came to tackling the Huns at the Catalaunian Plains in 451 Aëtius had Visigoths, Franks, Saxons and Sarmatians on his side, among other contingents. There is also a particularly telling example from the story of Gerontius, which, since he was British and presumably had other Britons in his command structure, is of particular interest. As touched upon in Chapter 1, when Gerontius rebelled against Constantine III, he persuaded the Vandals, Sueves and Alans who had crossed into the Empire in 406 to attack Constantine III, and when Gerontius managed to trap him in Arles, Constantine duly sent his general Edobichus, himself a Frank, to raise a relief army of Franks and Alemanni to fight for him. So one lot of Germans (plus the non-Germanic Alans) were supposed to fight a slightly different lot of Germans on behalf of two rivals for the imperial throne. Roman warfare in the fifth century was, in fact, fast becoming a drama played out by a high percentage of non-Roman actors.

Thus, if Vortigern decided that he needed some extra military muscle, then it would be no surprise if he went looking for Germanic mercenaries. And if, when reviewing his defence strategy, Vortigern needed any further persuading that outsourcing to the nearest available Germans was the route to follow, then he needed only to look at what his immediate neighbours were up to.

Just across the Channel, in an area that had had close contacts with Kent before the Roman invasion of Britain, and continued to have them long after Vortigern's time, a number of cities in northern France and Belgium were garrisoned by units of *laeti* and *gentiles*. The *Notitia Dignitatum*, in its typically bureaucratic way, lists the different units from different tribes settled in different towns. There were Batavian *laeti* and Suevian *gentiles* stationed at Bayeux and Coutances, Teutonic *laeti* at Chartres, Sarmatian *gentiles* in Paris, Lingonian *laeti* dispersed in Belgica Prima, Aeduan *laeti* at Epuso, Nervian *laeti* at Famars, Batavian *laeti* at Arras and Yvois-Carignan, unspecified *laeti* and *gentiles* at Reims and Senlis, Sarmatian *gentiles* between Reims and Amiens, and Lagensian *laeti* at Tongres. Archaeology also seems to confirm the presence of significant numbers of warriors equipped with a mixture of Roman and German equipment in the area at this time. At Vermand, Vron, Furfooz and Haillot male graves have been found containing Germanic weapons (notably curved *francisca* axes and *angons*, Germanic javelins with a long metal 'neck' attaching the spearhead to the wooden shaft) alongside distinctively Roman military kit like buckles and belt fittings.[1] Sometimes there are also female graves containing Germanic brooches. At Cortrat, for instance, among the graves of the local population were buried two men with belt-buckles and crossbow brooches of the type worn by the Roman military, and three women with triangular bone combs and Germanic brooches.[2] This may be archaeological proof of the *Notitia*'s evidence that *laeti* and *gentiles* were settled in the Empire to defend still-functioning Roman period towns, though this has recently been questioned.[3]

In Britain, as discussed, it seems that the early fifth-century Anglo-Saxon settlements to the north of Kent were deliberately planted in order to defend key strategic points along the border of the Catuvellaunian/Trinovantian confederation, suggesting that the authorities there had already adopted contemporary continental custom and recruited Germans to bolster their own tribal militia long before Vortigern did the same.[4] It was clearly an effective strategy, since the entry in the Anglo-Saxon Chronicle for the year 571 indicates that a swathe of this territory, including some of the areas of early Anglo-Saxon settlement, was still under some form of British control as late as the second half of the sixth century. The pattern seen on the European mainland of Germanic brooches appearing in cemeteries alongside fifth-century Roman belt fittings is repeated in and around Catuvellaunian/Trinovantian territory. Not surprisingly, considering that Britain was no longer part of the Empire by this time, the belt fittings are not found in such quantities here as they are across the Channel. Nevertheless, they are here, and they are of a distinctive type (a dragon buckle with fixed plate – *see colour plate 14*) that is probably of too late a date to have arrived in Britain before 410. They are therefore likely to have been brought from the continent by the newly recruited Germanic troops.[5]

What's more, as one might expect, bearing in mind the prevalence of the practice in mainland Europe, other British tribes/*civitates* also seem to have been operating their own German recruitment programme at the same time as, or possibly even before, Vortigern was making his fateful decision. In the territory of the Iceni and the Corieltauvi, and in the *civitas* of the Belgae, early to mid fifth-century Anglo-Saxon settlement echoes the distribution of Roman-period towns and settlements, and may have been arranged strategically to defend against attacks by neighbouring tribes. The earliest Anglo-Saxon settlement in Icenian territory is in the west, away from the North Sea coast, but it is at Spong Hill and very close to a Roman settlement as well as the linear earthworks known as Launditch and Panworth Ditch, which may be of post-Roman date (in their final form[6]) and seem to mark out a 'front line' facing the Fens. Judging by the Roman road network and ceramic evidence in the area, the Fens were at this time likely to have been controlled by the Corieltauvi or Catuvellauni.[7] Furthermore, mixed in with the cremation graves at Spong Hill are some inhumation graves which it has been argued might represent Britons living alongside the newcomers.[8] In Corieltauvian territory early Anglo-Saxon settlement clusters around the tribe's northern border with the Parisi and Brigantes, and around the tribe's southern borders. There is a particularly strong correlation in the area between Roman period settlements and early Anglo-Saxon cemeteries.[9] In the territory of the Belgae there is evidence of an early Anglo-Saxon presence at the *civitas* capital Winchester in the form of a cluster of supporting arm brooches found a long way from other areas of their distribution in Britain.[10] There is also evidence of early Anglo-Saxon settlement in the region around Salisbury, which is located on the western edge of the Atrebatic portion of the *civitas* of the Belgae and would have been close to both Durotrigan and Dobunnic territory. The presence of the late Roman or post-Roman Bokerley Dyke on the border between the Durotriges and the *civitas* of the Belgae marks this out as a zone of probable conflict and thus a good place to plant Anglo-Saxon mercenaries.

With all this going on in the territories around Kent, it would be frankly surprising if Vortigern had not invited in somebody like Hengest with his followers to add a little extra muscle to his forces in Kent. Equally, it would also be surprising, bearing in mind Kent's extremely close relationship with the continent, if Hengest and his followers were the first Germanic fighters recruited there. It comes as no surprise, therefore, to learn that indeed there are signs that Germanic warriors may have been in Kent in the post-Roman but pre-Hengest period.

For a start, a number of the early fifth-century Roman buckles associated with areas of early Anglo-Saxon settlement around the borders of the Catuvellaunian/Trinovantian confederation have also been found in Kent.[11] Assuming Hengest really did arrive in Kent some time around the dates suggested by Bede (AD 445), the Anglo-Saxon Chronicle (449) and one of the various dates suggested by the *Historia Brittonum* (the end of Roman Britain plus 40 years = 450), then the buckles may be too early to have arrived with him and his followers.

Then there is the question of the origins of Quoit Brooch Style. As mentioned in the last chapter, this is a style of metalwork that first appears in Kent in the early fifth century and seems to combine Dobunnic style with elements derived from continental Roman buckle and belt design of the period.

In the late fourth and early fifth centuries a style of decoration that has become known as chip-carving became common on buckles and belt fittings made along the Empire's German frontier (*colour plate 12*). It is called chip-carving because the individual design elements seem to have been chipped out when the original pattern was created, giving the final designs a markedly three-dimensional effect. As with Quoit Brooch Style, the origins of

*35* Anglo-Saxon chip carving.

chip-carving are controversial. Some of the patterns clearly feature classical elements, but the overall effect of chip-carving marks a clear break with the classical past and contemporary classical designs. It is worth noting, for instance, that chip-carved belt fittings remain very largely separate from late Roman dolphin and plain-loop buckle designs. There is little cross-fertilisation of design. Of the large numbers of chip-carved buckles I've seen, only two are hybrids that incorporate any dolphin elements.

Perhaps even more to the point, chip-carving also represents a clear break with the classical future (at least the future from the early fifth-century point of view). Chip-carving never became as popular in the Eastern Roman Empire, and while Byzantine buckle design retained other features of late Roman western buckle designs (such as the use of pairs of dolphins to form the top of the buckle loop), chip-carving never became a significant feature of Byzantine buckles and belt fittings.[12] It is also worth noting that chip-carving was never adopted on buckles and belt fittings made in fourth- and fifth-century Britain beyond Kent. By contrast, it became immensely popular throughout the Germanic world and became the bedrock of early Anglo-Saxon metalwork design, featuring on a wide range of items (*35*).

It's a controversial idea, but there do seem to be reasons to think that chip-carving should be associated not necessarily with late Roman soldiers in general,

*36* Fifth-century Quoit Brooch. *(After Suzuki, 2000)*

but perhaps mainly with late Roman soldiers of Germanic extraction. Traditionally, the Romans regarded it as one of the defining features of 'barbarians' that they had 'flashy' tastes,[13] and metalwork doesn't get much flashier than the large chip-carved belt sets of the late fourth and fifth centuries. In their original bright, shining metal, the densely packed swirls, borders and other design features of chip-carving raised into sharp 3D would have looked anything but understated, and the sheer size and quantity of belt fittings that made up some belt sets would have packed a huge visual punch. Whether chip-carving was originally designed to appeal specifically to Germanic troops in the Roman army or whether it was just rapidly adopted by them as their own isn't clear, but the comparative rejection of chip-carving in non-Germanic areas and its overwhelming acceptance in Germanic areas does suggest that where chip-carved belt fittings are found, there is a possible link to the presence of Germanic troops.

If this is true, then the influence of Germanic troops may be indicated by those Quoit Brooch Style items where chip-carving is more prominent than the typically Dobunnic incised lines. The presence at Alfriston on one Quoit Brooch Style item, probably dating from the period 420–450, of a ribbed, kidney-shaped buckle of a type that is also found in burials of Germanic warriors within the Roman Empire also seems to support the idea that chip-carved Quoit Brooch Style may indicate the presence of Germanic troops in Kent in that period.[14]

One interesting aspect of Quoit Brooch Style that differentiates it from other regional styles of metalwork in late and post-Roman Britain is the presence of a number of pieces in northern France, just across the Channel. An early Quoit Brooch for instance comes from Bénouville, and there's a Quoit Brooch Style buckle from Amiens.[15] As mentioned in Chapter 1, a few (non-Quoit Brooch Style) British buckles and belt fittings have been found in Europe, but these have almost all been in southern Europe and are likely to be related to the activities of Magnus Maximus and Constantine III. The presence of Quoit Brooch Style metalwork on the other side of the Channel suggests links between post-Roman Kent and early fifth-century Gaul. Considering that this part of Gaul was garrisoned by Germanic *laeti* and *gentiles*, it may even have been the case that Kent was drawing Germanic troops from this area at this time. The presence of *francisca* axes at Richborough might support this conclusion.[16] These curved axes were commonly used by the Franks, and since the Franks were to have a close connection with the Anglo-Saxon kingdom of Kent (Anglo-Saxon burials in Kent, for instance, display Frankish influence on dress, drink and weapons), it would seem not unreasonable for them to have had a connection with a pre-Anglo-Saxon British kingdom there.

Yet, if Kent had an existing pre-Hengest connection with suppliers of Germanic troops just across the Channel, it is hard to know why Vortigern would suddenly wish to introduce Anglo-Saxons into his military mix. Perhaps he was influenced by the use of Anglo-Saxons by the Catuvellauni and Trinovantes to the north. Perhaps the Anglo-Saxons were cheaper. Or it may be that Frankish soldiers with spare time on their hands had suddenly become in short supply. The whole area of northern Gaul and Belgium that could theoretically have been supplying Kent with Germanic recruits before Hengest was overrun by the Huns in 451, at almost exactly the same time as Hengest's traditional arrival in Kent. Even before that, Aëtius the Roman commander in Gaul and Attila had been supporting opposing factions in a civil war within Frankish territory. Situations like these could easily have prompted Vortigern to seek a new supplier. It is perhaps worth noting in this context the Anglo-Saxon Chronicle entry for 443, a few years before the alleged arrival of Hengest and Horsa, which remarks that in that year the Britons sought overseas help from the Romans but received none because

*37* Later Anglo-Saxon annular brooch.

of the war against Attila, and it was at that point that the Britons turned for help to the Angles.

The nature of this new supplier is, perhaps inevitably, slightly hazy. Bede describes Kent as being settled by Jutes, and certainly there is evidence of contact between Jutland and Kent in the late fifth century, not least in the form of bracteates and square-headed brooches from Kent which have close parallels in the Jutland area.[17] The earliest date for such square-headed brooches in Kent is, however, probably in the 470s or 480s, and the Anglo-Saxon Chronicle, for what it's worth on this point, does describe Hengest and his followers as Angles not Jutes. As it happens, the period between 450 and 470 in Kent is indeed dominated in terms of brooch finds by Anglian cruciform brooches (with a smattering of Saxon forms such as the late supporting arm brooch from Eastry, and probably, though the dates are a little uncertain, later examples of Quoit Brooch Style items).[18] Slightly confusingly, most of the Quoit Brooches themselves are among these later examples, even though the whole style, including earlier pieces such as the buckles with Dobunnic-type decoration, is named after them (*36*). These Quoit Brooches are round brooches made out of a flat ribbon of metal, either as a full circle or with a small break in the ring. As with so much concerning Quoit Brooch Style, the origin of the Quoit Brooch form itself is controversial. However, it has been suggested that the appearance of very similar brooches (though without Quoit

Brooch Style designs) across areas of Anglian settlement in East Anglia and the north in the late fifth and sixth centuries (*37*) might possibly suggest some kind of Scandinavian connection (though if so, the mechanics of the connection are obscure).

We should not, however, be too determined to label Hengest as either Jutish or Anglian (or anything else). As with many other periods of history that have witnessed almost continuous warfare and massive displacement of civilian populations, the fifth century was almost certainly a time when often quite ethnically mixed groups of armed men were ready to fight for almost anybody for the right money. On the continent, for example, large armed groups of different peoples were cooperating with one another. The Germanic Sueves and Vandals and the non-Germanic Alans crossed Gaul and entered Spain in a more or less coordinated movement in the early fifth century, and we have already mentioned the large number of different peoples found in the army of Aëtius at the battle of the Catalaunian Plains. We do not have so much information on the smaller armed groups of the time, but they must have existed and some would have been of equally mixed ethnic origin. And it is just possible that we have a snapshot of just such a mixed group, perhaps even incorporating Hengest himself, prior to his allegedly winning the contract with Vortigern.

Hidden within the English epic *Beowulf* is a story within a story, where Hrothgar's bard sings a tale about a battle at a place called Finnsburg. This story is backed up by another rare surviving fragment of Anglo-Saxon poetry, the Finnsburg Fragment. The overall story that can be pieced together from these two sources is a dramatic one of international treachery, murder and vicious combat, and at its heart is a character called Hengest.

As far as the story can be reconstructed, a Dane named Hnæf spends the winter with his brother-in-law Finn, a Frisian, at his hall known as Finnsburg. However, some kind of dispute takes place and there is a dramatic night attack during which Hnæf is left fighting for his life in the hall where he has been sleeping with his men:

> So the king, new to combat, spoke,
> There is no dawn rising nor
> dragon flying nor hall's beams blazing,
> but men attack, war birds scream,
> the grey wolf howls, spears shake
> and shields clang. Wandering moon
> shines through cloud and crimes
> will be done, causing our people's pain.
> Wake up, my warband, now.

Hold your shields and yourselves firm,
Fight at the front and have courage.

(The Finnsburg Fragment)

The defence goes well, according to the Finnsburg Fragment, but somewhere along the way Hnæf must have been killed, because in *Beowulf* he is depicted being burnt on a funeral pyre with Finn's son (presumably another casualty of the battle), while Hnæf's sister Hildebuh mourns. Hengest seems to have taken over what remained of Hnæf's war-band and negotiated some kind of deal with Finn. Ultimately, however, this deal too seems to have broken down and Hengest kills the Frisian Finn.

There is, of course, no way of proving that this Hengest is the same Hengest said to have been invited into Kent by Vortigern, but Hengest is not a particularly common name and it's certainly not impossible. The early cruciform brooches found in Kent, for instance, have parallels in both Frisia and Scandinavia,[19] which might fit with the kind of adventure described in the Finn story. One thing that is clear is that the world of Finnsburg was precisely the kind of world Hengest and his followers would have inhabited before striking it lucky in Kent.

It is interesting to note in the Finnsburg story the recurrent theme of broken deals, since a broken deal is of course one of the things Hengest is best known for in relation to Kent. In the words of Gildas:

> In this way the barbarians were imported into the island as soldiers, deceitfully stating that they were ready to tackle grave dangers on behalf of their generous hosts. They demanded, and received, supplies which for a time, as they say, kept the dog's jaws busy. Then they start complaining that their rations weren't generous enough, working the situation up into a crisis and threatening that, unless supplies are increased, they would tear up the contract and decimate the island. Shortly afterwards they put their threats into action.
>
> (Gildas, *On the Ruin of Britain*, 23)

The word Gildas uses for the contract between the *superbus tyrannus* and his mercenaries is the Latin word *foedus*. This is extremely significant because it explicitly marks them out as *foederati*, like so many of the Germanic troops fighting for the Romans in mainland Europe.

Earlier Quoit Brooch Style items extend into areas like Hampshire and Wiltshire, perhaps indicating the spread of Vortigern's empire. Later Quoit Brooch Style items, however, including most of the Quoit Brooches themselves, are mainly restricted to Kent, which would fit well with the notion of Kent being severed from its Dobunnic supply lines by Hengest's rebellion.[20]

*38* Faesten Dic, a probably post-Roman linear defensive earthwork, very close to the site of one of Hengest's battles at Crayford.

As touched upon in the last chapter, it is not entirely clear which specific enemy Vortigern would have had in mind when he started handing out rations to Hengest and his followers. It might have been the Picts, as Gildas implies, or the Catuvellauni, or perhaps Ambrosius to the west. However, very soon Hengest turned on his former employer and the Anglo-Saxon Chronicle for 455 records Hengest fighting Vortigern probably at Aylesford. The 457 entry, however, merely records Hengest fighting at Crayford against unspecified Britons who fled to London. Similarly the 465 and 473 entries simply record Hengest's victories over anonymous Britons. A location is given for only one of these battles, that at 'Wippedesfleote', and this is now unlocatable. The *Historia Brittonum* account insists that four battles were fought against Vortimer, Vortigern's son. However, assuming these are the same four battles, the *Historia Brittonum*'s account differs substantially from the Chronicle in making the last battle a clear victory for the Britons, while the Chronicle makes it a clear victory for Hengest. It is, of course, entirely possible for two opposing sides to claim victory in the same battle, especially if the outcome was rather indecis ive. Alternatively, it is possible that the writer of the *Historia Brittonum* chose to make his story more palatable to a Welsh audience and simply created a new account in which the Britons ended up triumphant, and assumed that all Hengest's battles were against Vortigern and his family, when a number of other enemies were probably just as likely.

The reference to Britons fleeing to London is an interesting one. Ptolemy, a second-century geographer, indicated that London was a town of the Cantii and therefore connected to Kent. However, it is more likely that by the second half of the fifth century the London area was controlled by the Catuvellauni. Certainly London was well within Catuvellaunian territory under Cunobelin, and the appearance of Anglo-Saxon settlements to the south of London, closing the strategic ring defending Catuvellaunian/Trinovantian territory, implies that it was again in the second half of the fifth century. So, the 457 battle may have been a clash with the Catuvellauni.

In his two subsequent battles Hengest could have been fighting either Vortigern and/or Vortimer or the Catuvellauni, or he could have been involved in fighting with a third enemy, perhaps against the *civitas* of the Regni in present-day Sussex. It is interesting to note that the Anglo-Saxon warlord Ælle is recorded by the Anglo-Saxon Chronicle as arriving in Sussex just four years after Hengest's last recorded battle. This may merely suggest that the Chronicler had two stories to tell and decided to slot one in after the other for ease of narrative, but equally it could indicate some kind of connection, perhaps with Ælle being invited in by the British authorities to counter Hengest.

Interestingly enough, the date of 473 for Hengest's last recorded battle is also roughly consistent with the arrival in Kent of the more distinctively Jutish brooches and artefacts mentioned earlier. It has been suggested, plausibly enough, that this represents a second wave of Anglo-Saxon immigration into Kent, a wave that might conceivably be connected with Oisc, the mysterious figure who is said to have succeeded Hengest.[21]

We have already mentioned the apparent discrepancy here. While the Anglo-Saxon Chronicle records Esc/Oisc as Hengest's son, and the later Anglo-Saxon kings of Kent did trace their lineage back to Hengest, they actually referred to themselves as Oiscingas, the descendants of Oisc, which perhaps indicates some kind of disconnection between the two. It has been suggested that Oisc was a Jutish leader who took over Kent from Hengest, and so was his successor in that way rather than inheriting the kingdom from him as a son.

How the assorted rulers of Kent in the fifth century were connected to one another is not entirely clear, nor can we tell at this distance how the local population reacted to them. However, there is evidence to suggest that it may all have been rather more complicated than the simplistic idea of war-crazed invaders running amok through a cowering local population. There may, of course, have been an element of that, certainly at the beginning of Anglo-Saxon control, but we should not necessarily assume it continued.

For a start, if and when Hengest rebelled against Vortigern, it is conceivable that the local Cantii might have sided with Hengest against Vortigern. A distant Dobunnic warlord controlling an expansionist Dobunnic/Cornovian confederation is unlikely to have been greeted with open arms by the Cantii, and just as the Atrebates and Iceni seem to have supported the Roman invaders under Claudius against the expansionist Catuvellaunian/Trinovantian confederation, so the Cantii may have seen the arrival of Hengest as a chance to dislodge Vortigern from their territory.

In his description of the Anglo-Saxon revolt Gildas paints a lurid picture of death and destruction among the Britons. For example, he writes:

> So the columns were flattened by blows from battering rams and the cities, together with their bishops, priests and people, were devastated amidst flashing blades and crackling flames. A sad sight, in the middle of the streets lay the tops of tall turrets thrown down, the stone of high walls, sacred altars. There were body parts, covered in a crust of crimson, looking as if they had been squeezed in some terrible press and with no hope of burial except in the ruins of houses or in the stomachs of birds or beasts.
>
> (Gildas, *On the Ruin of Britain*, 24)

However, one should probably take this with a large pinch of salt, certainly as it relates to mid fifth-century Britain. Gildas seems to know a fair bit about Britain before the end of Roman rule, but seems much hazier on later events. He seems to have used Anglo-Saxon saga sources to flesh out his knowledge, and his account here also appears to borrow heavily from classical or biblical

*39* St Martin's, Canterbury. The building contains much Roman material in its fabric and may represent some form of continuity from the Roman period.

literary descriptions of urban destruction. In addition, Gildas clearly loathed the Saxons, and was therefore unlikely to do anything but criticise the way they set up the first specifically Anglo-Saxon kingdom. Apart from anything else, he must have despised the fact that they were pagans. Among his stock descriptions of destruction, Gildas lays a notable emphasis on what the Saxons are supposed to have done to churches and churchmen.

Certainly the fact that Hengest's first two recorded battles were on the western borders of Kent would not suggest that he faced substantial internal opposition, and generally there seems to be a great sense of continuity in Kent from the Roman period into the Anglo-Saxon period, which again does not support the idea of the apocalyptic destruction described by Gildas.

The name Kent itself is, of course, a survival of the name of the Cantii, whose capital, Durovernum/Canterbury, may have remained a major centre from Roman times right through into Anglo-Saxon times. There is some evidence for a continued British presence in Canterbury into the fifth century, and a British church may have survived there under the early Anglo-Saxons. In addition, unlike in many other Roman-period towns, there is evidence of early Anglo-Saxon settlement inside Canterbury itself, with sunken-featured buildings dating to the fifth and sixth centuries being found there.[22] In the countryside round about, the major estates and the regions/lathes of the Anglo-Saxon period may reflect Roman administrative arrangements and it is noticeable that many Anglo-Saxon estate centres were located on the same sites as Roman-period villas or settlements.[23] The division of Kent into West Kent based on Rochester and East Kent based on Canterbury also seems to have survived from pre-Roman into Roman and then Anglo-Saxon times.

As elsewhere in Britain, it is true that it is hard to find specific archaeological evidence of Britons in Kent in the late fifth century. However, this is not just an issue with Britain. In areas like the Moselle valley we have good historical evidence for the local populations continuing in existence after the arrival of new Germanic overlords, but they are still largely invisible archaeologically.[24] It may be that we just have to accept that almost all the things that make Britons of the fourth century so archaeologically visible – the mass-produced artefacts of Roman culture – were suddenly gone.

It has been claimed that the fact this book has been written in English rather than in Welsh is evidence that few Britons remained in the east of England, the idea being that if many had, their language would have remained in England as well. Proponents of this argument point across the Channel to France's new Germanic invaders, the Franks, who adopted the local existing language rather than imposing their own language. One problem with this line of argument, however, is that the local language in question was not the original Gallic language of the locals' ancestors, but the Latin they had adopted from the previous invaders. A variant of the language argument points out that there are very few instances of Celtic words being adopted into early English. This is certainly true, but equally only about a hundred Celtic words were adopted into early French.[25] However, we do not even know if the Britons of southern, central and eastern England were speaking a Celtic language when the Anglo-Saxons arrived. It seems much more likely that, like their neighbours across the Channel, these culturally Roman Britons had also become linguistically Roman.[26] If they then changed language again, to become linguistically Anglo-Saxon, you would expect there to be even fewer Celtic words surviving here than in France where the language had only changed once. There are many Latin loan words in early English. Many were adopted before the Anglo-Saxons arrived in England. When the rest were adopted is not always entirely clear. Recent research into early English is focusing on Celtic structures in the language rather than vocabulary.

Even Gildas, in the midst of his anti-Saxon diatribe, is prepared to admit that a significant body of Britons stayed on under new Germanic management,[27] and it has to be said that the idea of large scale ethnic cleansing is not something that existed so much in the ancient world. Populations, of course, shifted and changed over the centuries, and there were plenty of invasions and conquests, sometimes including the attempted eradication of individual cities. But there are very few instances of new immigrants eradicating an entire race within a few years or decades of their arrival. It is certainly not something that any of the Germanic invaders of Western Europe and North Africa at the end of the Roman period even attempted. Relations with the locals were not always exactly warm, but there is no question anywhere of a policy of deliberate mass extermination or of driving an entire race into exile. People generally lacked the organisation, logistics and political/racial motivation needed for such a course. Even where an area was conquered by force, an accommodation would eventually be reached in which the new conquerors took over the top slots, imposed elements of their culture (if they came in large enough numbers) and in a fairly short time period intermixed with their new subjects.

In the light of all this we should almost certainly see Kent in the late fifth century as containing a good number of Britons who had adopted Anglo-Saxon ways and culture and effectively become, at least in archaeological terms, Anglo-Saxon, just as their ancestors had adopted Roman ways and become in archaeological terms Roman.

This is a conclusion that seems obvious but it was, and still is, often resisted on the grounds that Roman culture with its baths and sculpture and all the rest of it was so allegedly superior to early Anglo-Saxon culture with its sunken-floored huts that nobody would voluntarily swap one for the other. The argument, though, is false on a number of grounds. Most crucially, whatever culture the Britons may have had by the time the Anglo-Saxons arrived, it wasn't anything like the luxuries of Pompeii, and not all that close to the affluent lifestyle of a rich early fourth-century villa owner. By the time the Anglo-Saxons appeared on the scene, Roman buildings were almost all decaying fast and the more luxurious and modern aspects of Roman lifestyle were already just a memory. The low-tech Anglo-Saxon lifestyle was probably both more effective and more appealing in this context.

What is more, the new Anglo-Saxon culture may even have been more aesthetically appealing to the Britons. A number of aspects of early Anglo-Saxon culture (some of the brooches, for instance) are appealing enough. Perhaps more to the point, they could easily have carried attractive cultural messages. Part of the appeal of Roman culture to Britons in the period up to the mid-fourth century would have lain in its implicit message of power and wealth. But there are signs that in the late fourth century and increasingly in the fifth aspects of Germanic culture across the Empire were becoming more closely associated with power. It has even been argued that Roman soldiers of the period adopted elements of Germanic style in order to link themselves with perceived Germanic qualities of fierceness and success in battle.[28] Similarly, in the new Germanic kingdoms in mainland Europe, even though Roman culture survived there much more strongly than it did in Britain, there is plenty of evidence of locals adopting the culture of the new Germanic elites. Theoderic in Italy, for instance, is recorded as saying, rather wittily, that while rich Goths imitated Romans, poor Romans imitated Goths, and there is the interesting case of the Roman aristocrat Cyprian who learnt the Gothic language and had his sons trained in Gothic military matters.[29] Once Anglo-Saxons started becoming powerful and influential within British tribal territories, so a lot of the perceived attributes that had once belonged to Roman culture would rapidly have become attached to Anglo-Saxon culture instead.

# CHAPTER 4

# AMBROSIUS

Tracing the path of British history as it wends its way through the murkier parts of the fifth century is often a hazy occupation, with characters like Vortigern and Hengest lurking just on the margins of knowledge. When we turn to Ambrosius, though, a sudden burst of clear light blows away the fog. Or so it seems at first.

Gildas, writing probably less than a hundred years later, mentions Ambrosius Aurelianus quite explicitly, with no potentially ambiguous reference to a *superbus tyrannus*:

> So that they should not be entirely destroyed, they take up arms under the command of Ambrosius Aurelianus, a modest man, who perhaps alone of the Roman people had survived such a storm, even though his parents, of course robed in purple, had been killed in the same catastrophe. His descendants, in our times, have failed to live up to their ancestor's greatness but, under Ambrosius, the Britons challenged their previously victorious enemy and, with the Lord's assent, won.
>
> (Gildas, *On the Ruin of Britain*, 25)

The passage comes after Gildas' description of the rebellion by Hengest and his dramatic (and probably exaggerated) account of a Saxon rampage, and the basic sense is that under the command of Ambrosius the Britons gathered their strength, regrouped and took on the invaders.

However, Gildas does not content himself with making this particular point. In addition, he makes reference both to the origins of Ambrosius and to his descendants, and chooses to depict Ambrosius as almost the sole survivor of the Roman people, a rather curious description which has given rise to endless speculation about his connections with the continent and continental politics. However, to a monk writing in a sixth-century Britain that had deliberately rejected, or certainly lost, most of the trappings of Roman culture, the phrase could easily have meant no more than 'almost the last of those keeping to Roman ways'. Certainly, Ambrosius himself does not seem to have come from the continent as an adult, because Gildas says his parents were killed in the Saxon rampage, 'of course robed in purple'. This is another curious and controversial phrase. It has recently been argued that what Gildas is saying here could be a reference to martyrdom, with the purple (or crimson) representing blood.[1] This is certainly possible, though the fact that Gildas uses the separate word *occisis* to say bluntly and directly that Ambrosius' parents had been killed renders needless and repetitive an indirect comment about them being 'robed in scarlet' to denote their slaughter. Therefore, it seems best to accept the traditional understanding that being 'robed in purple' is a reference to the parents exercising some kind of administrative authority somewhere in Britain. The description of Ambrosius as *vir modestus*, 'a modest man', does not prevent this interpretation. It has been argued that this phrase suggests Ambrosius had humble origins, but it is more likely that Gildas is using *modestus* here in direct contrast to his earlier description of Vortigern as *superbus tyrannus*. Gildas portrays Ambrosius as a respectable and respected leader against the Saxons, a man who epitomises Christian modesty. Vortigern, on the other hand, is shown as proud and arrogant, the ruler who invited the Saxons into Britain. This approving approach is supported by the way in which Gildas describes the descendants of Ambrosius, who have 'failed to live up to their ancestor's greatness' (or possibly ancestors' greatness, since the Latin here could mean either).

Gildas' Latin becomes rather unclear at the end of this section, but it seems to make most sense if the reference to a victory over the invaders is attributed to Ambrosius himself, rather than to his descendants.

In the paragraph after his description of Ambrosius Aurelianus, Gildas makes a reference to the British victory at the siege of Badon Hill:

> From that time, sometimes the citizens conquered, sometimes the enemy, so that the Lord might, in his usual way, find out whether this nation, the Israel of today, loves Him or not. This was the situation up to the year of the siege of Badon Hill, almost the most recent, and not the least, of the slaughters suffered by these rogues.
>
> (Gildas, *On the Ruin of Britain*, 26)

However, despite the assumption of many that Ambrosius Aurelianus must have been the British commander at Badon, there is nothing in Gildas' original text to justify such an assumption. His mention of Badon comes after his description of Ambrosius, and he seems to locate it in the period *after* the fight-back under Ambrosius, a period in which both Britons and Saxons had military successes. Of course, Ambrosius could have been the commander at Badon, but Gildas does not say so specifically and, bearing in mind his obvious admiration for Ambrosius, it seems likely that he would have done so, if Ambrosius was.

Sadly, despite Gildas' comparatively full (by the standards of post-Roman historiography) description of this particular sequence of events, there is no evidence at all of where Ambrosius was conducting his operations. There is a reference just before the Ambrosius passage that refers to Britons taking refuge in 'mountains, steep places, thick forests and sea rocks'. This at first sight looks interesting but is in fact a fairly stock description by Gildas of wild places, and he uses rather similar phrases, earlier in his diatribe, about Britons fleeing the Picts:

> Meanwhile, a terrible and infamous famine afflicts the wandering and uncertain people, forcing many of them to surrender to the bloodthirsty bandits so that they could find a little nourishment to keep them alive. Others, though, managed to avoid this and rather continued to fight back from hills, caves, valleys and thick forests.
>
> (Gildas, *On the Ruin of Britain*, 20)

What's more, even if Ambrosius was present at the battle of Badon, or it took place in roughly the same area as his sphere of operations (which at least seems likely from the text), this does not help much. There is no agreement today on where the battle of Badon was located, with proponents of different regions identifying a wide variety of potential sites with names somewhat similar to Badon Hill. And since the proposed sites range all the way across Britain from south to north, west to east, we are no further forward.

Fortunately, however, we are not entirely reliant on Gildas in tracking down Ambrosius Aurelianus. There is evidence from other sources which could suggest not only where Ambrosius was located, but also potentially some significant details about who he was and what he was up to.

We have, of course, met Ambrosius before, as the opponent of Vitalinus at the battle of Guoloph/Wallop. This tradition of conflict between Vortigern's family and Ambrosius seems to be amplified by a brief aside in the *Historia Brittonum* to the effect that during Vortigern's reign the Britons (presumably Vortigern's Britons rather than Britons in general) lived in fear of Ambrosius. If, therefore, it is correct to see Vitalinus and Vortigern as representatives of an aggressive Dobunnic/Cornovian confederation expanding into Atrebatic territory, then it seems logical, bearing in mind the probably tribal nature of post-Roman politics and war in Britain, that Ambrosius might be an essentially Atrebatic figure.

As discussed in Chapter 2, it seems possible that the Dobunni overran the Atrebatic area around Silchester at some time around the end of the Roman period. This area, however, was only a part of the vast territory occupied by the Atrebates in pre-Roman times, which was divided up by the Romans into three separate administrative areas or *civitates*. The region around Silchester possibly occupied by the Dobunni would correspond to the Roman-period *civitas* of the Atrebates. Directly to the south of this, though, lay the *civitas* of the Belgae, which was unique among Roman-period British *civitates* in that it seems to have been cobbled together from two separate units, with a western half carved from formerly Dobunnic territory and tacked on to an eastern, ethnically Atrebatic half (*40*).

*40* Milestone erected by *R(es) P(ublica) Belgarum*, the *civitas* of the Belgae.

*41* Dobunnic buckle plate from Silchester. *(After Hawkes & Dunning, 1961)*

There is evidence – in the form of hoards, buckle distribution, the collapse of the massive New Forest pottery industry and a string of burnt villas lying along very much the same line as Wansdyke, that great defensive linear earthwork,[2] of conflict along the border between the *civitas* of the Belgae and the Dobunni towards the end of the Roman period (*colour plate 16*). Subsequently, judging by the cultural differences that are evident to the south and north of Wansdyke (to the south hillforts are reoccupied and imported Mediterranean pottery is found, while to the north neither of these apply, but grass-tempered pottery, which is very rare to the south of Wansdyke, is found), the western half of the *civitas* of the Belgae seems to have been absorbed by the Durotriges from the south.[3]

This carve-up, however, still left the eastern, Atrebatic half of the *civitas* of the Belgae. What happened in this area at the end of the Roman period is far from clear. However, the cemetery at Lankhills, Winchester has produced rare evidence of what appear to be Pannonian troops billeted here in the 370s or 380s, well before the end of Roman control. In a cemetery where late Roman-period burials largely consisted of individuals buried in winding sheets without clothes or dress accessories, one group of burials stood out. Males were buried with military crossbow brooches, military belt sets and knives at the waist. Females were all buried wearing bead necklaces and bracelets. Among the beads were hexagonal blue cylinder beads, found nowhere else in Britain but occurring on the continent along the Danube frontier, and some of the females wore large numbers of bracelets on the left arm, a practice only found otherwise in Pannonia, an area on the Danube.[4] We have literary evidence of Germanic prisoners being sent to Britain for garrison duties. For instance, in 277 Probus is said to have sent Vandal and Burgundian prisoners to settle in Britain, where they are described as being useful to the emperor 'if anyone rebelled'.[5] It is possible, therefore, that the unusual deployment of Pannonian warriors at Winchester may have something to do with potential or actual Dobunnic hostilities against the area. A small cluster of early fifth-century Anglo-Saxon supporting arm brooches (*42*) from the Winchester area may also represent the presence of *foederati* (after all, there is nothing to say that Ambrosius did not have small numbers of Anglo-Saxons on his side), or perhaps even the presence of Anglo-Saxon prisoners of war.[6] The Roman settlement outside Salisbury also seems to have survived into the post-Roman period as a focal point of some description, with fifth-century Anglo-Saxon settlement in the area. The Anglo-Saxon Chronicle records a battle in 552 between Cynric and the Britons at Old Sarum, the hillfort adjoining the Roman period settlement.

Evidence of some form of continuity from the Roman into the post-Roman period at these two sites is particularly interesting because the small cluster of villages in Hampshire bearing the name Wallop are almost equidistant from Winchester and Salisbury, although a little to the north. Both towns would be likely objectives for any Dobunnic force that reached Guoloph on its route south.

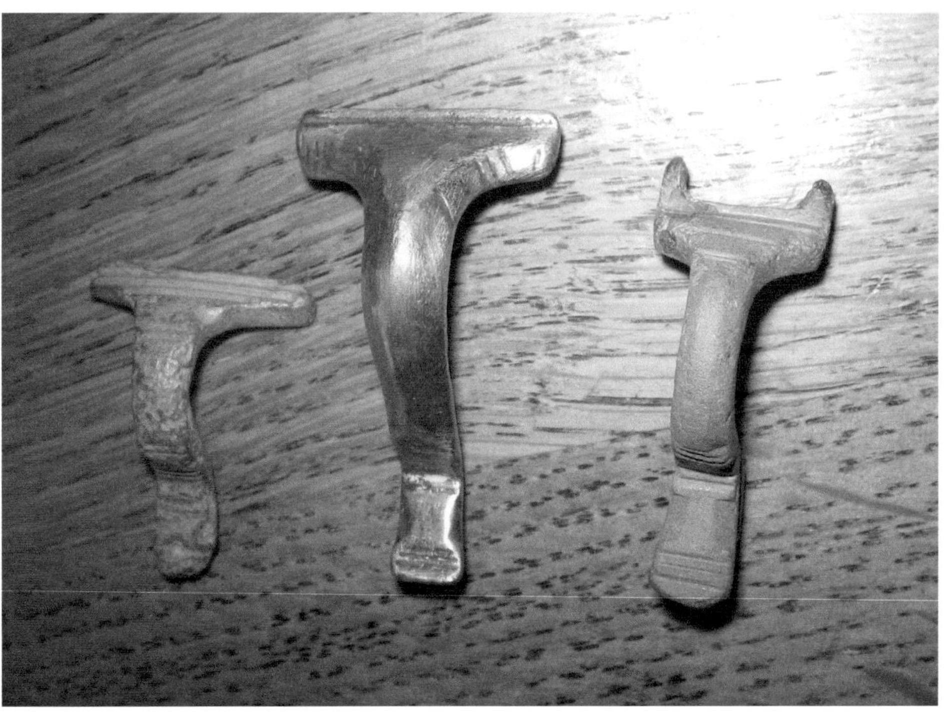

*42* Supporting arm brooches.

If it is correct, then, to see Ambrosius as an Atrebatic figure, this puts a rather different light on the comment by Gildas that Ambrosius was almost the last survivor of the Roman people, and perhaps makes it more understandable. The Atrebates' love affair with Rome went back a long way. They were one of the British tribes most eager to adopt Roman culture even before the invasion of 43 AD. Their coinage from the last few decades before the invasion (*43*) carries a wide variety of classical motifs (at a time when Icenian, Corieltauvian, Dobunnic and Durotrigan coins showed much less Roman influence) and their king ,Verica, was probably responsible for inviting the Romans into Britain in the first place. The Atrebates became thoroughly Romanised during the occupation and it is quite conceivable that this close connection with and affection for Rome would have carried over into post-Roman times as well. For instance, it is worth notingthat in the late Roman period, when Dobunni, Catuvellauni, Corieltauvi and Iceni all seem to have been developing specific tribal styles of belt buckle, the Atrebates apparently continued to manufacture their version of Roman belt buckles as used in mainland Europe, without adding any specific extra stylistic elements that might distinguish their buckles as Atrebatic. It's also worth bearing in mind that the Atrebates of Britain had, at some stage, links with the Atrebates of northern Gaul, just across the Channel, and in the post-410 period, when northern Gaul was at least nominally still part of the Roman Empire, such links

*43* Coin of Verica showing the adoption of Roman style by Atrebates in the period just before the Roman invasion.

could perhaps have helped to retain pro-Roman sentiments among the Atrebates in Britain.

It is even, of course, possible that Ambrosius himself might have been a descendant of pro-Roman kings like Verica. As touched on in Chapter 1, from the evidence of high-status Roman villas established on the same sites as high-status pre-Roman dwellings it seems very likely that British tribal aristocracies largely survived the arrival of Rome intact. A British king even seems to have survived in Atrebatic territory after the invasion in the shape of the client-king Togidubnus, who is mentioned both by Tacitus and in an inscription from Chichester. If the Atrebatic aristocracy survived the arrival of Rome intact, they may well also have survived the departure of Rome relatively intact. If the reference in Gildas to Ambrosius' parents being robed in the purple is some indication of their having some kind of administrative authority, perhaps even royal powers, then it may be that Ambrosius inherited the power they had. Certainly, the reference by Gildas to the qualities of Ambrosius' ancestors seems to show that they were still very much in the public eye in Gildas' time, and may even have still been in power.

If Ambrosius was effectively the ruler of the Atrebatic half of the *civitas* of the Belgae, then his conflict with Vortigern would suddenly become very understandable. At the end of the 'forty years of fear' and after the battle of Guoloph, Vortigern seems to have failed to defeat Ambrosius. On the contrary, it is even possible that Ambrosius managed to inflict some kind of significant defeat on Vortigern. Here we encounter a new potential source of information in the shape of Roger of Wendover. Although he was writing later, and his work contains much poetic/mythical material, he apparently had access to some early records, for instance, in relation to the founding of the Anglo-Saxon kingdom of Essex. Roger of Wendover says that Ambrosius actually killed Vortigern. In addition, the *Historia Brittonum* suggests that Vortigern's son Pascent ruled in Builth and Guorthegirnaim by Ambrosius' consent, suggesting that Ambrosius had extended his political influence far into what had previously been Vortigern's territory. We are, however, very close to, and quite possibly well over, the border between myth and history here, so it would be extremely unwise to place too much reliance on the evidence in question. Having said that, if Ambrosius did, in some sense, replace Vortigern as the pre-eminent warlord in central Britain, this would fit neatly with the way in which Gildas introduces Ambrosius into his story just as Vortigern disappears from his narrative.

Ironically, it is slightly harder to understand how Ambrosius interacted with the Saxons than with other Britons, despite the fact that it is only because he rallied a force of Britons against the Saxons that he makes it into Gildas' work at all.

As indicated earlier, the best guess that we can make about where Gildas was writing is probably somewhere in the West Country, perhaps in Durotrigan territory.[7] If so, then this would fit very well with the idea of Ambrosius as leader in the *civitas* of the Belgae, because any British leader defending that area against Saxons from the east would also, in the process, be preventing them from reaching Durotrigan territory, something for which Gildas would presumably have been very grateful.

A letter from Gaul of a date that must be almost contemporary with Ambrosius gives an account of another aristocrat raising a local militia against Germanic invaders, and we can imagine something rather similar in the case of Ambrosius, though, if Gildas is to be believed, on a rather larger scale:

Sidonius – To his dear Ecdicius

It is something never to be forgotten by the citizens, men and women of all ages and ranks, who thronged on to our half-destroyed walls to watch as you crossed the plain between us and the enemy. In the middle of the day, in an act future generations will find hard to believe, you rode with your troop of barely eighteen cavalrymen through the heart of the enemy, thousands of Goths. Hearing your name, seeing you, those battle-hardened hordes were stunned. Their leaders were bemused and could not figure out how many their troops were, and how few yours were. Immediately they withdrew their whole line to the pinnacle of a steep hill and, having once besieged the town, they were now not even able, because of you, to deploy their forces. You killed some of their best men, at the back not because they were slow but because they were too brave. Without having a single one of your own men killed in this crucial clash, and with fewer companions around you than normally fill your dinner table, you were master of the now empty plain.

I can better show with my vows than with my words how the people flocked to greet you with salutes, cheers, and tears of joy as you made your way towards the city in a leisurely fashion. We saw the most fortunate ovation of your return amidst the crowds, with the courtyards of your large house packed. Some of those who came to greet you

*1* Typical late Roman infantry equipment. *Courtesy of John Conyard and www.www.comitatus.net.*

*2* Gothic cavalryman with late Roman cavalryman, illustrating the regular use of Germanic troops by Roman commanders. *Courtesy of John Conyard and www.comitatus.net.*

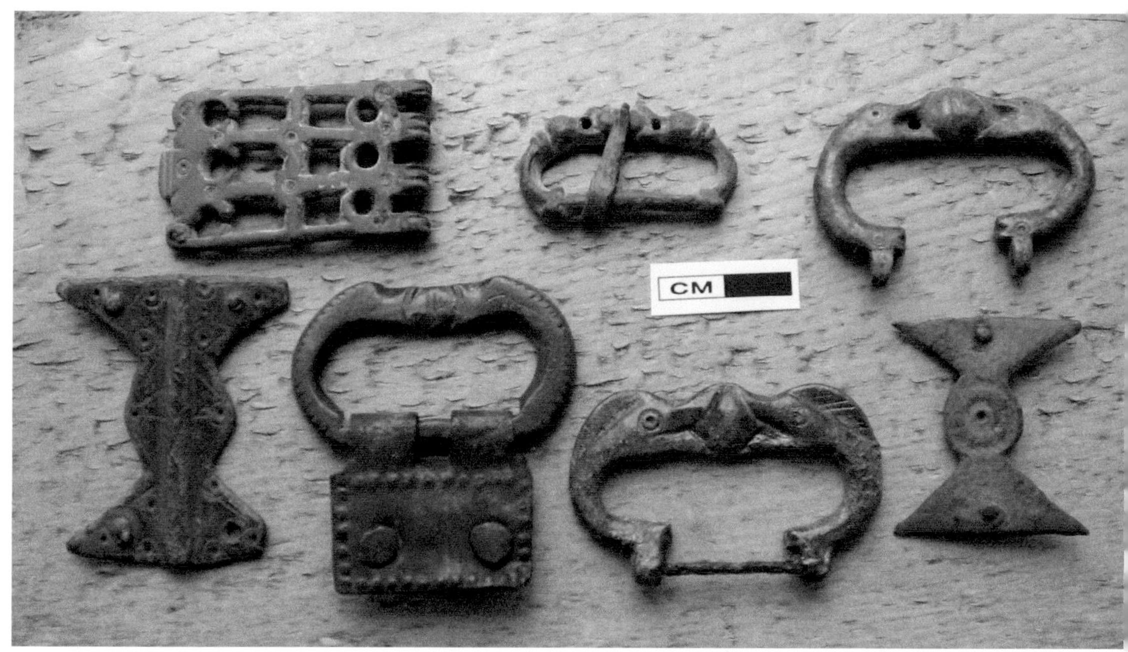


*3* Late Roman belt fittings showing buckles, a buckle plate and typical propeller-shaped belt stiffeners.

*4* Typical late Roman infantry outside earlier fortifications. *Courtesy of John Conyard and www.comitatus.net.*

5 The walls of Tarragona where Gerontius established Maximus as emperor.

6 Late Roman mosaic from Tarragona.

7 The Roman walls of Arles. Gerontius besieged Constantine III here, before being forced to retreat.

*8* Christianity in late Roman Britain. The font at Richborough.

*9* Bastion at Caerwent. Could Caerwent have been an outpost of Vortigern's territory?

*10* British militiamen of the early fifth century would probably have been lightly armed with knife, spears and shield. *Courtesy of John Conyard and www.comitatus.net.*

*11* The walls at Silchester, capital of an area possibly annexed to Dobunnic territory in the fifth century.

*12* Chip-carved late Roman strap end, showing palmette motif also characteristic of Quoit Brooch Style designs.

*13* The fort at Richborough.

*14* Fifth-century Roman fixed plate dragon buckle of a type associated in Britain with early Anglo-Saxon arrivals. From Bassingbourn.

*15* St Martin's Church Canterbury. A building that contains Roman fabric and may represent some form of survival of British Christianity in early Anglo-Saxon Kent.

*16* Wansdyke.

*17* The walls of Chichester, Roman-period capital of the Regni.

*18* Detail of the wall at Pevensey, site, according to the Anglo-Saxon Chronicle, of a victory for Ælle in 490.

*19* Post-Roman inscription from Wareham in Dorset, reading IUDNNE FIL QUI.

*20* Late fifth-century British warrior.
*Courtesy of John Conyard and www.comitatus.n*

*21* Looking across the site at Tintagel. Possible seat of the kings of Dumnonia.

*22* Post-Roman inscription from Rialton in Cornwall recording Tribunus. It is probably here a name but could be a survival of the Roman rank, Tribune.

*23* The Roman Newport Arch at Lincoln. Some argue the reference to Linnuis in the *Historia Brittonum* links Arthur to the area around Lincoln, Roman Lindum.

*24* Barbury Castle. Thought to be the site of the battle of Beranbyrig in 556 in which Cynric and Ceawlin fought unspecified Britons (probably Dobunni).

*25* Roman and Anglo-Saxon. The Jewry Wall at Leicester, the remains of a Roman bath building, with, in the background, the partly Anglo-Saxon Church of St Nicholas which incorporates much Roman material.

*44* Late Roman horseman. Ecdicius in action probably looked rather similar, and so maybe did Ambrosius. *(Courtesy of John Conyard and www.comitatus.net)*

> washed off the dust of battle with their kisses, while others took off the bridles greasy with foam and blood, and others laid out the saddles wet with sweat, unfastened the cheek-pieces of the helmet you were eager to be rid of, and untied your leggings. We saw people counting the nicks on blades made blunt by much killing and measuring with trembling fingers the size of gashes torn in your armour…
>
> (Sidonius Apollinaris, *Letters*, 3,1)

The question of which Saxons Ambrosius might have been confronting, however, is far from clear. Gildas, in his description of events after the revolt, talks about rampaging Saxons reaching the western ocean. However, he does not set any clear timescale in what is, after all, a furious diatribe against the Saxons rather than an attempt at accurate history. In reality, it is more likely that in this reference he is talking more about his own time than about the time of Ambrosius. The only dating (however reliable or not) specifically attached to Ambrosius is that connected to the battle of Wallop. The *Historia Brittonum* places this 12 years after the start of Vortigern's reign and 8 years after the arrival of the Saxons in Britain, and there is no evidence of Saxons reaching anywhere near 'the western ocean' at that time.

Hengest is one possible enemy of Ambrosius. The Atrebates, after all, had a pre-Roman history of conflict with Kent. Another possible enemy is Ælle, the founder, according to the Anglo-Saxon Chronicle, of the South Saxon kingdom in the 470s and 480s. We don't know on what authority, unless it is a rough calculation from Gildas, but Bede places Ambrosius Aurelianus in the reign of the Emperor Zeno (474–491), so that is perfectly conceivable. Roger of Wendover, for what it's worth, has Ambrosius fighting Hengest, Aelle and Pascent, son of Vortigern, all at the same time. This could well, of course, be a literary device, simply dragging in all and sundry for an impressive fictional punch-up, but equally, in the chaotic state of mid to late fifth-century Britain, it would hardly be surprising if it were true.

A final and intriguing possibility, in terms of identifying Ambrosius' Anglo-Saxon enemies, is the potential resurrection of another pre-Roman conflict. In the last decades before AD 43 the Catuvellauni seem to have expanded south from their territories in the Upper Thames area, since around AD 35 the coins of one Epatticus appear in the northern part of Atrebatic territory, in the area around Silchester. It is not entirely clear who Epatticus was. However, it seems fairly certain that his coins represent a major extension of Catuvellaunian influence into Atrebatic territory. The reverses of his coins may maintain Atrebatic design traditions, but the obverses are based on Cunobelin's coinage, and on his coins Epatticus calls himself the son of Tasciovanus, the powerful Catuvellaunian leader.[8] The evidence of a probably post-Roman ditch north of Silchester and the fact that the Roman road in this area fell out of use suggests that this could well have become a conflict zone again in the post-Roman period. As discussed previously, any Anglo-Saxons heading south from the Upper Thames region in the mid to late fifth century would probably have been, at least theoretically, under the control of the Catuvellauni. However, as we shall see in Chapters 5 and 6, the answer to the question of exactly who was a Saxon and who was a Briton was beginning to become increasingly blurred in eastern Britain by the late fifth century. It is, for instance, perfectly conceivable that Gildas regarded as a Saxon any Briton who was not a Christian and who adopted elements of Anglo-Saxon culture, no matter whether it was Germanic or British blood (or a mixture) that ran through their veins. In around 440 or 441 Salvian wrote of the situation in Spain that 'a great part of the Spaniards' had become 'barbarians'.[9]

How and where the battle of Badon fits into all this is very hard to determine. As discussed above, there is probably no particular reason to think that Ambrosius Aurelianus was actually present at Badon and the battle may well have taken place decades after the time of Ambrosius. Gildas' reference to an apparent relative date for Badon is notorious for being incomprehensible:

> From that time, sometimes the citizens conquered, sometimes the enemy so that the Lord might, in his usual way, find out whether this nation, the Israel of today, loves Him or not. This was the situation up to the year of the siege of Badon Hill, almost the most recent, and not the least, of the slaughters suffered by these rogues,

45 Bath. A city probably in the *civitas* of the Belgae and a frequently suggested location for the battle of Badon.

> and this was, as I know, in the 44th year (plus one month) which was also the year of my birth.
>
> (Gildas, *On the Ruin of Britain*, 26)

Does this mean, as some claim, that the battle of Badon took place 44 years and one month before Gildas was writing, or does it mean, as Bede assumed, that the battle took place 44 years and one month after the arrival of the Saxons? Either way, since we can't reliably date either the arrival of the Saxons or the date at which Gildas was writing, we can only suggest that Badon took place probably some time around the end of the fifth century. The *Annales Cambriae* date the battle to 516, but the *Annales* date is not generally thought to be very reliable, particularly since, if one takes the first meaning of Gildas' opaque comment, it would leave Gildas writing very late (after, for instance, the *Historia Brittonum*'s date for the death of Maglocunus whom Gildas addresses as a living person in his diatribe); similarly, if one follows Bede's interpretation, then it would leave the Anglo-Saxons arriving in Britain in 472, which seems much too late.

In terms of location, we can at least say that the battle of Badon is likely to have taken place not too far from the activities of Ambrosius and, judging by the importance Gildas attributes to it, not too far from where he himself was writing. This, however, leaves a whole swathe of the West Country that could be the site of the battle and a significant number of surviving place names that could be linked to it (including Bath, Baydon, and the assorted hillforts called Badbury). However, without knowing for certain the participants on the other side of the battle or the date (with any degree of confidence), tracking down its location and meaning may rely on the chance future discovery of a war grave close to some relevant site. It is, in any event, worth pointing out that despite the prominence that the battle of Badon Hill has acquired (mainly because it is the only battle Gildas mentions by name and the only clearly identified British victory of the period), in reality it may have been a battle of no more than local significance. Gildas himself says of Badon that it was 'not the least slaughter' of the Saxons, which, of course, is not quite the same as saying it was the greatest, though it has often been interpreted that way. It has also been pointed out that Badon does not figure largely in other early British texts, which it might have been expected to if it was the crushing, large-scale victory that many people have tended to assume it was.

Nothing is known about the later career and death of Ambrosius (unless the suggestions in the *Historia Brittonum* of his taking control of at least part of Vortigern's territory are true), but we shall return to the later history of his probable territory in Chapter 9. By that stage Old Sarum was still ruled by a man with a British name, but in a sign of things to come he had an Anglo-Saxon identity and he called his soldiers Saxons, though they probably still included many people of British descent.

# CHAPTER 5

# RIOTHAMUS

> Euric, king of the Visigoths, saw how quickly Roman emperors changed and decided to take control of Gaul himself. Hearing of his plans, the Emperor Anthemius asked for British help. So the British king Riothamus travelled by way of Oceanus to the state of the Bituriges with twelve thousand men, and he was received as he disembarked from his ship. Euric, king of the Visigoths, then attacked the Britons with a huge army and, before the Romans could come to their aid, he routed Riothamus, king of the Britons, after a long struggle. Having lost a large part of his army, Riothamus then fled with all the men he could still muster to the Burgundians, a neighbouring tribe, at that time allied with the Romans.
>
> (Jordanes, *The Origins and Deeds of the Goths*, 45, 237–8)

One British warlord, Gerontius, had been instrumental in the early stages of the collapse of the Western Roman Empire, and another was to play a part in its final, dramatic, dying days.

Around the year 470, just six years before the Western Roman Empire disappeared forever, the Visigothic king Euric, seeing the writing on the wall, decided to make a grab for power in Gaul. The Western Emperor of the time was one Anthemius (reigned 467–472), an experienced military man, but one who was struggling to cope with a crumbling administration and with internal disputes both with Ricimer, his *magister militum* ('master of the soldiers') and son-in-law, and with Arvandus, his prefect in Gaul (who was probably colluding with Euric and was later tried for treason). Anthemius sought help where he could find it, appealing to Riothamus, a king of the Britons.

It has been suggested, because of the location in Gaul of Riothamus' encounter with Euric, that the Britons in question must have been more specifically Britons from Brittany, where a distinctive British identity was emerging around this time rather than from Britian itself. However, the reference to Riothamus arriving via Oceanus, the Atlantic Ocean, does seem

*46* Anthemius.

to indicate that, whatever connections he may have had with the Bretons, Riothamus was probably primarily a British warlord actually from Britain. The territory of the Bituriges as mentioned by Jordanes, lies just to the south and west of Brittany and it is hard to see why Riothamus would have gone to all the time, trouble and expense of embarking his twelve thousand men for an Atlantic cruise if he could just have strolled a short distance down one of the Roman roads in the area. Equally, as we saw with Gerontius, there is nothing strange about a British warlord seeking to extend his power by a European venture; indeed, by the second half of the fifth century, depending on where exactly Riothamus came from, it might have seemed a perfectly logical choice and a much better bet than scrapping with other British tribes and their Germanic mercenaries.

It is widely assumed that once the Britons had kicked out the Roman authorities, and Honorius had accepted the *fait accompli* with as much imperial dignity as he could muster, contact between Britain and the Roman Empire ceased entirely. But as we have already seen in the case of Kent and Quoit Brooch Style, this is not true. In addition, there is a smattering of historical evidence that also indicates continued contacts across the Channel.

47 Looking through the walls of Verulamium to the shrine of St Albans. St Germanus visited here in the period after the end of Roman rule.

Some time in the 430s or 440s St Germanus, Bishop of Auxerre, travelled to Britain on one or perhaps two occasions. According to an account of the saint's deeds that was written probably around 480 and therefore has a certain credibility, Germanus debated with Pelagian heretics, visited the shrine of St Alban at Verulamium and led locals in a battle against invaders (*47*). Some of the elements in the story – there are a couple of instances of miraculous healing, and Germanus and the British forces he was leading defeated their opponents just by shouting Alleluia very loudly – look rather more like hagiography than history. Nevertheless, there is no particular reason to entirely reject the idea that Germanus did travel to Britain in the post-Roman period.

Equally, Gildas gives what seems to be a rather garbled account of 'the groans of the Britons', in which he says that, in the period after the departure of the Romans and before the settlement of the Anglo-Saxons in Britain, the Britons appealed for help against their enemies to 'three times Consul Agitius'. Gildas here seems to have confused the Roman war leader Aëtius, who was indeed made consul three times, and the later independent warlord Aegidius, who was operating in northern Gaul in the 460s. Aegidius is an interesting character in his own right and it is at this point worth briefly mentioning the highlights of his career, not least to illustrate once again how Roman commanders were perfectly happy to use Germanic allies to achieve their goals. Aegidius was made *magister militum* by Aëtius around 450. However, he was a keen supporter of the Emperor Majorian, and when Majorian was forced out of power in 461, possibly on Ricimer's orders, Aegidius rebelled, establishing his own independent Domain of Soissons and allying himself with Childeric, King of the Franks. He may, in fact, even have done rather more than that. Gregory of Tours claims that he actually replaced Childeric as King of the Franks for eight years. Whichever character Gildas really had in mind when describing the 'groans of the Britons', his comments are certainly indicative of continued links between the Britons and the slowly expiring Western Roman Empire.

Both these incidents of cross-Channel communication are, however, a far cry from a Roman emperor inviting a British warlord and twelve thousand warriors to come to his rescue. Once again, therefore, in order to understand Riothamus better, we need to work out where he came from and explore the situation there at the time he was summoned to Gaul.

This is a period after the Anglo-Saxon settlements in Catuvellaunian territory and elsewhere in eastern England, after the rebellion of Hengest, and possibly at a time when Ambrosius Aurelianus may have been active. Is this anything more than a simple coincidence? Some people have made much of it, suggesting that Riothamus was really a title rather than a name, and that Riothamus was really Ambrosius Aurelianus himself (or even, in other versions of the 'Riothamus is just a title' approach, Arthur).[1]

Riothamus, or Rigothamus, could be construed as a Latinisation of a British phrase meaning 'highest king'. However, it is also a perfectly reasonable British proper name of the fifth century. There is no particular reason to view it as a title and indeed, there are good reasons not to. References to kings and lords are a not uncommon feature of British names of the time. Rigocatus, a name also featuring the Rigo– ('king') element, is for instance that of a fifth-century British bishop mentioned by Sidonius Apollinaris (about whom more later in this chapter) and the element 'tigern', meaning 'chief' or 'lord', appears in a number of names, including Tigernacus, Tegernomalus and, of course, Vortigern.

Equally, the evidence suggests that if a fifth-century British warlord was looking for a title, he would be more likely to use a Roman one than a British one. Vortipor, for instance, ruler of the Demetae and target of some of Gildas' barbs, is described in an inscription as 'protictor', the Latin *protector*, while in the account of St Germanus' voyage to Britain, he is shown curing the son of a man 'with tribunician power'. Furthermore, the word '*tribuni*', 'of Tribunus', appears either as a name or as a rank on a post-Roman inscription from Rialton in Cornwall (*colour plate 22*).[2]

What is more, if Ambrosius Aurelianus really was Riothamus and had led a (by the standards of the day) large British expeditionary force to France only to lose it and end up taking refuge with the Germanic Burgundians, one can't help feeling that Gildas might just have mentioned something about it. Again, it seems hard to believe that a king of any state that was heavily involved in fighting either with other Britons or with Anglo-Saxons in the 470s would have decided to take himself off across the Channel with what must have been a large proportion of his fighting men at a time when his own British power base might be under threat.

In our search for the home territory of Riothamus then, we almost certainly need to look further west than Atrebatic territory, to an area that in the fifth century might have had the motivation, the means and the opportunity to send a seaborne expeditionary force of twelve thousand men to Gaul, or at least send a force of sufficient size that a writer could, through the common practice of exaggeration, describe as consisting of twelve thousand men.

To the west of Ambrosius' probable power base in the territory of the *civitas* of the Belgae lay the tribal territory of the Durotriges. This tribe controlled a substantial length of coastline and there is plenty of evidence of a thriving British community in the area in the post-Roman period. Burials at Studland, Worth and Ulwell are probably post-Roman,[3] and a number of post-Roman British inscriptions were found at Wareham when most of the walls of the old Saxon church of Lady St Mary were demolished in the early nineteenth century. To the north are the famously reoccupied hillforts at South Cadbury and Cadbury/Congresbury, and there is also Glastonbury Tor, where there is evidence of fifth- and sixth-century activity. However, as discussed previously, it seems probable that, certainly by the time of Riothamus, the Durotriges had became deeply involved with the conflict in the western, previously Dobunnic, half of the *civitas* of the Belgae. In addition, the construction of the late or post-Roman linear defensive earthwork of Bokerley Dyke suggests the Durotriges were becoming nervous about their eastern neighbours some time probably in the late fourth and fifth centuries.

Even further to the west, however, beyond the Durotriges, lay the territory of the Dumnonii. In the first half of the first century BC the territory of Dumnonia, in Cornwall and Devon, was probably one of the more affluent places in Britain. It was linked into the Atlantic trade routes both directly, through sites such as Mount Batten, Plymouth, and probably indirectly too. For instance, there is evidence that suggests Dumnonian sites such as Mount Batten having contact with the large Durotrigan hubs of cross-Channel trade in the Solent.[4] The Dumnonii probably supplied a range of items, including cattle and metals (tin, lead, silver, copper).

There is evidence too of close cultural links between Dumnonia and Armorica in the pre-Roman period. It has even been argued that culturally the Dumnonii had more in common with Armorica than with any of their British neighbours. Characteristic cliff castles and fogous (underground rooms), for instance, are found in both areas and there is evidence of close cross-Channel links in the ceramic tradition of the two areas as well. The South-Western Decorated Ware Style found in Dumnonian territory, for instance, seems to be derived from Armorican styles.[5]

The cross-Channel trade route through Durotrigan territory was not, however, to last. There is a sudden drop-off in imported Gallic pottery at Hengistbury Head after around 50 BC, and it has been suggested that this should be linked to Caesar's attack on Armorica in 56 BC. In the second half of the first century BC the trade routes seem to have moved east to the much shorter sea-crossing across the straits of Dover, and in the last decades before the Roman invasion of AD 43 it was the south-central and south-eastern parts of the country that were filled with Roman goods and Roman culture.[6]

This pattern continued under the Roman occupation with the centre, south and east of Britain becoming thoroughly culturally Romanised. The Dumnonii, by contrast, like Wales to the north, seem to have largely resisted Romanisation. The Dumnonii did have a Roman-style *civitas* capital at Exeter (*48*), and some of the smaller and more portable elements of Roman lifestyle (such as Samian ware, glass and metalwork) are found there. However, throughout most of the tribal territory, life seems to have continued under the Roman occupation in many ways much as it had before it. There is only one known villa in the west of Dumnonian territory, at Magor Farm, and while the shape of houses generally did show a broad change from round to oval or elongated, perhaps under Roman influence, a new type of non-Roman dwelling appeared in West Cornwall during the Roman period. This was the so-called courtyard house, which consisted of an array of rounded rooms built with massive stone walls, grouped round a central courtyard to create an enclosed unit.[7]

In the late fifth century (from about the 470s onwards), though, things changed once more. Suddenly, with the collapse of security in Gaul and the centre and east of Britain, it was the west, in the shape of Dumnonian territory, that became the focus of the trade routes from the Mediterranean, with quantities of Mediterranean pottery appearing on sites in Dumnonian territory (*50*).

Generally speaking, late fifth-century Dumnonia gives the impression of being one of the most thriving parts of Britain at the time, and was quite probably capable of supplying and equipping a reasonably strong force of warriors; with its long coastline and maritime tradition, it was almost certainly capable of transporting them across the Channel and around Brittany with ease, as well.

*48* The walls of Exeter, the Roman-period capital of the *civitas* of the Dumnonii.

*49* Post-Roman inscription from Dumnonia.

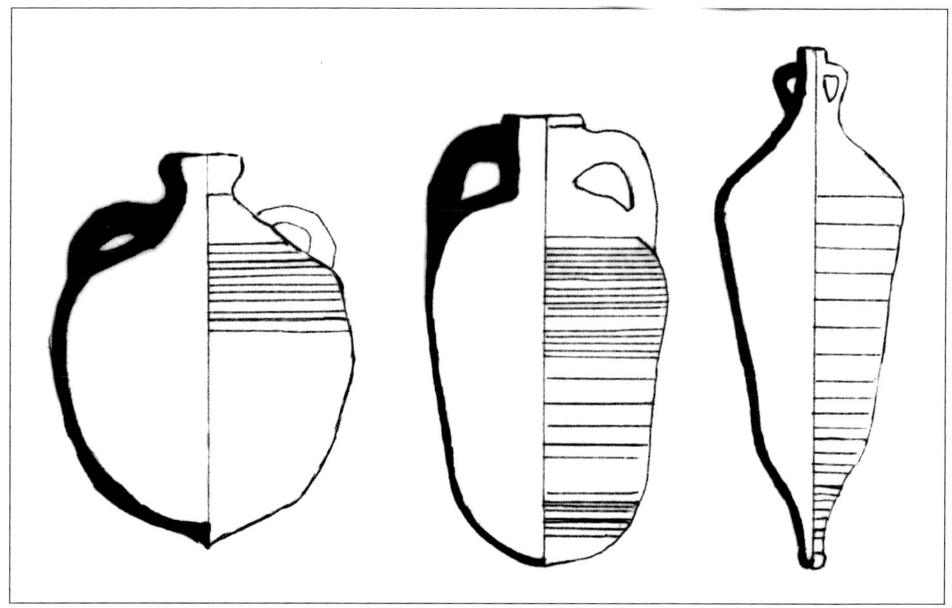

*50* Types of Eastern Mediterranean pottery imported into Dumnonia in the late fifth and sixth centuries. *(After Dark, 2000)*

However, the quantities of late fifth- and sixth-century Mediterranean pottery found in Dumnonia are so large that it has been calculated that something more than just simple trading in minerals must have been going on (although trading in tin was no doubt part of the picture). Some of the arrays of Mediterranean amphorae found in Dumnonian territory from this time are comparable with the quantities and types found on sites in the Eastern Roman Empire that are thought to have been in receipt of official government supplies, and this has raised the question of whether Dumnonia had some kind of official or quasi-official connection with the Byzantine authorities.[8]

It has been suggested that such contacts could be connected with the activities of the Emperor Justinian (*51*). With our knowledge of later historical developments we regard Justinian (reigned 527–565) as a Byzantine emperor, but he saw himself as emperor of the whole Roman Empire and he made serious and extensive attempts to reconquer significant parts of the Western Roman Empire and take them back from their new Germanic rulers. At huge cost he succeeded in destroying the Vandal kingdom in North Africa, thus bringing that territory back into the Empire. He then got bogged down in a lengthy and costly war to retake Italy for the Empire but finally succeeded after two decisive victories over the Ostrogoths in 552. Justinian, though, almost certainly had ambitions beyond the recapture of Italy and a chunk of North Africa. He managed to take control of territory as far west as the Atlantic coast of Spain, through an interesting reversal of one of the military

*51* Justinian.

norms of the fifth century. Instead of a Roman usurper calling in Germanic assistance against other Romans, this time a Visigothic usurper named Athanagild called in Byzantine assistance against the Visigothic king Agila. It is also known from Procopius that Justinian sent gifts to rulers in Britain at this time. It has therefore been suggested that the mass of Mediterranean pottery in Dumnonian territory should be associated with diplomatic activity by Justinian in the area, in addition to any commercial links.[9]

This is certainly quite likely. However, the pottery starts appearing in Dumnonian territory around the 470s, well before the time of Justinian but pretty much around the time of Riothamus and Anthemius.[10]

There are other reasons to consider the possibility of a connection between Anthemius and the start of fifth-century Mediterranean trade and political contacts with Dumnonian territory. Much of the imported pottery found in Dumnonia seems to have come from the Eastern Mediterranean, but the same is true of pottery found in Italy itself dating to the late fifth and early sixth centuries, with, for instance, the relative quantities of one important Eastern type of amphora at Rome rising sharply in the period after 450 (well before Justinian's attempt at reconquest began).[11] Anthemius may have been emperor of the Western Roman Empire but he was an easterner in origin, born and bred in Constantinople. He was put on the western throne by the Eastern Emperor Leo, and once there he remained in close cooperation with Leo. Anthemius' son Marcianus, for instance, married Leo's younger daughter Leontia. In addition, during Anthemius' reign, instead of each half of the Empire appointing two consuls, each half appointed one, and the two thereby appointed were recognised across both Eastern and Western Empires. This close cooperation meant that in 468 (probably just a few years before Riothamus' expedition to Gaul), in a precursor to Justinian's later attempts to reconquer the west, Anthemius and Leo jointly mounted an expedition to reconquer the areas of the Mediterranean and North Africa held by the Vandals. This is exactly how Justinian's attempt to reconquer the west started. A huge amount, probably in excess of 64,000 pounds of gold, was spent on assembling the force and for a time it paid off as things went well for the expedition. Tripoli fell, and to the north forces working for Leo and Anthemius recaptured Sicily and Sardinia. However, it all ended in disaster for the emperors when their commander in Sicily and Sardinia was assassinated and the Vandals destroyed the Roman fleet with fire-ships. There was to be no further attempt to reconquer North Africa until Justinian.

There is no specific evidence that the plans of Leo and Anthemius ever extended significantly beyond the reconquest of the part of North Africa held by the Vandals, plus Sardinia and Sicily, but it is certainly possible. It has, for instance, been suggested that an attack by the Goths on the Sueves in Lusitania at the same time might have been another prong of the campaign.[12] It is even more possible that Leo and Anthemius were building diplomatic links with previously lost parts of the Empire, just as Justinian would do in the next century. Certainly, given the vast amounts of money being spent on the main expedition, the cost of a little extra diplomacy in Dumnonia would have been fairly insignificant.

If Anthemius was going to appeal for help with his problems in Gaul from anywhere in Britain, then it seems logical that he would do so from the part with which he and the government in Constantinople had the most extensive contacts. Bantham in Devon is about the only site in Britain where excavation has revealed significant quantities of imported Mediterranean pottery dating from around the mid-470s,[13] while Tintagel has produced by far the largest collection of Byzantine pottery north of the Mediterranean region.[14] Such finds are indicative of the kind of close contacts which might have allowed Anthemius to call on the aid of the local warlord.

But there is a whole set of additional reasons for thinking that Riothamus, the British warlord fighting in central Gaul, is most likely to have come from Dumnonia. We have already mentioned Brittany, and of course the end of the

Roman period is precisely when we see the development of a specifically British political and cultural identity in Armorica.

The origins of the emergence of this identity are, however, both obscure and controversial. The *Historia Brittonum* attributes the origins of the Bretons to British troops left in Brittany by Magnus Maximus after the end of his brief usurpation:

> Maximus, refusing to send his comrades-in-arms back to their wives, children and homes in Britain, handed over to them many areas, from the lake on top of Mons Jovis to the city called Cant Guic, and to the western tumulus, in other words, to Cruc Occident. These are the Armorican Britons, and they are there to the present day.
>
> (*Historia Brittonum*, 27)

As discussed in Chapter 1, it is likely that Magnus Maximus did take British militiamen with him to mainland Europe and it is therefore possible that some may have settled in Brittany in the 380s and 390s. Some French historians have taken the story seriously enough to try to identify the landmarks specified – with varying results.[15] However, it is hard to see why Maximus personally would disband his British contingent and send them to Brittany (unless as a garrison), and since his final defeat took place in Aquileia in northern Italy, it is unlikely that any stragglers from that battle would have ended up in Brittany. Similarly, there is little mention in the historical sources of Britons living in Armorica in the late fourth and early fifth centuries. There are, however, references to Britons there in the late fifth century and it is probably best to see the real origins of Brittany in this period, the period of Riothamus.

In Gildas there is a reference to Britons fleeing over the seas to escape the rampaging Saxons, and there has sometimes been a tendency to view Brittany as a safe haven created by British refugees to protect them from the Saxons. Some Britons almost certainly did flee abroad to escape violence in this period. However, as we have already seen, Gildas was probably rather prone to exaggeration when it came to the Saxons, and there are good reasons to see the creation of Brittany as more closely connected to British tribal politics than to any Anglo-Saxon misdeeds.

Brittany was divided into several separate areas, and at some stage in its early history two of the main ones were probably named after regions in Britain. An area on the north coast of the Breton peninsula became known as Domnonée (the local equivalent of Dumnonia), while an area on the south side of the peninsula near its tip became known as Cornouaille. Cornouaille is, of course, the local equivalent of Cornwall, also a part of Dumnonia at this time.

We have already seen in terms of the pre-Roman Atrebates how a political entity from one side of the Channel could extend its identity and its power base across to the other side, and we have touched on the possibility of Frankish power also extending across the Channel into Anglo-Saxon Kent. Something similar is quite likely to have been happening here.

*52* The Drustan stone, mentioning one Cunomorus.

As discussed above, Dumnonia had very extensive contacts with Armorica in pre-Roman times. Indeed, the cultural similarities were so close that previous generations of scholars assumed that they must represent an extensive movement of people across the Channel (although this is now thought unlikely). It is probable that close contacts between Dumnonia and Armorica continued throughout the Roman and into the post-Roman period. We have already seen, for example, that when Britain threw out the Romans in 409, the Armoricans did so too, and Zosimus tells us that the Armoricans acted in imitation of events in Britain, suggesting clear cross-Channel influence.

If Dumnonia, perhaps made newly self-confident by renewed Mediterranean trade contacts and with its ambitions boosted by the patronage of the Roman and Byzantine authorities, was looking to emulate the Dobunni and expand its power base, then a cross-Channel venture would be an obvious choice. Breton genealogies and stories seem to retain memories of rulers who exerted power on both sides of the Channel, including perhaps one Cunomorus (a sixth-century Breton named Chonomor is mentioned by Gregory of Tours and could be the Cunomorus father of Drustan named on the famous inscription from Cornwall; *see fig. 52*). And in the case of Domnonée they contain another interesting name: Riothamus.[16] These genealogies are hardly the most reliable of sources. However, in the light of the supporting circumstantial evidence it doesn't seem unreasonable to to give some weight to their assertion that Riothamus was king of a Dumnonia that existed in the fifth and sixth centuries on both sides of the Channel.

Interestingly, this idea would fit very neatly with another fascinating piece of evidence, nothing less than a letter written to Riothamus himself. An astonishing survival, this is the only known letter addressed to any post-Roman British warlord, and it was written by Sidonius Apollinaris, a diplomat, poet and bishop in fifth-century Gaul. Let's take a peek into Riothamus' inbox:

> I will write to you once again in my usual way, mixing compliments with complaints. I do not in the least want to follow opening words of greeting with an unpleasant subject, but things always seem to happen which a man of my position and in my situation cannot mention without unpleasantness, and cannot omit to mention without dereliction of duty. Nevertheless I always try to bear in mind your keen sense of honour which makes you always ready to take responsibility for others' faults. The person bearing this letter is such an ordinary person, so harmless and helpless, that he almost seems to invite trouble. He complains that the Britons are secretly luring his slaves away. Whether that is true, I cannot myself say. However, if you could just confront the parties involved and examine the issue on its merits, then I believe this unfortunate man may be able to convince you, that is assuming that a stranger from the country, unarmed, downtrodden and poor as well, has a fair chance against opponents with the advantages that he lacks, in other words, weapons, cleverness, aggression, and the courage of men who know they have plenty of friends behind them.
>
> (Sidonius Apollinaris, *Letters*, 3, 9)

The implication of Sidonius' letter is perhaps that Riothamus exerted some kind of control in mainland Europe beyond what might normally be expected of the mere commander of a roving band of raiders. If, on the other hand, Riothamus was also king of the continental part of Dumnonia as well as of the British part, and an official ally of Anthemius as well, then he could, no doubt, have exercised the kind of authority Sidonius indicates.

With the sparse evidence available, we can only speculate as to Riothamus' exact intention in responding to the pleas of Anthemius and taking a Dumnonian army into the military and political turmoil of central Gaul around the year 470. We cannot know for sure whether he saw his operations as simply a defence of his territories in Brittany, or whether he saw himself more in the mould of Gerontius, dominating large areas of Western Europe and playing a major role in imperial politics. What would have happened if the

Roman forces had turned up in time to support Riothamus and his Britons in their prolonged struggle against (by the sound of it) overwhelming numbers of Visigoths will remain one of history's mysteries.

Whatever his original plan, Riothamus' downfall holds its own interest too. For instance we are already seening that any notion of the fifth century being a straightforward struggle between Britons and Germanic groups is far too simplistic, and we have the same situation with the end of the Riothamus story. For a start, a supposedly Roman faction was probably working against Riothamus and Anthemius. Sidonius Apollinaris mentions in another letter that Arvandus, the Praetorian Prefect of the Gauls, was alleged to have encouraged Euric, the Visigothic king, to attack the Britons beyond the Loire, which could be a reference to Riothamus and his forces. Equally, it is worth noting that after his defeat by Euric's Visigoths, Riothamus was happy to take shelter with another group of Germanic warriors, the Burgundians, who were friendly with Anthemius.

Brittany had a long future ahead of it as a politically independent British region and it still retains its British/Breton cultural identity to this day. British Dumnonia survived as a powerful kingdom until the seventh century, unthreatened by Anglo-Saxon expansion. The Mediterranean trade routes survived until the late sixth century but largely seem to have broken off after that, possibly in response to the discontinuation of Byzantine attempts to reconquer the West.

We shall return to Dumnonia in Chapter 7 to consider one of Gildas' five 'tyrants', Constantine of Dumnonia, who could have been a descendant of Riothamus.

# CHAPTER 6

# ÆLLE

In the case of Hengest we can potentially link the warlord featured in the Anglo-Saxon Chronicle to the story of a rebellious Saxon mercenary in Gildas and possibly to the roving warrior playing a starring role in the story of the fight at Finnsburg. For evidence of the existence of our next Anglo-Saxon warlord, however, we are reliant on a brief reference in Bede and a handful of entries in the Chronicle which refer to the kingdom of Sussex and record events there which it dates between 477 and 490.

Bede says that Ælle was the first Anglo-Saxon king to hold *imperium*, or power, over all the provinces of Britain south of the Humber. The Anglo-Saxon Chronicle amplifies this comment by attributing to Ælle the title of *Bretwalda*. This title has been the subject of fierce debate; indeed, some have questioned whether it should be called anything as formal as a title. However, the term seems broadly to have been used to indicate an Anglo-Saxon ruler who exerted wider authority than any other in his own lifetime. Bede, however, was writing some time in the eighth century and it is very unclear at what date the concept of the *Bretwalda* developed. There is no real question of any single Anglo-Saxon warlord in the late fifth century being able to control all the provinces of Britain south of the Humber. There is no other historical or archaeological evidence that might suggest any kind of unified political control over such a vast area at this time. By contrast, as already discussed, there is a lot of evidence which suggests that Britain was fragmented into much smaller political units. It seems best, therefore, to see Bede as taking here a highly anachronistic view of fifth century warlords, one much better suited to his own time in the eighth century. Ælle may well have been a key figure in southern Britain in the late fifth century, but he wasn't running events in, for instance, Lincolnshire at the time.

If, therefore, we are going to try to understand who Ælle may have been and what he was up to, we will have turn to the Anglo-Saxon Chronicle and analyse the evidence there. As already touched on in the cases of Vortigern and Hengest, the Chronicle is not always the firmest evidence to rely upon, particularly in its earlier sections dealing with the fifth and sixth centuries. Recent research has, for instance, demolished any Victorian idea that the Chronicle's account of this period represents careful contemporary record-taking. Nevertheless, as Gildas himself demonstrates, Anglo-Saxon accounts (probably in poetic saga form) were clearly already widely known not long after the events in question and it seems likely that the Chronicle for the period represents a distillation of the core facts of these accounts even if overlaid with a later gloss. As with any record based on memory, the chronology is unlikely to be very exact and occasionally events may end up in slightly the wrong order, but the basic outline of the facts still remains. It therefore seems more likely than not that the sparse details concerning Ælle in the Anglo-Saxon Chronicle do, in fact, record something authentic about the career of a genuine late fifth-century warlord. Bede may have lost the plot slightly in terms of allotting Ælle all the territory south of the Humber, but his brief reference does at least help confirm that Ælle was viewed in the early eighth century as a genuine historical figure and not as some mythical hero.

The Anglo-Saxon Chronicle's account of Ælle's career indicates that he landed at a place called Cymenesora in 477, fought the Britons there and subsequently drove them into a forest called Andredeslea. In 485 Ælle is recorded as fighting Britons at a location referred to as Mearcredesburnansted, and finally the Chronicle says that he besieged Andredesceaster in 490 and then killed all the Britons inside.

On the face of it the Chronicle account seems to tell a simple story of an Anglo-Saxon invader landing in Sussex (which at that stage was the territory of the British *civitas* of the Regni), slaughtering assorted Britons in assorted battles and subsequently establishing an Anglo-Saxon kingdom to replace the British *civitas*, this kingdom being the kingdom of the South Saxons or Sussex. This is certainly how Ælle's exploits were viewed in Victorian days and, indeed, for most of the twentieth century as well.

There is, however, evidence both within the Anglo-Saxon Chronicle account and in the history and archaeology of Sussex for a very different view. There are good reasons for thinking that if he is a red figure, Ælle should in fact be seen, like the Saxons of the *superbus tyrannus* and the *foederati* in Catuvellaunian/Trinovantian territory, as representing Germanic military assistance specifically invited by Britons, and it is logical to suspect that at least some of the Britons he was fighting would therefore be the enemies of the Britons who originally sponsored his arrival.

It is perhaps the geography of events as described in the Anglo-Saxon Chronicle, combined with the archaeological information gleaned from early Anglo-Saxon sites in Sussex, that most strongly argues for this interpretation. Cymenesora, where Ælle is said by the Chronicle to have first landed in 477, is identified in a tenth-century charter as being near Selsey and Chichester in the far west of Sussex.[1] Admittedly the charter in question is probably a fake but even so it is a fake from the Anglo-Saxon period and it can still therefore be relied on for geographical information. In any convincing fake, it's important to get the small details correct.

*53* Mosaic from Bignor in the *civitas* of the Regni.

The pre-Roman tribal capital of the Regni was located near Selsey (the site itself has been lost to coastal erosion, but some impressive linear earthworks remain and rich finds have been washed up), while the Roman-period capital of the *civitas* of the Regni was located at Chichester (*colour plate 17*). It would therefore make sense for foreign recruits coming to fight for the Regni to land at this spot. However, in the Anglo-Saxon Chronicle account Ælle is shown as storming ashore here and slaughtering the first Britons he came across. This seems largely incompatible with the archaeological evidence which locates almost all Anglo-Saxon activity in Sussex in the fifth century in the far east of the region, in the area bordering the *civitas* of the Cantii and subsequently a mixed Saxon and British Kent.

The rest of the Anglo-Saxon Chronicle account, though, is entirely consistent with the idea of these far eastern borderlands being Ælle's main zone of operation. The Chronicle records him chasing Britons into the forest called Andredeslea. Andredeslea, or as it later became Andredesweald, was the Anglo-Saxon name for the Weald, a region of greater extent at that time than today, but which included the territory to the north of the area of early Anglo-Saxon settlement and divided it from Kentish territory to the north and east. The Chronicle also records Ælle fighting at Mearcredesburnansted in 485. This name is widely thought to indicate a place by a reedy river which marked a border, so again we are in border territory. Finally, there is the attack on Andredesceaster in 490. Andredesceaster was the Anglo-Saxon name for Pevensey Castle, the imposing Roman fort that lies just to the east of Eastbourne.

*54* Pevensey, the site of a victory for Ælle in 490, according to the Anglo-Saxon Chronicle.

Today Pevensey lies well within the borders of Sussex, but in pre-Roman times the ceramics of the area just to the east of Pevensey show closer links with those in the territory of the Cantii, while the Roman road system in the area seems designed to link more closely to Kent than to Sussex. Anglo-Saxon charters also suggest large shifts in the border between Kent and Sussex in this area (a charter of Offa, for instance, granting land at Icklesham, which is only about 15 miles from Pevensey and today lies well within East Sussex, refers to the 'cantwara mearc', the border with Kent[2]). Pevensey should therefore probably be seen as a point on, or very close to, the eastern border of the *civitas* of the Regni at the time of Ælle's arrival (*54*).

It is, of course, conceivable that the two later battles are the result of Ælle carving out a chunk of marginal Regni territory here and occupying it, in conflict with the Regni. However, the combination of his alleged arrival near the capital of the Regni in the far west of Sussex, and then his settling down in the far east of Sussex while focusing his activities probably to the north and east would strongly suggest a figure working in conjunction with the Regni, not against them. As mentioned in the chapter on Hengest, the Anglo-Saxon Chronicle does not record which Britons Hengest was supposed to be fighting in his last recorded battle but it does say that he took large quantities of booty and plunder and this could conceivably have been from a raid against the Regni. As already discussed, it is not wise to take the Chronicle's fifth-century chronology too seriously, but it is mildly interesting nonetheless to note that the battle in question is dated 473 and Ælle is said to have turned up in Britain just four years later in 477. Could the arrival of Ælle and his followers be the response by the Regni to the events of 473?

Aside from such speculation, the possibility of Ælle working in cooperation with the Regni rather than spending his time attempting to drive them out is supported by archaeological evidence of British and Anglo-Saxon customs mingling in the areas of Sussex first settled by the Anglo-Saxons. At Beddingham Villa, for instance, near the eastern borders of the Regni and of the kingdom of Sussex, an apsed masonry shrine was hollowed out possibly for the creation of an Anglo-Saxon sunken featured building and the fill of the cut contained mixed late Roman and early Anglo-Saxon pottery, suggesting continuity. Equally, at Thundersbarrow, Old Shoreham, early Anglo-Saxon cremations are found that include late Roman pottery and nearby is a Roman period settlement, where occupation seems to have continued up until at least the fifth century. At Rookery Hill, Bishopstone, it has been argued that some of the many inhumations of late fifth- and sixth-century date buried in a crouched position and aligned north–south may represent a form of British cultural continuity.[3]

It is obvious, though, that at some stage, whether or not Ælle and his followers did arrive at the invitation of the Britons, the British *civitas* of the Regni was somehow transformed into the Anglo-Saxon kingdom of Sussex. It may be, of course, that as probably happened in Kent, at some stage Ælle simply stopped taking orders from the Regni and started giving them. However, there are signs that the transition may have been rather more complex and protracted than that.

One curious feature of the Anglo-Saxon Chronicle's account of Ælle's activities that is often overlooked is that at no point does the Chronicle actually say Ælle took over power or made himself king in his area of operations. The position of king was, of course, a key feature of Anglo-Saxon society (certainly by the time the Chronicle was being compiled) and in most other cases where the Chronicle gives details of major fifth- or sixth-century leaders, it seems very careful to mark the point at which the person in question 'took over the kingdom' or simply 'became king'. There is no such reference in the case of Ælle. In fact, apart from the anachronistic reference in Bede, and the Chronicle's description of him as a *Bretwalda*, and presumably therefore a sort of king, there is no evidence that Ælle ever controlled Sussex (or even a chunk of it) in his own right. This might be nothing more than a simple omission, but might also indicate that Ælle's status was not kingly but something rather different.

Another strange thing about Ælle is that, apart from the three sons listed in the Chronicle (including the elusive Cissa to whom we will return shortly), he appears to have no known descendants. No complete king list survives for the kingdom of the South Saxons and it seems unclear whether later south Saxon kings were really descended from him. What is more, the earliest known Anglo-Saxon king of Sussex (unless Ælle or any of his sons were kings) has the name Æthelwalh. *Walh* or *wealh* is the Anglo-Saxon word for Briton or Welshman, and also meant slave or servant. It seems inherently unlikely that any king would have a name proclaiming slave or servant status and in this context therefore it seems likely that this name

55 The walls of Chichester, a town possibly named after Cissa.

probably means 'noble Welshman' or 'noble Briton'.[4] This interpretation seems to be supported by the fact that in other cases where the *walh* element appears in a royal name, it can arguably be connected with a British element in the royal family. Thus, for instance Cenwalh is a king of Wessex (from a royal house containing a number of British names, including Cerdic and Cædwalla) and Merewalh is king (or sub-king) of the Magonsæte territory in the Welsh borderlands, an area where significant British influence could be expected to have persisted. Assuming that Ælle is a real character, it may conceivably be that he never, in fact, took control of the Regni at all, but simply became part of the existing hierarchy of the Regni, perhaps through marriage.

If we are looking for the development of a specifically Anglo-Saxon identity in Sussex, and perhaps for the origin of Bede's claims that Ælle had influence over other Anglo-Saxon kingdoms, we may instead have to turn to Cissa, one of the three characters listed by the Anglo-Saxon Chronicle as Ælle's sons.

As with Ælle himself, we are not overburdened with evidence concerning Cissa. In fact, the only evidence for his existence takes the form of two entries in the Anglo-Saxon Chronicle and a place name with mysterious origins. The first Chronicle reference to Cissa is the entry for 477, which says Ælle was accompanied to Britain by his three sons Cymen, Wlencing and Cissa. The second reference is the entry for 490 that placed Cissa at Ælle's side as he massacred the Britons at Pevensey. The disputed place name is Chichester, which in its earliest form appears as Cisseceaster, which should mean Cissa's Roman town/fort. One of the 'poetic' aspects of the Chronicle noted earlier is that it occasionally seems to make up minor characters in order to explain significant place names. Thus, for instance, the Anglo-Saxon Chronicle entry for 501 states: 'This year Port and his two sons, Bieda and Mægla, came to Britain, with two ships, at a place called Portsmouth.' It is assumed here that Port is a fictional character made up in an attempt to explain the origin of the name Portsmouth.

On this basis it has been argued that Cymen, Wlencing and Cissa are also made-up characters created to explain away difficult place names. In this way, the argument goes, Cymen would be derived from Cymenesora (Ælle's alleged original landing place), Wlencing would be derived from Lancing and Cissa from Chichester. With Cymen and Wlencing this may or may not hold true. These two characters do not appear again in the Chronicle and could, therefore, conceivably be names just slipped in to pad out the narrative. Cissa, however, does appear again, taking part in the battle at Pevensey, so he is less likely to be a completely fictional character. Equally, Cissa is a real Anglo-Saxon name. There seems, for instance, to have been a Wessex sub-king of that name operating somewhere in the Wiltshire area during the reign of King Ine (688–726).[5] And the name Chichester does seem to be derived from the name Cissa. Attempts have been made to find different origins for the name Cissesceaster but none has been entirely convincing.

We therefore have to face the possibility that Cissa was a real person. If he did exist, and if he arrived in Britain with Ælle in 477, he would presumably have come to most prominence some time after his father's final Chronicle appearance in 490. As indicated above, we should not take the Chronicle dates too precisely, but again the date in question, around the end of the fifth century, is an interesting one in the area and one where other evidence suggests that something of significance was happening.

The map of Anglo-Saxon cemeteries dating from the fifth century in Britain shows a comparatively small number of them, mostly clustered on *civitas* borders, as in the case of those situated around the borders of the Catuvellaunian/ Trinovantian confederation, or those on the eastern borders of the Regni or on the western borders of the *civitas* of the Belgae (*56*). The great exception is Kent, where the widespread expansion of Anglo-Saxon cemeteries across the east Kent heartlands in the second half of the fifth century suggests the spread of an Anglo-Saxon identity under perhaps Hengest and Oisc. As discussed in Chapter 3, this expanding Anglo-Saxon identity probably included a large number of Britons who adopted Anglo-Saxon culture and an Anglo-Saxon lifestyle, just as their ancestors had adopted Roman culture and a Roman lifestyle.

In the early sixth century, however, Anglo-Saxon cemeteries become far more widespread (*56*). This is particularly true in a number of areas, most notably the western part of Sussex, including the area around the pre-Roman tribal capital of the Regni at Selsey and the Roman period capital of the *civitas* of the Regni at Chichester. This sudden explosion of Anglo-Saxon culture across Sussex presumably marks the effective point at which the *civitas* of the Regni became the

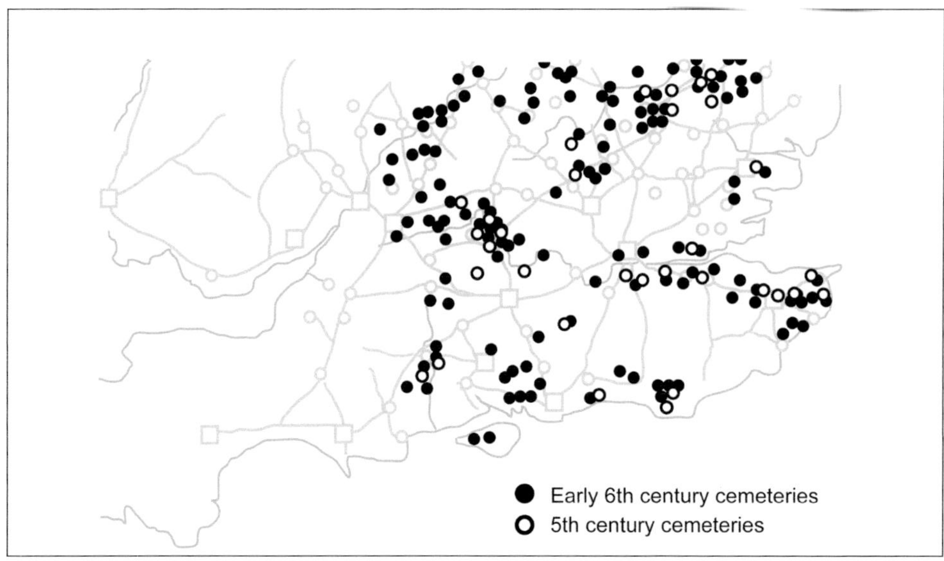


*56* The spread of Anglo-Saxon cemeteries from the fifth to early sixth centuries, set against towns and roads of Roman Britain. *(After Dark 2000 et al.)*

Anglo-Saxon kingdom of the South Saxons. Again, as with Oisc, this sudden expansion of Anglo-Saxon identity may have involved a number of new immigrants. However, we should also probably imagine a large number of those adopting Anglo-Saxon identity at this time as being ethnically British. Mixed Anglo-Saxon and British practices in individual burials suggest as much. For instance, at Apple Down, Compton, a number of burials featuring Anglo-Saxon grave goods also contain Roman coins, unpierced and apparently left as obols in the Roman fashion.[6]

There is plenty of evidence in British history that a change of name for a political entity need not imply a complete break with an area's past. In the pre-Roman period the British tribe in Hampshire and Berkshire acquired the Gallic name Atrebates, and, as we shall explore further in Chapter 10, a British tribe in East Yorkshire picked up another foreign name, the Parisi, along with some foreign cultural customs. In the post-Roman period some tribal areas kept their name when they became kingdoms (the territory of the Dumnonii, for example, became the kingdom of Dumnonia), but some seem to have changed their name (as the territory of the Cornovii probably became Powys), though the same people were still occupying the land.

The point at which the Regni became the South Saxons would mark a suitable point for an Anglo-Saxon warlord to rename the Roman period capital with his own name. It is unclear exactly what happened at Chichester in the post-Roman period, though a supposedly late Roman cemetery outside the town's Eastgate does appear to contain pottery that is associated with post-Roman occupation at Chilgrove Villa. This suggests that the cemetery too may date to the second quarter of the fifth century or later.[7] Certainly the fact that Selsey and Chichester became the seats of the kings of the South Saxons again indicates a good deal of continuity from Regni to South Saxons.

It may also be that the westward shift of explicitly Anglo-Saxon settlement seen in the early sixth century marked a new self-confidence in Sussex and a new shift of focus which may have brought about conflict with the kingdom's western neighbours. Going a step further, perhaps this was the ultimate origin of the *Bretwalda* story.

The strongest archaeological indication that something significant was happening in Sussex at this time comes from the strange settlement patterns of the Jutes. As discussed in Chapter 3, after the early, more culturally mixed years that were probably associated with Hengest's period, Kent developed a more explicitly Jutish cultural aspect from about the 470s onwards. Then, about 30 years later, there is evidence of Jutish culture and settlement spreading to another area of southern Britain. However, the area in question was not, as one might logically expect, an area adjacent to Kent, but instead lay on the other side of Sussex, in southern Hampshire and the Isle of Wight.

All this could, of course, be coincidence. Perhaps the Jutes were just looking for land anywhere it was available. However, the chronology and the geography do suggest that the pattern of Jutish settlement on either side of Sussex may in some way be related to the appearance of an explicitly Anglo-Saxon identity right across Sussex at around the same time.

Though a small independent Jutish kingdom was formed in the Isle of Wight, there is no evidence that the Jutes of south Hampshire ever constituted a separate independent Jutish kingdom. Two main possibilities, therefore, present themselves. Either an Anglo-Saxon warlord in Sussex, perhaps Cissa, or perhaps (if the Chronicle has got the dates really wrong) Ælle himself, was moving Jutes from a Sussex-dominated Kent to the other end of his realm to guard his western borders, or alternatively, perhaps the British authorities in southern Hampshire, in the *civitas* of the Belgae, were looking for additional Germanic support against a newly confident and expansionist Sussex.

The evidence, such as it is, rather tends to suggest the latter. A type of spearhead with fullered blades (with stepped or helicoidal section) is found across the area of south Hampshire and the areas to the north and west in late fifth- and sixth-century Anglo-Saxon contexts (57).[8] The fact that this type appears to be more closely related to British rather than to Anglo-Saxon antecedents seems to suggest Anglo-Saxons (and Jutes) on some level cooperating militarily with Britons in this area at this period. This type of spearhead, is, however, hardly found at all in either Sussex or Kent. All of this seems to suggest that the Jutes of southern Hampshire were more closely connected with Britons from the *civitas* of the Belgae and the Atrebates than with the Regni or South Saxons to the east. Equally, Wulfhere of Mercia is recorded as giving the Meonware (the Jutish area of south Hampshire)

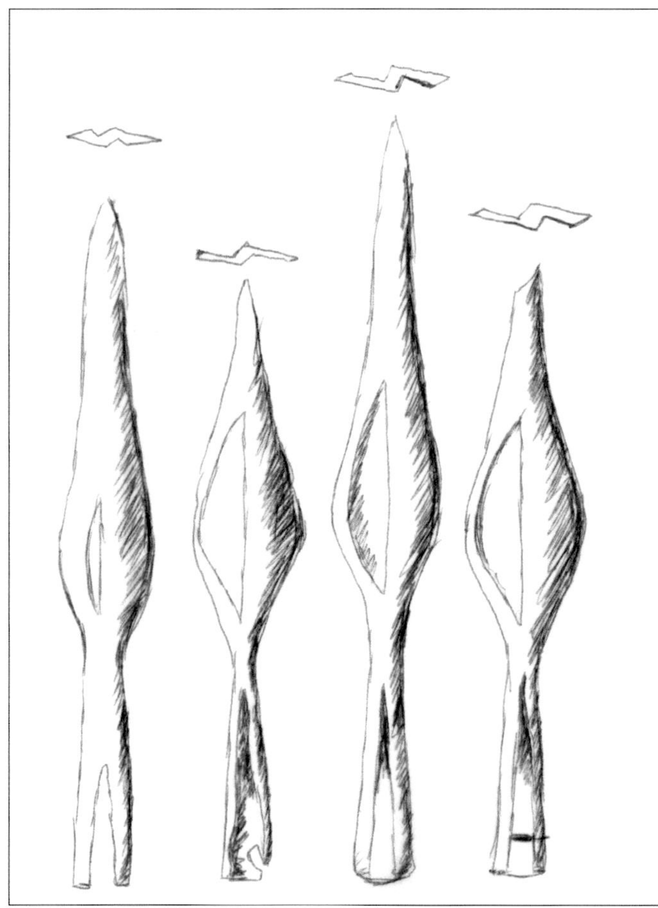

57 The distinctive type of post-Roman spearhead (Swanton Type I1) found in and around areas of Jutish settlement in southern Hampshire, with stronger stylistic links to British spearheads than to Anglo-Saxon types. *(After Swanton, 1973)*

and the Isle of Wight to Æthelwalh of Sussex in the late seventh century, which indicates that it was, prior to that point, not part of Sussex. Presumably it had been a part of Wessex.

If Sussex did go through an expansionist phase under Ælle and Cissa, it was not to last. The next *Bretwalda* listed after Ælle is a king of the West Saxons, which just about sums up the South Saxons' fate. While Wessex steadily grew in importance, Sussex steadily diminished. The next Anglo-Saxon Chronicle reference to Sussex after the period of Ælle is an entry for 607 which records Ceolwulf of Wessex fighting the South Saxons. It was a sign of things to come as the kingdom of Sussex was indeed eventually taken over by the kingdom of Wessex.

# CHAPTER 7

# THE FIVE WARLORDS OF GILDAS

So far, while getting to know something about the dynamics of the struggle for power in post-Roman Britain, what has been rather lacking is a sense of daily life for the average, hard-working fifth- or sixth-century warlord. Fortunately the daily life of the contemporary warlord was Gildas' specialist subject and the picture he paints offers a fascinating and unique insight into what it was really like to live life as a British warlord in the post-Roman period. His version is admittedly highly coloured and one-sided but he is not indulging, as far as we can tell, in posthumous tittle-tattle. He at least purports to be addressing his comments to actual living warlords, so if anything he said about the lifestyles of such high-profile figures was outrageously and obviously untrue, it would have presumably invited disbelief from his readers rather than the pious shock and horror that he was presumably aiming for. His version is also lent a fair amount of credibility by the very fact that it is entirely consistent with the behaviour of other warlords all the way through history up to the present day. Violence, sex, loot: it's all here in industrial quantities.

The five warlords on the receiving end of Gildas' tongue-lashing are Constantine, Vortipor, Cuneglasus, Maglocunus and Aurelius Caninus. Gildas tells us that Constantine ruled Dumnonia and that Vortipor ruled the Demetae, or Dyfed. Amazingly enough, what may be a memorial stone for this very Vortipor has survived (found at Castell Dwyran near Narberth) on which he is described as *Protictor* or Protector – the sort of title warlords love to take. Cuneglasus seems to be linked to the slightly mysterious kingdom of Rhos, which probably originated in the tribal territory of the Deceangli and later became part of Denbighshire. From later sources it seems likely that Maglocunus ruled Gwynedd in the north-west of Wales. Various genealogies place him there, and the *Historia Brittonum*, which was probably composed in Gwynedd, refers to a 'great king' of Gywnedd called Mailcun.[1] Cuneglasus and Maglocunus may have been related (a medieval genealogy makes them both great-grandsons of Cunedda), which would not be unreasonable bearing in mind the proximity of their territories (and the fact that Rhos was later swallowed up by Gywnedd).[2] There is unfortunately no agreement on where Aurelius Caninus was based. Assorted attempts have been made to link him to Ambrosius Aurelianus because of the vague similarity of their names, or to one of various characters in Welsh genealogies known as Cynan, a Welsh name that could conceivably be Latinised as Caninus. Sadly, though, unless new evidence turns up, like a conclusive inscribed stone, Aurelius Caninus will probably have to remain as 'address unknown'.

The biggest problem with understanding the context of these five characters is the difficulty of tying them (and indeed Gildas) down to a particular date. We have already touched upon this problem in Chapter 4 and it recurs here. Traditionally it has been accepted that Gildas must have been writing before 547 because an entry in the *Annales Cambriae* records Maglocunus as dying of the plague in that year. Since it would seem rather to defeat the object of the exercise for Gildas to be berating a dead warlord (though admittedly berating dead warlords is generally a safer occupation than berating dead ones!), it has been assumed that the five warlords were probably active some time in the first half of the sixth century. This may well be the case. However, the *Annales Cambriae*, dating in its final form from long after the period in question and including disputed references to Arthur and the battle of Camlann, is hardly the safest source if we are talking about sixth-century dates.

As discussed in Chapter 4, the only other potentially fixed point in Gildas is equally elusive. In a garbled and essentially incomprehensible passage, Gildas refers to the British victory at Badon Hill, his own birthday and the period of 44 years. Modern authors have tended to interpret this strange passage as meaning that Gildas was born in the same year as the battle of Badon, and that the battle took place 44 years before he was writing. Bede, by contrast, obviously understood Gildas to mean that the battle of Badon Hill took place 44 years after the initial arrival of the Anglo-Saxons, and since Bede is likely to have been more familiar both with the events and with the Latin of the period, his view carries some weight. If we add to this central element of confusion the fact that we don't have agreed dates either for when Gildas was writing (from which we could work back to Badon) or for the initial arrival of the Anglo-Saxons (from which we could work forwards), it becomes almost impossible to tie these five warlords down to any chronological period more exact than somewhere around the end of the fifth and the beginning of the sixth century.

We have already touched upon this period in Dumnonia in connection with Riothamus. This was a time in which the economic backwater that Dumnonia seems to have become under the Romans rediscovered its pre-Roman connections with the Atlantic trade routes to the Mediterranean. It was a period in which Dumnonia turned from being one of the most backward regions of Britain into probably the most cosmopolitan part. Major quantities of exotic ceramics from the Eastern Mediterranean were being shipped to the

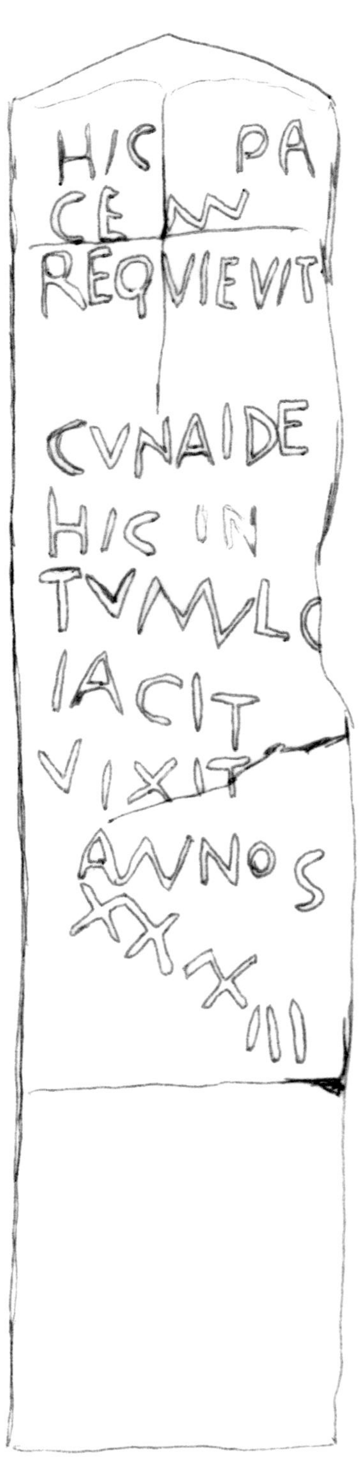


*58* Funerary inscription of Cunaide from Dumnonia. *(After Thomas, 1994)*

*59* Post-Roman inscription from Dumnonia recording one *IVSTVS*.

area, as part of either commercial or diplomatic traffic. Dumnonia has produced few inscriptions from the Roman period, but suddenly in the post-Roman period large numbers of Latin memorial inscriptions were being erected. Some of these use complex formulae suggestive of contact with the continent. An example from Carnsew in Cornwall, for instance, carries the inscription *HIC PACE NVP(er) REQVIEVIT CUNAIDE HIC (IN) TVMVLO IACIT VIXIT ANNOS XXXIII* ('Here recently went to rest in peace Cunaide. She lies in this grave. She lived 33 years').[3] Dumnonian authority, at least for a time, probably bridged the Channel to Dumnonée in Brittany. Some pre-Roman hillforts seem to have been reoccupied in Dumnonia, just as they were further east, in Durotrigan territory, but this is also the heyday of Tintagel (*colour plate 21*). For all its windswept, ruinous grandeur today, in the late fifth and sixth centuries this was a genuine small town with a form of street system and a concentration of multi-room and rectilinear buildings unlike anything found throughout western Dumnonia in the Roman period. It has been argued from the sheer quantity of Mediterranean ceramics found at Tintagel and the sophistication of its layout compared to other post-Roman sites in Dumnonia, as well as from its central position along the coastline of the later Hundred of Trigg, that Tintagel should be seen as the seat of the overall kings of Dumnonia.[4] If so, and if Constantine ever got to hear the less-than-complimentary remarks that Gildas was making about him, then it may have been on this very spot that he heard them.

The famous *Elegy for Geraint* is another literary source that may shed some light on Dumnonia at around the time of Gildas' Constantine. Geraint is specifically identified in the piece as a warrior from Dumnonia and the reference to Arthur in the poem might suggest that the work was intended to refer to a battle sometime in the early sixth century. The poem's battle is located at a place called Llongborth, but it is not unfortunately possible to identify either the enemy, whether British or Anglo-Saxon, or where Llongborth was supposed to be assuming it was a real battle. Suggested locations for Llongborth have included Portchester, Portsmouth, where the Anglo-Saxon Chronicle mentions a battle taking place in 501, and Langport in Somerset, which has an obviously similar name. It is, though, worth briefly quoting some of the elegy for what light it may shed on a Dumnonian's experience in battle in the post-Roman period:

> In Llongborth I saw a frenzy of killing
> And graves beyond counting
> And men red-drenched from Geraint's thrust.
> In Llongborth I saw blades clashing,
> Frightened men, heads bleeding,
> In front of Geraint the Great, worthy son.
> In Llongborth I saw cavalry spurs
> And men who did not fear the spear,
> Who drank wine from sparkling glass.
> In Llongborth I saw Arthur's
> Heroes who sliced with steel,
> Arthur the emperor, directing our work.
> In Llongborth Geraint was cut down,
> A brave man from the land of Dyvnaint,
> And before they died, they killed.
>
> (*Elegy for Geraint*)

The situation in Dumnonia around the beginning of the sixth century seems to have been similar in a number of ways to that in another kingdom featured in Gildas' diatribe, the kingdom of the Demetae, or Dyfed. Here, as in Dumnonia, there had been only limited Romanisation during the occupation. The Demetae did have a Roman-style *civitas* capital at Carmarthen, but apart from a few changes like the appearance of a few Roman trinkets and the introduction of rectilinear instead of curvilinear farmsteads, for most Demetae folk life in the Roman period was probably relatively little different from life in the pre-Roman period.

*60* Stone from Dyfed commemorating Vortepor and attributing to him the title *Protictor*.

However, just as in Dumnonia, Dyfed in the post-Roman period seems to have witnessed the sudden and rapid introduction of a more cosmopolitan culture. The sites at Brawdy and Gateholm are reminiscent in some ways of Tintagel, and significant quantities of Mediterranean pottery from this period are also found across the kingdom.[5] There is a strange reference in Gildas where amidst his tales of death, destruction and despair he says that:

> However, with the attacks subsiding, the island was flooded with such an abundance of supplies as has never been known and, as a result, licence and luxury of every kind grew.
>
> (Gildas, *On the Ruin of Britain*, 21)

Across most of Britain there is very little sign at all of luxurious living in the post-Roman period and it has been suggested that what Gildas is referring to in these lines is the appearance of these exotic Mediterranean ceramics along stretches of the western coast of Britain, along with whatever more perishable items accompanied them.[6] Chronologically Gildas seems to place this brief period of luxury just before the arrival of Hengest, rather than after it, but as already discussed above, where historians are relying on memories passed down orally, it would hardly be surprising if some events got slightly out of the correct order.

In addition to the Mediterranean ceramics, large numbers of Latin memorial stones also appear across Dyfed just as they do in Dumnonia. Among them are a number where the inscription suggests some continental influence. One of these is the probable inscription of Vortipor himself, '*MEMORIA VOTEPORIGIS PROTICTORIS*', 'to the memory of the Protector Votepor(ix)' (*60*).

In addition to Latin text, some Dumnonian inscribed stones feature inscriptions in ogam script, traditionally regarded as Irish, and the use of ogam script is even more widespread in Dyfed. Taken in conjunction with the appearance of a number of Irish place names in the area and the survival in an eighth-century Irish text of a story about an Irish dynasty founding the kingdom of Dyfed, the presence of the ogam inscriptions has traditionally been taken to indicate that Dyfed should be regarded as a part-Irish, part-British kingdom. The story known as 'The Expulsion of the Deisi' recounts the alleged adventures of a sept or sub-clan of Tara who were expelled from Tara by Cormac mac Airt. One part of the sept is said to have sailed across the sea from Ireland to Britain and founded a dynasty in Dyfed. A genealogy gives the alleged descent of Vortipor himself from the Irish leader Eochaid.[7]

Recently, however, the trend has been to question this interpretation, viewing the story as a later myth and the evidence of Irish place names as perhaps representing a much older connection across the Irish Sea.[8] This is certainly possible, but there is at least some evidence of Irish raiders crossing the Irish sea in the late fourth and early fifth centuries, with a proportion of them being taken into the Roman army, just as was happening with Germanic forces on the other side of the Empire at exactly the same time. There is, of course, St Patrick's own account of how he was taken by Irish raiders across the sea to Ireland, plus there is the case of the rather mysterious Attacotti. These people are mentioned in the description of the so-called 'Barbarian Conspiracy' raids across Britain in 367–369, and are most plausibly viewed as raiders from Ireland. The name Attacotti is most likely a Latin version of the Irish word *aithechthuatha*, a word meaning a client tribe, and four units of Attacotti are subsequently listed in the *Notitia Dignitatum*, fighting as part of the Roman army. They include the *Honoriani Atecotti Seniores*, the *Honoriani Attecotti Iuniores* and the *Attecotti Iuniores Gallicani*.[9] The story of an Irish dynasty taking over a British kingdom and giving it an Irish identity is also strikingly similar to the probable situation in the east of Britain, where Anglo-Saxon warlords were busy taking over British kingdoms and giving them an Anglo-Saxon identity. For these reasons it may be that there is at least a core of truth underlying the Deisi story, even if it is overlaid with fictional elements.

Moving north across Wales we come to Gywnedd, the territory of Maglocunus. This area had seen even less Romanisation than either of the *civitates* of the Dumnonii or the Demetae during the Roman period, and the Roman occupation probably had even less impact on life among the Ordovices than it did with either the Dumnonii or the Demetae. In fact the Ordovices, the tribe whose territory seems to have formed the basis for the kingdom of Gwynedd, may never have formally become a *civitas* at all. There was no Roman-style *civitas* capital for the Ordovices and the most significant outpost of Roman lifestyle in this region was the fortress at Segontium/Caernarfon. It is not, therefore, surprising to see occupation of hillforts in the region during the Roman period and probable occupation in the post-Roman period as well.[10]

However, despite its resistance to Romanisation, Gwynedd did not remain unaffected by the spread of a more cosmopolitan culture up the west coast of Britain in the fifth century. Mediterranean pottery is rarer in this area than further south but it does appear, and a Byzantine intaglio was found at Cefn Cwmwd.[11] Also present are large numbers of inscribed memorial stones. In addition, there is another story of a warlord coming from far away to take over a kingdom.

In this case the *Historia Brittonum* records a certain Cunedda, allegedly the great-great-grandfather of Maglocunus, coming 146 years before his time from the territory of the Votadini (today in north-east England and south-east Scotland) to push out some foreigners and found the kingdom of Gwynedd. The reference to foreigners being in the territory of Gywnedd gets some limited support from evidence of connections between Ireland and the Lleyn peninsula. There is, however, little specific evidence of connections between Votadinian territory and Gwynedd at the time, and it has been suggested that the story of Votadinian founders is a myth created around the time of the writing of the *Historia Brittonum* by a Gywnedd dynasty keen to emphasise its connections with the north.[12] This is certainly possible. However, the references to Cunedda in the *Historia Brittonum* are very brief and simple and do not particularly have about them the ring of bombastic dynastic propaganda.

There is also the fact that at some stage at the end of the Roman period the tribal territory of the Ordovices does seem to become the kingdom of Gwynedd, with the name of the tribe only living on in minor forms, as in the name of an area known as the Cantref Orddwy 'the cantref of the Ordovices'.[13] The origins of the name Gwynedd are unclear, but as we have seen elsewhere (with a British tribe adopting the Gallic name Atrebates, and with the *civitas* of the Regni becoming the kingdom of the South Saxons) a new name could potentially mean new, partly foreign management. It is true that the absence of Votadinian material is a slight worry in terms of complete acceptance of the Cunedda story, but arguing from an absence of material in a period as archaeologically obscure as the fifth century carries its own risks. If it did occur at all, and if the *Historia Brittonum*'s chronology has any validity, then Cunedda's arrival in Ordovician territory would have been earlier than the arrival of the Anglo-Saxons and might therefore have been on a slightly different basis. Cunedda might effectively have been the leader of some kind of Roman unit, which might mean that any artefacts that did arrive with him were more Roman than Votadinian. Alternatively, he might have been accompanied by fewer colleagues than other post-Roman warlords – similarly, when the British tribe acquired the continental name of the Atrebates, they did so probably through a takeover by the continental Atrebatic leader Commius and without any archaeological sign of cultural change. It may be that there is actual archaeological evidence of a Votadinian connection, but it just has not been found yet.

To the east of Gwynedd lay the territory of the Deceangli and the kingdom of Rhos, which may have developed out of it, areas probably both linked to Cuneglasus. The Deceangli could have been slightly more Romanised than the Ordovices, in the sense that they might actually have been regarded as a *civitas* – inscriptions on Roman-period lead ingots may suggest as much – though if so, it is unclear where their *civitas* capital was located. Ffrith and Prestatyn are both possibilities, but equally both these Roman-period sites may have been more closely linked to mineral extraction.[14] A large hillfort at Dinorben shows occupation in the Roman period and there is evidence of occupation in the post-Roman period too. It is also possible that the hillfort of Bryn Euryn was occupied in the fifth and sixth centuries. This hillfort lies above a medieval manor house called Dineirth (Welsh for 'the fort of the bear'), a name that may originally have been attached to the hillfort itself. Gildas opens his attack on Cuneglasus with another of his typically convoluted sentences which nonetheless makes two clear references to bears:

> And, Cuneglasus, why have you thrown yourself into the filth of your old sins from your teenage years, you bear, riding on many and driving your chariot at the fort of the bear, scorning God and upsetting His order, you whose name means brown butcher.
>
> (Gildas, *On the Ruin of Britain*, 32)

The unusual comment about a chariot has caused some comment. Can Gildas really be talking about some kind of war-chariot centuries after they seem to have fallen out of use, or should we imagine a more ceremonial version? However, it is the reference to bears that has drawn most interest. In particular it has been suggested that Gildas' reference to a '*receptaculi ursi*' or 'stronghold of the bear' might link Cuneglasus to Dineirth, 'the fort of the bear'.[15] Equally, the references to bears have also been used to attempt to link Cuneglasus and Dineirth to Arthur, a name that, if it is British in origin, could mean something like 'bear-man'. By contrast to the Roman period, when the Deceangli/Rhos may have been more closely connected to continental culture than the Ordovices/Gwynedd, in the post-Roman period the situation seems to have been reversed. Mediterranean ceramics hardly seem to have reached this area and even incised memorial stones are in much shorter supply than they are either to the west or to the south. This may be some kind of cultural indication of the post-Roman political balance of power between its two neighbours. The Ordovices/Gwynedd would eventually swallow up the area, with the name of the Deceangli only living on in the Cantref of Tegeingl, an administrative division in the region. Even Dinorben, which must have been one of the main sites in the tribal territory of the Deceangli, became known by another name meaning 'the fort of the Ordovices'.[16]

This then is the broad context for the world of the five warlords described by Gildas, which is interesting enough in itself. What the text of Gildas' diatribe does, though, in extraordinarily intimate detail, is shed light on what it really might have meant to live life as a post-Roman warlord.

If Gildas is to be believed (and as discussed above, it seems likely that, in his basic description of the warlords, he is), these were men for whom war against neighbouring Britons was a way of life. Of British warlords in general, Gildas writes: 'They make war but the wars they make are unjust wars, wars against their own countrymen' (*On the Ruin of Britain*, 27). And he doesn't get any more complimentary when it comes to his treatment of individual warlords. Of Aurelius Caninus he says: 'Have you not, by hating the peace of your country like some deadly snake, and thirsting for civil wars and constant plunder, shut the gates of heavenly peace and rest against your soul?' (*On the Ruin of Britain*, 30). Cuneglasus likewise is addressed in the following terms: 'Why have you started such a conflict against both men and God, against men who are your own countrymen, with your lethal weapons, and against God, with your infinite crimes?' (*On the Ruin of Britain*, 32). And he does not beat around the bush with Maglocunus either: 'And you also, dragon of the island, have robbed many tyrants of their kingdoms and of their lives as well' (*On the Ruin of Britain*, 33).

Caesar himself seems to imply that prior to the Roman arrival Cassivellaunus had been at war with all his neighbours, and judging by the warlike motifs that are regularly seen on pre-Roman British coins and in pre-Roman British art, it is likely that warfare and raiding across tribal borders was common in pre-Roman Britain. Gildas' comments about his five warlords suggests that this might well have been the situation in post-Roman Britain too. The various Irish annals that record events in Ireland in this period, for instance, also offer an almost constant list of battles and the Anglo-Saxon Chronicle of course paints a rather similar picture.

To be fair to the warlords in question, Gildas had for his day a rather highly developed view of a united British identity, in which he thought Britons should unite to face a common pagan enemy. The warlords themselves, by contrast, like their ancestors, probably viewed neighbouring kingdoms not mainly as fellow Britons, their countrymen, but more as foreigners, rivals and potential targets. Only occasionally, and doubtless where self-interest dictated, were neighbours seen as potential allies. Their attitude is perfectly in line with the idea that the Anglo-Saxons first settled in the east of the island not as unwelcome raiders but primarily as extra Germanic military muscle brought in by British warlords to fight other British warlords. Perhaps it was purely a matter of geography that prevented Gildas' five warlords from also hiring a few Anglo-Saxons. Perhaps, in their part of the country, Irish or Votadinian mercenaries were more readily accessible. Judging by the rest of Gildas' description, it certainly seems unlikely that they were taking a principled moral stand in not hiring Saxons.

It is interesting to note that Gildas particularly associates territorial aggression with Gwynedd, even at this comparatively early stage in the period after the end of Roman control. As noted in Chapter 2, in an echo of probable Catuvellaunian expansionism in the immediate pre-Roman period and possible Dobunnic expansionism in the immediate post-Roman period, the aggressive expansion of Gwynedd was to be a key feature of early Welsh history. At a fairly early stage Gwynedd took over the kingdom of Rhos. It absorbed Powys in the mid ninth century and Ceredigion in the late ninth century, while Dyfed came under its control in the early tenth century.[17] In his life of King Alfred, Asser (originally a monk at St David's in Dyfed and therefore presumably quite knowledgeable on events in Wales) indicates that in the ninth century Elisedd, the king of Brycheiniog, placed himself under Anglo-Saxon over-kingship in the face of aggression from Gwynedd, thus once again demonstrating that British kings simply did not see it as unacceptably 'unpatriotic' to team up with Anglo-Saxon allies against other British leaders.

If Gildas' warlords were tough on their neighbours though, they seem to have been just as tough on their own subjects, frequently exploiting them in the pursuit of personal gain. There is nothing particularly surprising here. The people may starve but warlords rarely do. Gildas, of course, starts off his diatribe with a comprehensive accusation about the nature of British kings, and obviously sees their kingdoms essentially as kleptocracies in which the strong and powerful pretty much just take what they want:

> Britain has kings but they are tyrants, and it has judges but they are corrupt. They spend their time terrorising and robbing the innocent while protecting and promoting bandits and criminals.
>
> They pursue criminals in their lands but they also have criminals to dinner, cosying up to them, rewarding them.
>
> (Gildas, *On the Ruin of Britain*, 27)

It is interesting to note that the warlords appear to have been working within societies that did have some kind of civil structures although whether these were survivals from the Roman administration or tribal practices or a combination of both is not clear. We have already noted references to judges, courts and judgements. However, it is even more evident that Gildas did not think the warlords paid enough attention to such niceties. Aurelius Caninus is described as 'swallowed up in the murk of terrible murders'.[18] Vortipor is described as 'seated on a throne of lies, and from head to toe stained with murder'.[19] And Constantine gets a special mention for not only committing murder, but doing so in a sacred setting:

> This year he made a solemn vow, in which he swore, first by God and then by the choir of saints and the Mother of God, that he would treat his countrymen fairly. Having done that, he then wounded and tore with spear and sword as if with teeth, in the habit of a holy abbot, in the presence of both their earthly mother and their spiritual mother the church, two royal youths with two attendants.
>
> (Gildas, *On the Ruin of Britain*, 28)

However, it has to be said that what really grabs the attention of many modern readers, and presumably would have had quite an impact in Gildas' day as well, is the sheer soap opera aspect of the warlords' private lives. Gildas is obviously shocked and horrified, but these are clearly men (and women) who didn't exactly regard lifelong monogamy as a major goal in their lives. Once again Gildas starts with a scene-setting general condemnation: 'They have plenty of wives but also mistresses and lovers' (Gildas, *On the Ruin of Britain*, 27).

Then we get down to the individual nitty-gritty. Constantine is first up:

> For many years before he had been stained with the filth of numerous adulteries, after rejecting his lawful wife contrary to the words of Christ Lord of the Nations, who said, 'what God has joined together, let no man separate' and 'men, love your wives'.
>
> (Gildas, *On the Ruin of Britain*, 28)

Vortipor seems to be accused of incest:

> Why, after the honourable death of your rejected wife, did you heavily weigh down your miserable soul with lust, almost the worst of all sins, and with the shamelessness of your daughter?
>
> (Gildas, *On the Ruin of Britain*, 31)

Cuneglasus gets no bonus points at all for chucking out his wife and going after her nun sister:

> Why, in addition to your other countless lapses, did you, after expelling your own wife, pay attention to her delinquent sister, who had promised to God perpetual chastity, the highest tenderness of heaven, as the poet says? You pursued her with all the energy of your mind, or rather with all its stupidity, contrary to the words of the apostle saying that adulterers cannot gain access to heaven.
>
> (Gildas, *On the Ruin of Britain*, 32)

But it's Maglocunus who really takes the biscuit with a private life that would not look out of place in any modern soap opera:

> For you scorned the marriage of your first wife (though, after you violated your vow, she was not yours lawfully but only because of the time she was with you) and took up with another woman, the wife of a man still living, and the wife not of a stranger but of your own nephew. Because of this your stiff neck, already burdened with sins, is now weighed down by the burden of two horrifying murders, one of your nephew and the other of your former wife, and you have now descended down into the very depths of sin, from low to lower and bad to worse. Following this, you then publicly married the widow who was responsible through guile and plotting for such a weighty crime and took her to be, as the tongues of flattering parasites say, your lawful, wedded wife, though we say, it is a sin.
>
> (Gildas, *On the Ruin of Britain*, 35)

Sex, murder, marriage: it's got the lot. Of course, when compared to many other powerful men throughout history, Gildas' warlords are far from being the worst. In times when the rule of law is loosened and the power of the sword is everything, powerful men tend to act as they please. Nonetheless, it is good to have such vivid details from a period where it can be hard to find the personal, human touch among the post-holes and sometimes rather unspectacular archaeological evidence.

# CHAPTER 8

# ARTHUR

No study of warlords in post-Roman Britain would be complete without at least a small section on Arthur. Having said that, it is hard to know if Arthur belongs anywhere near a history book. With some of the previous characters we have looked at, question marks have been raised over their authenticity as genuinely historical figures. However, nowhere do those question marks loom larger than with Arthur.

Hengest, for example, has references in Bede and the Anglo-Saxon Chronicle, links to Gildas, and a firm and understandable context and geography. It is possible that he is mythical, but on balance it looks more likely that he was a real historical figure around whom more poetic and mythical stories later clustered.

By contrast, the situation with Arthur looks to be just the opposite: he was essentially a figure of myth who later became regarded as historical. There is plenty of early evidence for an essentially mythical Arthur. He is mentioned in earlier Welsh stories like Culhwch and Olwen, for example, and has a starring role in the later Arthurian and Grail romances. In Culhwch and Olwen, for instance, Culhwch falls in love with Olwen, the daughter of a giant, but can only marry her if he fulfils a series of near-impossible tasks. Arthur offers to help Culhwch, and the story of how they accomplish a number of the feats is then told, including the hunting of the great boar Twrch Trwyth, the rescue of Mabon ap Modron (perhaps a figure derived from the Celtic god Maponus and only found after an encounter with a talking eagle and a talking salmon), and the quest for the cauldron of Diwrnach. It doesn't get much more mythical than this.

By contrast, early evidence for an essentially historical Arthur is thin on the ground. What may be the earliest reference to Arthur is contained in a stanza in the 'Y Gododdin', which mentions that a certain warrior was powerful 'but no Arthur':

He gave food for ravens on fort walls,
Though he was no match for Arthur,
Among the mighty on the battlefield,
Gwawrddur was a bastion in the front line.

('Y Gododdin')

Unfortunately the date of this reference is problematic. There has been much debate over the date of the 'Y Gododdin' itself, and even if an early date (of around 600) is accepted for the core of the poem, it is hard to prove conclusively whether this mention might be a later interpolation or not. Even more to the point, though the mention does at least appear to confirm Arthur's status as a warrior, it does nothing to indicate whether he was seen by the poet as an essentially mythical or a genuinely historical figure.

The reference to Arthur as emperor in the *Elegy for Geraint* (see Chapter 7) may at least indicate that this poet did regard Arthur as historical on some level, but again the poem is of uncertain date, plus the Arthur reference could have been inserted after the original poem was composed, and the very suggestion that Arthur was some kind of emperor may make it of questionable historical validity. Generally speaking, we would expect a character described as an emperor to be a figure of some stature and it seems unlikely that such a figure could have existed even in the Britain of the fifth and sixth centuries without more explicit evidence of him being found elsewhere. Having said that, a minor Moorish warlord called Masties did style himself *Imperator* in an inscription of the late or post-Roman period, so the terminology used in the elegy may not be entirely beyond possibility.[1]

With Geoffrey of Monmouth having long since been dismissed by most scholars as basically an early historical novelist (certainly he added his own large fictional element to the mix) rather than a proper historian, that pretty much just leaves the strange section on Arthur in the *Historia Brittonum*. This is essentially the basis for any view of Arthur as an understandable historical figure and the one source to which proponents of a historical Arthur keep coming back. As such, it is worth quoting the relevant section in full:

In that time the mighty Arthur fought against the Saxons, with the kings and warriors of Britain. And, though there were others more noble, he was twelve times the commander in battle and won twelve victories. The first battle he fought was at the mouth of the River Glein. The second, third, fourth and fifth battles were on another river, that the Britons call Dubglas, which is in the region of Linnuis. The sixth battle took place on the River Bassas. The seventh battle was in Celidon Wood, which the Britons call Cat Coit Celidon. The eighth battle was near the fort of Guinnion, where Arthur carried on his shoulder a picture of our Lord Jesus Christ and of the holy Mary, and he chased the enemy the whole day and killed

*61* The amphitheatre at Caerleon which is linked in legend with Arthur.

> many. The ninth battle was at the City of the Legion. The tenth battle was on the banks of the River Tribruit. The eleventh battle was on the Breguoin Hill, which we call Cat Bregion. The twelfth battle was a very fierce engagement, when Arthur came to Badon Hill. In this battle he himself killed nine hundred and forty, with the Lord's help alone. In all these battles the Britons were the victors, for no power can prevail against the will of God.
>
> (*Historia Brittonum*, 50)

At first glance this paragraph has a certain air of credibility about it. Arthur is not identified as an emperor or a king (as he is in the *Elegy for Geraint* and most later Arthurian literature). Instead he is identified as a warlord. A list of battles is given with names and some added detail which lends a certain sense that this is history being recounted.

However, there is also a sense that the author is deliberately trying to build up Arthur as a major figure and the trouble really comes when we take this detailed list and make a serious attempt to fit the Arthur of the *Historia Brittonum* into what is known about the politics and the geography of post-Roman Britain. The chronology is hard to pin down (though admittedly, as we have seen with Gildas and his warlords, that can be true even of historical figures of this period). The writer sandwiches this Arthur section between a reference to Hengest and Octa in Kent and a reference to Ida son of Eoppa in Bernicia. This could place Arthur anywhere between around 490 and around 550. We have already discussed the difficulties of fixing any kind of date more precise than 'some time around 500' for the battle of Badon. For what it is worth (which on early dates like this, probably not very much), the *Annales Cambriae* (a series of chronicles put together in Wales and dating in their final form perhaps from the late tenth century) date the battle of Badon to 516 and the battle of Camlann, the supposed site of Arthur's death to 537 (though it is not even mentioned in the *Historia Brittonum*).

Even more problematic than pinning down the chronology is any attempt to reconstruct the geography of the passage. For a number of the battles there is no single generally accepted identifiable location, and where locations do seem identifiable they place the battles right across Britain. The battle of the Wood of Celidon is usually associated, not unreasonably, with the Caledonian Forest in Scotland. By contrast, the battle of the City of the Legion is presumably either York, Chester or Caerleon, while the battle of Badon (judging by the general context of the politics of the time and Gildas' reference to the battle) is almost certain to have been somewhere in the south or south-west. In the light of the fragmented political geography of post-Roman Britain, it seems unlikely that any one British leader could have commanded battles in all these locations.

One possible explanation for such geographical diversity is that the author of this section has simply added other famous battles to a list of Arthur's original battles in order to fill out the list and make it more impressive. Thus, it has been argued that the battle of the City of the Legion could be a reference to the battle of Chester, which was fought in 605 or 606 according to the Anglo-Saxon Chronicle between King Æthelfrith of Northumbria and Welsh forces, probably mainly from Powys and Rhos. The battle of Celidon Wood could be derived from an early Welsh poem 'The Battle of the Trees', in which animated trees fought for the magician Gwydion. The battle of Breguoin could be a reference to a battle in the Cells of Brewyn mentioned in a Welsh triad and linked there to Urien, ruler of Rheged.[2] Finally, the battle of Badon would, of course, come from Gildas and be linked to the resistance by the British in the time of (or after) Ambrosius. This approach to interpreting the *Historia Brittonum*'s list of battles does simplify things but, of course, does nothing to reassure anyone that the passage should be seen as essentially historical.

And there are other reasons to doubt the idea of Arthur as a historical figure. Gildas makes no mention of him, even in connection with the battle of Badon (unless, as has been claimed by some historians, Cuneglasus is Arthur under another name, and the *ursus*/bear references in Gildas are a reference to the *Arth*/bear element in the name Arthur). Plus, as a figure in Welsh and British culture, he seems, in some sense, to appear from nowhere and leave no trace after he has gone. Genealogies were very important to medieval Welsh dynasties, as a way of establishing their claim to the land they occupied, and we have already seen how major historical figures like Magnus Maximus and Vortigern do appear in these genealogies. Arthur, however, does not (as one might expect from his high profile in the Middle Ages) feature prominently in early Welsh dynastic genealogies[3] and there is little in the way of an agreed genealogy for Arthur himself. The mysterious figure of Uther may have been his father, but apart from that there is no agreed line of descent for Arthur. Similarly, while there are occasional references to the sons of Arthur, these are elusive figures and do not seem to connect in any convincing way to later dynastic genealogies.

Apart from the few references already mentioned, the one thing that might conceivably suggest Arthur was a genuine historical figure is that a number of probably historical characters named Arthur do appear in the late sixth and seventh centuries. Thus, a great-grandson of Gildas' warlord Vortipor, presumably born in the late sixth century, was given the name Arthur in a genealogy of the kings of Dyfed. A son of the Dal Riadan king Aedan, probably born also in the late sixth century, was referred to as Arturius. An Irish king was killed in the mid-620s by someone called Arthur, who was therefore born either in the late sixth or very early seventh century.[4] These characters are almost certainly too late to be the Arthur of the *Historia Brittonum* (even if they came from appropriate parts of Britain, which they don't), but they could, at least theoretically, point to his existence. There is no evidence of Britons called Arthur before this period and the idea has been put forward that the sudden appearance of this cluster of names argues for a famous historical prototype. This is certainly possible, but we should remember that just because we have no evidence of Britons called Arthur in the pre-Roman or Roman period, it does not prove there weren't any.

All in all, the evidence for a historical Arthur looks decidedly thin. There is, however, one possible reason why a genuine historical Arthur might have left such light traces in early British records. He might, of course, not have been British at all. This is the route taken by those who claim that the name Arthur is not in fact derived from a British root meaning something like 'bear man' but is in fact derived from the Roman name Artorius.[5]

The drawback with this Artorius approach is that the only major known historical Artorius connected with Britain is Lucius Artorius Castus, a figure from the second half of the second century AD. He, though, is mainly linked to Dalmatia and his connection to Britain largely consists of his having spent time on Hadrian's Wall as *praepositus* of *Legio VI Victrix*; he is also known to have led a military force from Britain to put down a rebellion across the Channel in Armorica. This is a very far cry in all sorts of ways from the Arthur of the *Historia Brittonum*. It is conceivable that stories about this historical character could in

*62* Magnus Maximus. Spanish by birth, he was adopted as a major figure in British legend.

some way have become conflated with later stories about fighting Saxons, but it does nothing to establish Arthur as a genuine post-Roman warlord.

If we are looking for foreigners who might have been around in Britain at the time of the Saxons, and might have produced an Arthur figure, then we have to look elsewhere.

One approach might be to view Arthur as an Irish warlord operating in Britain. As touched on in the last chapter, Irish warlords may have seized power in a number of locations in the far west of Britain in the post-Roman period, and it is worth noting that the sixth- and seventh-century Arthurs seem to be connected either to Ireland or to areas of potential Irish influence.[6] The problem with seeing the original Arthur (if such a person existed) as Irish, though, is that the main areas of Irish influence at the time of the *Historia Brittonum* Arthur would have lain far from any Anglo-Saxon settlement. In that sense, the idea of the Saxons as Arthur's main enemy would probably be anomalous. The only conceivable context for an Irish Arthur consistent in any sense with the *Historia Brittonum* would be one with him working for a power

*63* Post-Roman stone inscription of Latinus. It lies at the evocatively named Slaughterbridge in Cornwall and was once thought to refer to one of Arthur's battles.

like Vortigern's possible Dobunnic/Cornovian confederation. The tombstone of Cunorix at Wroxeter, the capital of the Cornovii, dates from the late fifth century and has been suggested to indicate the presence of Irish fighters there.

In fact, when we consider the evidence, if Arthur was a foreigner and if he fought the Saxons on behalf of British rulers, then his most likely ethnic identity would have been Germanic or Anglo-Saxon. At first, the idea of the great British hero of the fight against the Saxons as himself an Anglo-Saxon or German seems incongruous. However, it is not. As we have already seen, it was regarded as the most natural thing in the world in the late Roman Empire for Romans in need of some extra military muscle to hire Germanic groups, even if they were going to end up fighting other Germanic groups, and we have already considered a number of probable examples of this phenomenon in post-Roman Britain. Not only this, but the Britons and Welsh were perfectly capable of making an originally foreign figure into a leading character in British story and legend. Thus Magnus Maximus, though originally Spanish, features largely in medieval Welsh stories because of his rebellion based in Britain and probably because of his utilisation of British militiamen (*62*).

If Arthur was Germanic or Anglo-Saxon, it would certainly explain why he never gets a mention from Gildas, who, judging by his comments about the *superbus tyrannus*, presumably viewed any other British authority hiring Anglo-Saxon mercenaries with the gravest suspicions.

It might also, for what it's worth, explain the strange appearance of one Osla 'Big Knife' in the Arthurian stories. Osla is an Anglo-Saxon name, and 'Big Knife' is assumed to be a reference to the *seax*, the large dagger often used by Saxons. Because of his clearly Saxon features, it is no surprise to find Osla Big Knife billed in one early Welsh story as Arthur's enemy at Badon Hill. It is, however, rather more of a surprise to find Osla in the much earlier story Culhwch and Olwen, portrayed as one of Arthur's close companions hunting the boar Twrch Trwyth. As already described, Culhwch and Olwen is a decidedly mythical tale, so we should not take the list of Arthur's companions in it as any kind of muster list of a real Arthur's lieutenants. However, considering Arthur's fame as a fighter against the Saxons, it is curious and interesting to find him in such company in such a relatively early poem.

Arthur's name could also itself conceivably be Germanic or a basically Germanic name given a more British look by Britons telling stories about him. A sixth-century Lombard king was, for instance, called Authari. Arnthorr is a Scandinavian name. There is an Artor Presbiter recorded in Yorkshire in 1066.[7] The Anglo-Saxon name Eadhere, though it doesn't look much like Arthur when written down, seems to have been pronounced something like Ather. Thus, for example, the modern place name of Atherington in Devon is either derived from Eadhere or from a similar name.[8] Uther's name too could be derived from an Anglo-Saxon name like Ohthere. There is even a neat (probably far too neat to be true, but still mildly entertaining) explanation of Arthur's and Uther's names that might, theoretically, substantiate the idea of Uther as a foreign Germanic mercenary and Arthur as his son born in Britain. *Uthere* is an (admittedly rare) Anglo-Saxon word that means foreign military force.[9] Eardhere is a theoretically possible (though no instances actually survive) Anglo-Saxon name composed of the name elements *Earda* ('earth'), which appears in names like Eardwulf, and again *Here*, meaning military force. It would be pronounced something like 'Earther', or maybe even Arther (bearing in mind how Eadhere, for instance, becomes Ather). Earda can be taken to mean not just 'earth' but more specifically 'homeland',[10] and probably has that meaning in a name like Eardwulf. If Uthere was a foreign soldier who came to fight in Britain, then his son Eardhere would be the soldier born in his new homeland.

If Arthur was originally a Germanic name, then at some stage it would have to have been adopted also as a Welsh and Irish name. There is no particular problem with this. As we have already seen, the foreign (originally Greek) name of Gerontius was adopted as the Welsh name Geraint, and there are a number of instances of Anglo-Saxon names probably being adopted as Welsh names

*64* Badbury Rings, one suggested site of the battle of Badon.

in the pre-Norman period. Thus the Anglo-Saxon Eadwine becomes Welsh Edwin, Anglo-Saxon Æthelstan probably becomes Welsh Elystan, Anglo-Saxon Wærstan probably becomes Welsh Gwerystan, Anglo-Saxon Eadred probably becomes Welsh Edryd and Anglo-Saxon Uhtræd probably becomes Welsh Uchdryd.[11]

When it comes to the potential geography of a Germanic Arthur, it would seem most reasonable to assume that such a figure would fit into one of the gaps (both geographically and chronologically) where there is evidence suggesting early Anglo-Saxon settlement under British control, but where we do not have evidence of another known Anglo-Saxon warlord playing a dominant role.

One possible area to explore on these grounds might be the territory of the *civitas* of the Belgae in the period after Ambrosius Aurelianus and before the rise of Cerdic, probably in the early sixth century. A base in the *civitas* of the Belgae would place Arthur within striking distance of a number of suggested locations for the battle of Badon, including Bath, Baydon and a number of hillforts called Badbury (*64*). It is mildly interesting to note that the Anglo-Saxon Chronicle lists Cerdic's grandfather as Esla, a name, at least in Anglo-Saxon terms, that is very similar to Osla (though bearing in mind that Cerdic's own name is British, at least one of his grandfathers is likely to have had a British, rather than an Anglo-Saxon, name). Such a location might tie in with the rather cryptic comment in

65 Early Anglo-Saxon funerary urns from Cleatham in Lindsey. *(Courtesy of Kevin Leahy)*

Gildas that Ambrosius' descendants (presumably living at very roughly the same time as the Arthur of the *Historia Brittonum*) were, in Gildas' eyes, much inferior to Ambrosius himself. If the descendants were indeed relying on a Germanic warlord, then Gildas would certainly have regarded them as much inferior. Having said that, as we shall explore in the next chapter, depending on when exactly Gildas was writing, this comment might equally refer to the transformation by the probably British, or part-British, Cerdic of a British *civitas* into an Anglo-Saxon kingdom.

There are, however, two other important candidates for the potential location of a Germanic Arthur. Recently claims have been made that Arthur might originally have been linked with the kingdom of Lindsey.[12] This slightly mysterious early medieval kingdom was based around Lincoln, and probably formed the northern half of the tribal territory of the Corieltauvi when it broke in two in the post-Roman period. There is significant evidence of continuing British influence in the area. The name Lindsey itself derives from the Roman name for Lincoln, Lindum. The first of Lindsey's Anglo-Saxon kings doesn't seem to have taken power in Lindsey until probably around the middle of the sixth century. Even then, one of Lindsey's subsequent 'Anglo-Saxon' kings had a British name, Cædbæd. Post-Roman penannular brooches, common in the west of Britain and generally reckoned to represent British influence, are, by the standards of eastern Britain, common in Lindsey. Examples found there include what appear to be locally made examples, demonstrating a continuing cultural tradition in this area.[13] In Lincoln it is thought that a Roman-period church, on the site of today's church of St Paul in the Bail, remained in continuous use until it was replaced in the early seventh century by an 'Anglo-Saxon' building.[14] The evidence for British survival at a time when Anglo-Saxons were settling in the area suggests a possibly British kingdom surviving with the help of Anglo-Saxon mercenaries until the middle of the sixth century, so perhaps Arthur could have been the commander of these.

Further supporting the idea of Arthur in Lindsey is the possibility that some of the battle locations from the *Historia Brittonum*'s list (among those that do not seem to have been 'borrowed' from elsewhere) may refer to this part of the country. Four of his battles are said to have taken place on a river called Dubglas, in the region of Linnuis. It has often been suggested that the region of Linnuis refers to Lindsey itself. This is certainly possible. There are, however, other candidates (for example, the area around Ilchester, Roman Lindinis, in Somerset), and there is currently no River Dubglas in the Lindsey area, nor any river with a similar name (though the name could, of course, have been replaced by a later one). Equally, the River Glen in the south of Lincolnshire is one of the two usually suggested candidates for the location of the battle at the mouth of the River Glein mentioned in the *Historia Brittonum*.

One of the potential drawbacks in looking for Arthur in Lindsey, though, might be that Lindsey itself was relatively isolated from the main thrust of the expansion of Anglo-Saxon culture westwards into central and western England. So the question is, could a warlord busy fighting the Saxons in such a backwater be raised to national prominence as the archetypal defender of Britain?

There is, however, an area of British political survival to the south of Lindsey which was much more central to the conflict with expanding Anglo-Saxon political control. We have already mentioned the probable planting of Anglo-Saxon mercenaries around the borders of the Catuvellaunian and Trinovantian confederation as one of the first acts of Anglo-Saxon settlement in this country. Yet this is an area that, according to the Anglo-Saxon Chronicle (in one of its entries for the later sixth-century, when it is probably becoming much more reliable) remained mostly under British political control as late as 571. For that year the Chronicle states: 'This year Cuthwulf fought against the Britons at Bedcanford and captured four towns, Lenbury, Aylesbury, Benson and Eynsham.' Bedcanford may or may not be Bedford, as is often suggested, but the location of the other towns captured is clear and they stretch across much of Catuvellaunian tribal territory. The fact that they were all taken after one battle suggests that much of Catuvellaunian territory remained united and under Catuvellaunian control well into the second half of the sixth

*66* Post-Roman penannular brooch found at Caxton in Catuvellaunian territory.

century. The idea of the survival of a British political entity in this area is supported by a range of other facts as well. As touched upon previously, there is evidence here of Roman-period practices and artefacts in Anglo-Saxon cemeteries. Also, as in Lindsey, post-Roman penannular brooches are found comparatively commonly (*66*) and the Catuvellaunian capital of Verulamium shows some of the strongest post-Roman survival of any Roman-period city in Britain. A sequence of construction in *insula XXVII* there seems to extend well into the fifth century, with a carefully dug trench holding a timber water pipe still in use at a very late date. Post-Roman occupation in timber buildings has been identified at a number of places in the city.[15] The shrine of St Alban on a hill outside the city remained an important Christian centre well into the fifth century (being visited by St Germanus sometime in the 420s) and quite possibly into the sixth century and beyond as well. It is one of only a very few locations in Britain mentioned by Gildas. We know, however, almost nothing about historical events within this politically British territory in the late fifth and early sixth centuries. If we are looking for a historical hole to fill with our Arthur, then this is in many ways an ideal one: it is important enough, central enough and mysterious enough to have potentially created the Arthur legend.

Some of the *Historia Brittonum*'s battles could also conceivably be linked to this area. South Lincolnshire's River Glein lies just to the south of Lindsey, but

*67* The walls of Verulamium.

it also lies just to the north of the borders of Catuvellaunian territory. Equally, if Linnuis is Lindsey, then a battle there is not inconceivable for a warlord based in Catuvellaunian territory. The Chilterns have been suggested as one possible location for the battle of the forest of Celidon. The location of the River Bassas has proved typically elusive, but one theoretical candidate is Bassingbourn ('the stream or little river of Bassa's folk'), which lies at a strategic spot just to the north of where Ermine Street meets the Icknield Way as it runs along the Chilterns. Here a rare buckle of a type used by fifth-century Germanic *foederati* was found (*see colour plate 14*). Possible locations for the battle of Guinnion Fort include the Roman fort of Vinovium near Hadrian's Wall or any of a number of Roman cities called Venta (such as Venta Silurum/Caerwent, Venta Belgarum/Winchester and Venta Icenorum/Caistor by Norwich), because a Roman 'V' equates to an early Welsh 'Gu'. There is, however, an equally good candidate on the northern border of Catuvellaunian territory. The Roman town called Magiovinium lay near modern-day Milton Keynes. Its 'Magio' element seems to mean 'Great', so effectively this is Great Vinium or Great Guinium.[16]

None of this, of course, at all proves that Arthur was a historical character. On balance, the evidence still seems to suggest that he was an originally mythical character who came in some way to be linked to the course of history. However, if he was a historical character, then the idea of him as a Germanic or Anglo-Saxon warlord fighting on behalf of British Catuvellaunian leaders would answer at least some of the more puzzling questions about this elusive and perennially intriguing figure.

# CHAPTER 9

# CERDIC

Compared with the elusive Arthur, we find ourselves back on slightly more solid ground with our next warlord, Cerdic. He appears as a major figure in the Anglo-Saxon Chronicle and was viewed by later kings of the West Saxons as the founder of their dynasty. This is not definitive evidence for his existence and his career, but it's much more promising than the situation with the elusive Arthur. The dates, as usual in the Chronicle, are admittedly probably rather unreliable. It has been pointed out that the king lists of Wessex give slightly different dates from those in the Chronicle[1], and the arrival of Cerdic and his son Cynric does also seem to be recorded twice in the Chronicle. Hence, the entry for 495 states: 'This year two leaders came into Britain, Cerdic and Cynric his son, with five ships, at a place called Cerdicesora.' This is followed by an entry for 508 which states: 'This year Cerdic and Cynric killed a British king called Natanleod, and five thousand men along with him. After this the area was called Netley, because of him, as far as Cerdicesford (Charford).' This is fair enough, except that it is followed by an entry for 514 which states: 'This year the West Saxons came into Britain, with three ships, at the place called Cerdicesora', and an entry for 519 which states: 'This year Cerdic and Cynric took over ruling the West Saxons. In the same year they fought with the Britons at a place now called Cerdicesford (Charford).'

The recurrence of Cerdicesora and Charford does seem to indicate that somehow the same basic facts have slipped in twice. Other evidence, including the lists of the kings of the West Saxons, suggests that Cerdic and Cynric are much more likely to have started their careers in 514 than in 495, and possibly even later then that.[2]

There is, however, one detail in the Chronicle that it is extremely unlikely the writer would have made up. It is probable that the Anglo-Saxon Chronicle in its final form was put together by chroniclers in Wessex around the ninth century. By this stage Wessex had for a long time been an explicitly Saxon kingdom and was keen to emphasise its Saxon identity. Clear proof of this is found in the issuing of laws (the Code of Ine) which discriminate against those still professing a British identity by fixing different amounts of *wergild* (money payable in compensation for a death) for Britons and Saxons. According to this code, Saxons were, literally, worth more than Britons. This code was issued around the end of the seventh or the early eighth century and does not reflect the situation in the early years of Wessex. What it probably does reflect is a period in which Wessex was in the process of conquering new British territories to the west of the original Wessex, and bringing new culturally British people under its control. It is exceedingly unlikely, therefore, that any West Saxon chronicler in the centuries immediately after the creation of the Code of Ine would have invented a founding father of the West Saxon dynasty with a British name.

Cerdic is basically the same name as Caradoc, which in turn is the same name as Caratacus, the great British warlord of the period of the Roman invasion. Cerdic's name is found in exactly the same form and about a century later attached by Bede to the ruler of a British kingdom in the north, Elmet. Equally, a British Ceredig is celebrated in the 'Y Gododdin':

> Ceredig, a beloved leader,
> A rampaging hero in the fight,
> Battle shield fretted with gold,
> Spears smashed to pieces, to splinters,
> The strike of his sword, strong, fierce,
> He held the front like a true man.
>
> ('Y Gododdin')

And Caradoc Vreichvras (or 'strong arm') was one of Arthur's supposed close comrades, who was described, for instance, in a Welsh triad as Arthur's chief elder at Celliwig in Cornwall. He might also be the same character known as Caradoc ap Ynyr who may have been a ruler of Gwent in the sixth century. There is no getting round it. Cerdic's name is about as British as it could be and that fact goes a long way towards supporting his historical existence.

It is even possible that the names of two of Cerdic's principal successors, Cynric and Ceawlin, are also British. Cynric could be Anglo-Saxon, but it could also easily be of British derivation. Thus it may incorporate the same *cun*/'hound' element as a large number of other British names, since 'Cun' becomes 'Cyn' in early Welsh, as Cunobelin becomes Cynfelyn. Such *Cun-* names are extremely common in the post-Roman period, with a whole host of them being found on fifth- and sixth-century inscriptions (including Cunacus, Cunatamus, Cunegnus, Cunocennus, Cunogenus, Cunomorus, Cunovalus,[3] plus, of course, Gildas'

Cuneglasus). It has even been argued that Cynric should be specifically equated with the British name Cunorix. Ceawlin, in turn, may be an early version of the British name Colin.

Cenwalh, a seventh-century king of Wessex and an unquestionably historical figure mentioned in Bede, has a name that incorporates the element *walh* or *wealh*, which was used by the Saxons of the Britons. What's more, another equally historical seventh-century king of Wessex, Cædwalla, also bears a name that could not be more British if it tried, and which has a long history as a personal name in Wales. The powerful Cadwallon of Gwynedd in the seventh century, who will be considered in more depth in Chapter 10, is one obvious example. (This is also the name from which was derived that of the most powerful British tribe of the pre-Roman era, the Catuvellauni.)

All this cannot be coincidence. Even more strongly than the vague suggestions of a British element within the Saxon royal house of Sussex, these names seem clearly to indicate that not only was there an even stronger British element in the Saxon royal house of the West Saxons, but that a Briton probably founded it. In the last chapter we discussed the possibility of a Saxon being adopted as a hero by the Britons. This seems to be the opposite situation, with a Briton becoming a hero and leader for the Anglo-Saxons.

There is, of course, nothing inconceivable in historical terms about a Briton leading an ostensibly Anglo-Saxon army and kingdom. As we have already seen, Roman generals had long been leading Germanic armies and one, Aegidius, may even have become specifically king of the Franks. According to Gregory of Tours, Aegidius replaced Childeric as king of the Franks for eight years.

Bearing Cerdic's hugely significant British identity in mind, we now need to turn to the Anglo-Saxon Chronicle's account of what Cerdic and Cynric are actually supposed to have done. For a start (ignoring the probably duplicated account of a landing at the same place in 495), it is recorded that the original West Saxons (presumably Cerdic and Cynric as in the 495 entry) landed at a place called Cerdicesora in 514. There is unfortunately no general agreement on exactly where this was, though it is assumed, on the basis of subsequent events, to have lain somewhere to the west of Southampton. However, five years later Cerdic and Cynric are recorded as fighting Britons at Charford and in the same year taking control of the West Saxon territory. The pair are recorded fighting a subsequent battle in 527 at the unidentified Cerdicesley. Cerdic is recorded as dying in 534, with Cynric taking over power among the West Saxons. There is then a subsequent gap in recorded fighting until 552, when Cynric on his own is listed as fighting the Britons at Old Sarum, outside Salisbury (*68*). Cynric and Ceawlin then fight the Britons together in 556 at Beranbury, usually identified as Barbury Castle on the northern edge of the Marlborough Downs (*69*), and in 560 Ceawlin is recorded as taking over the kingdom, by which time Cynric was presumably dead.

*68* Old Sarum.

*69* A view across Barbury Castle.

If we take the Anglo-Saxon Chronicle account literally, Cynric was fighting the Britons in 519 and reigned until 560, over 40 years later, which suggests quite a long career by the standards of the sixth century. There are three possible explanations for this. First, it is conceivable, even in a period when life expectancy was much lower than today, that he could have lived this long. Rulers are, after all, generally much better fed and better looked after than those being ruled, though the chances of a sudden and violent death were quite high for the average post-Roman warlord. Secondly, as touched upon previously, it is perfectly possible that the Chronicle dates for the early West Saxon kings may be slightly wrong. Working from Wessex king lists, alternative dates for Cerdic taking power among the West Saxons have been calculated, which would place the event in the 520s or even 530s. In addition, there is the intriguing possibility of a disappearing son. In one Wessex genealogy Cynric is listed as Cerdic's grandson rather than his son, while another figure named Creoda is the son of Cerdic and father of Cynric.[4] For whatever reason he went missing, Creoda might explain Cynric's otherwise rather lengthy career.

Cerdic's 'landing' poses a few questions. Since he seems to have been British, his arrival would have been more of a homecoming than an invasion. If it took place at all; rather than being a literary device introduced by a later chronicler to show him as a conqueror, presumably he brought Anglo-Saxon reinforcements with him. Regardless of the nature of his landing, we are then told a story of fighting along a line from Charford north to Salisbury and on to Barbury Castle near Marlborough. The basic course of this line could be hugely significant in terms of understanding Cerdic and Cynric because it roughly marks the western borders of the pre-Roman territory of the Atrebates, particularly that part of it which later formed the eastern half of the *civitas* of the Belgae in the Roman period. In other words, Cerdic is fighting on the western borders of what could well have been the home territory of Ambrosius Aurelianus. This is also an area that saw limited Anglo-Saxon settlement in the fifth century, followed by an explosion of Anglo-Saxon cemeteries in the first half of the sixth century at around the same time as Sussex was developing a distinctive Anglo-Saxon identity, and also, of course, at the same time as Cerdic and Cynric are recorded as being active. As discussed previously, this switch to an Anglo-Saxon culture and identity may even have been what Gildas had in mind when he wrote around this same time that the descendants of Ambrosius were much worse than Ambrosius.

We have already noted examples of early Anglo-Saxon settlements being placed in what look like strategic locations along tribal/*civitas* borders. The Anglo-Saxon settlements along the western borders of the tribal territory of the Atrebates and of the *civitas* of the Belgae, when taken in conjunction with the battles said to have been fought by Cerdic and Cynric, seem very much to fit into this pattern.

*70* Bokerley Dyke.

For a start, as pointed out by others, the fifth and sixth centuries in eastern Wiltshire seem to show a blending of British and Anglo-Saxon cultural elements rather than a straightforward replacement of a British culture by an Anglo-Saxon one. At Ashton Keynes, Avebury, Highworth, Liddington and Swindon, for instance, early Anglo-Saxon settlements are found very close to (sometimes actually on top of) British settlements of the Roman period. It is also, for example, now becoming clear that organic-tempered pottery of the period which appears on Anglo-Saxon settlements and burials in this area, and which used to be thought to demonstrate an exclusively Anglo-Saxon presence, does not in fact do so. This material is also found in association with a significant number of Roman-period British settlements. At Coombe Down, for instance, a sunken-featured building was found associated with organic-tempered pottery and Roman artefacts on the outskirts of a significant Roman-period British settlement.[5] Like Cerdic himself, the archaeology suggests a society of mingled British and Anglo-Saxon elements rather than one where the Anglo-Saxons simply pushed the Britons out.

The geography of the Anglo-Saxon Chronicle account would fit in very neatly with the idea of early Anglo-Saxons being brought in by the Atrebates to aid them in conflicts with other British tribes. A battle at Charford would presumably have been fought against the neighbouring Durotriges. The late or post-Roman Bokerley Dyke, which cut the Roman road from Dorchester to Salisbury, lies close to the border between the territory of the Durotriges and the *civitas* of the Belgae and suggests a history of hostility between the two areas at this stage (*70*). The fact that Durotrigan territory remains almost entirely without Anglo-Saxon settlement for up to two centuries after the initial Anglo-Saxon settlement in the territory of the *civitas* of the Belgae also clearly suggests a distinct break in communication between the two areas. A battle at Salisbury could also have been against the Durotriges, but it could just as well have been against the Dobunni, the logical enemy of Cynric and Cewlin at the battle of Barbury Castle.

Such a confrontation in the sixth century would have followed a probably long history of conflict between the Dobunni and the Atrebates in exactly this area. Shifting patterns of pre-Roman coinage in this area suggest possible conflict in the pre-Roman period. Early Dobunnic coinage is found to the west of Marlborough but then seems to disappear, to be replaced by Atrebatic coinage.[6] This is followed by evidence of conflict along this same border in the late fourth century (see Chapters 2 and 4), and this in turn is followed by the battle of Wallop in the fifth century. This interpretation of Cerdic and Cynric's actions as a continuation of earlier conflicts between the Atrebates and the Dobunni in the area seems to be confirmed by one of the next Anglo-Saxon Chronicle entries for Ceawlin after the battle of Beranbyrig. In 577 the Chronicle states that:

> This year Cuthwin and Ceawlin fought with the Britons and killed three kings, Commail and Condida and Farinmail, at the place called Deorham, and took from them three cities, Gloucester, Cirencester, and Bath.

It seems fairly clear that what Ceawlin was confronting in this battle was an essentially Dobunnic force. Deorham is thought to be the village of Dyrham, just to the north of Bath. Dyrham lies within the territory of the Dobunni. Cirencester was the capital of the Dobunni, and Gloucester was another of their biggest cities, and one potentially linked to Vortigern himself. Bath was a Dobunnic site in pre-Roman times and though it became part of the *civitas* of the Belgae in Roman times (probably thereby helping to ensure post-Roman conflict), it lies just north of Wansdyke and therefore almost certainly became Dobunnic again in post-Roman times. Whether the three cities really had separate kings by 577, or whether the Chronicle is simply recording the commanders of separate contingents from the three separate cities is not clear. However, the fact that all three figures were fighting alongside each other at a single battle, and that all their cities fell together after the defeat, clearly suggests a Dobunnic political entity still retaining, at the very least, a considerable degree of unity. The battle of Deorham can be seen therefore as effectively marking the final victory of Atrebatic forces over the Dobunni in a very long-running tribal conflict.

This is, of course, assuming that it is really legitimate to see Cerdic and Cynric as turning an Atrebatic political entity into the Anglo-Saxon kingdom of the West Saxons, just as Ælle may have turned the *civitas* of the Regni into the Anglo-Saxon kingdom of the South Saxons.

The exact origins of the kingdom of the West Saxons have recently become extremely controversial because of the trend to reject a key feature of the Anglo-Saxon Chronicle's account of its founding and to look instead to the Upper Thames region for the original birthplace of the kingdom. This is based on the idea that there was, in the first half of the sixth century, an independent Jutish kingdom in southern Hampshire.[7] The argument then goes that, if this was the case, then this area could not have been controlled by the West Saxons at this stage, and that the Chronicle account is the result of a Wessex dynasty with its origins in the Thames Valley area wanting to legitimise its later takeover of the Jutish area by rewriting earlier history.

It is certainly theoretically possible. However, as we have seen, the Anglo-Saxon Chronicle's account of Cerdic and Cynric fits very well with the archaeology and previous history of the relevant area, and we should probably only look to reject it if there are extremely strong and persuasive grounds for doing so, and there aren't.

The only evidence for early links between the kings of the West Saxons and the early Anglo-Saxon settlements in the Upper Thames area is that the first bishop to minister to the West Saxons or Gewissae (the political entity seems to have been known by this name in its earliest period, but as we have seen in a number of other instances, names could easily change) established his base at Dorchester-on-Thames. However, as already discussed in Chapter 2, it is much more likely that the early Anglo-Saxon settlements in the area, certainly those north of the Thames like Dorchester, were mainly linked eastwards to Catuvellaunian territory, not southwards, and only became part of the territory

*71* The abbey at Dorchester-on-Thames.

of the West Saxons after the battle of Lygeanburg in 571. In addition, the Gewissae are also recorded by Bede as being located around Winchester and the see of the Gewissae was transferred to Winchester after only some 25 years at Dorchester-on-Thames. Why exactly the original see was established at Dorchester-on-Thames is not clear, but it may have had something to with the specific situation at the time of its creation.

Bede's account of the establishment of the see reads as follows:

> At that time, when Cynegils was king, the West Saxons, who used to be called the Gewissae, embraced the Christian faith through the preaching of Bishop Birinus. He came to Britain on the instructions of Pope Honorius, having promised to him that he would spread the word of the holy faith in parts of the interior beyond English control, where no other teacher had previously been. Asterius, Bishop of Genoa, gave him episcopal consecration and when Birinus first came to Britain, he arrived in the territory of the Gewissae. Finding that they were all definitely pagan, he decided it was best to preach the word of God to them, instead of going further and looking for others.

> So, as he preached in this province, the king himself, having been catechised, was baptised along with his people. Oswald, the most holy and victorious king of the Northumbrians, was there and received Cynegils as he came out from baptism, and in an alliance pleasing and acceptable to God, he adopted the reborn Cynegils as his son, and married his daughter. The two kings gave to Bishop Birinus the city called Dorcic, so that he could establish his episcopal see there.
>
> (Bede, *Ecclesiastical History* 3, 7)

Cynegils' conversion seems to be intimately tied up in some way with his relationship with Oswald, the already Christian king of Northumbria. The establishment of Birinus at Dorcic/Dorchester is clearly seen as a sign of the alliance between the two kings and it is not just Cynegils who is recorded as giving Dorchester to Birinus, but Oswald too. In this context, it would seem reasonable that the two kings decided to find a location for Birinus in that part of Wessex closest to Northumbria. Bearing this in mind, in addition to the fact that the location of the see was relatively quickly transferred south to one of the main seats of West Saxon power at Winchester, its presence at Dorchester-on-Thames in the early seventh century certainly cannot be taken to indicate that this was where the West Saxons originated over 100 years earlier.

Equally, there are strong reasons to doubt the idea that the Anglo-Saxon Chronicle's account of Cerdic and Cynric's activities was deliberately faked in order to legitimise a later Wessex takeover of Jutish territory. For a start, if this was what was happening then it would be logical for the chronicler to locate Cerdic and Cynric's activities firmly inside Jutish territory. However, to the extent that it is possible, from the few literary references and from a smattering of relevant place names, to identify where Jutes were living in Hampshire, this seems to be simply not the case. The two battles that can be located, Charford and Salisbury, lie either on the edge of the Jutish area or outside it entirely. Then again, as already touched on, there is little or nothing to demonstrate that those Jutes who did live in southern Hampshire were ever politically independent of Wessex. We know of a Jutish kingdom in the Isle of Wight and there is evidence for a region settled by Jutes in South Hampshire, but there is nothing to indicate that these Jutes ever formed a separate kingdom there. As we have seen in many cases already, Anglo-Saxon settlement does not necessarily indicate Anglo-Saxon political control.

There is the possibility that Jutes were settled here to counter any threat of expansion by the South Saxons under Ælle (and possibly Cissa). Certainly the evidence of British-style spearheads found across the region in the late fifth and early sixth centuries suggests that the Jutes were here under the control of some form of British (or in the later stages Anglo-Saxon/British) authority, rather than as independent settlers and conquerors. The spearheads in question are of the type with corrugated blades briefly discussed in Chapter 6. They have very few

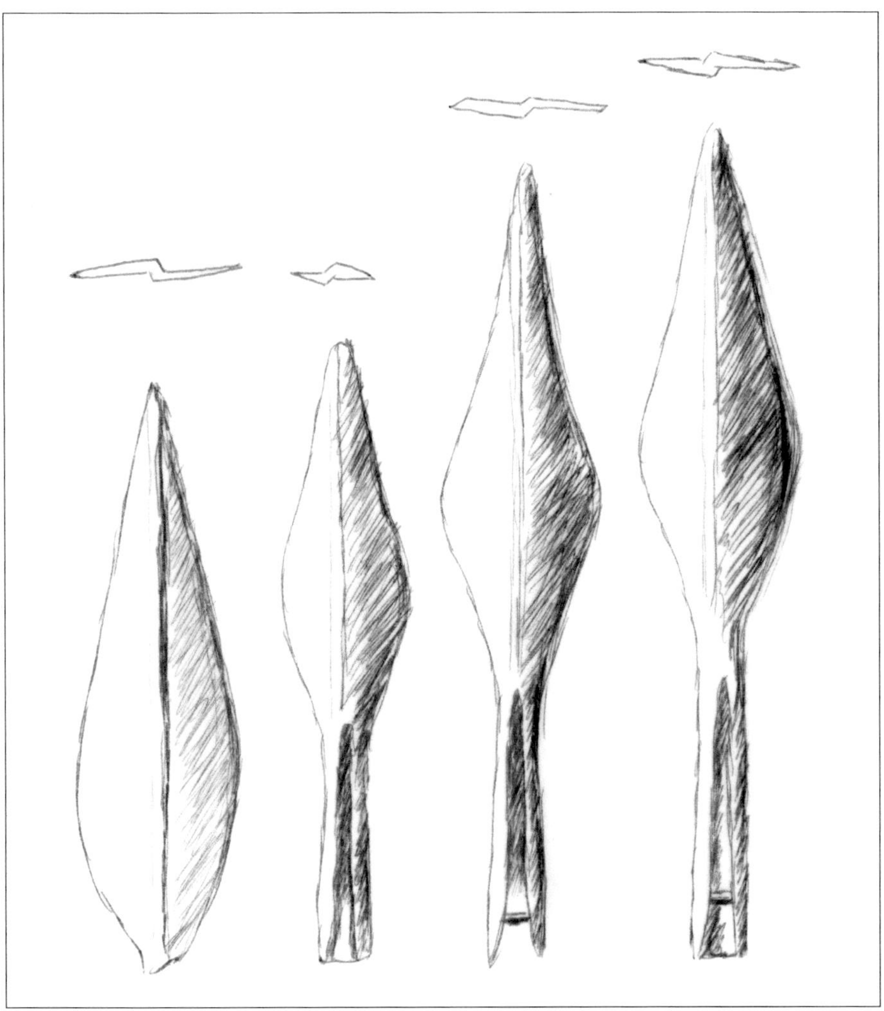

*72* A type of post-Roman spearhead (Swanton Type K1) with links to British types. The type is found across the probable territory of Wessex at the end of the sixth century. *(After Swanton, 1973)*

parallels among spearheads in the continental homelands of the Anglo-Saxons, but seem to have close links with earlier British spearheads.[8] Their appearance in Anglo-Saxon burials in a given area, therefore, seems to be a strong sign of military cooperation in the region between culturally Anglo-Saxon and culturally British people. This interpretation is supported by the appearance of these spearheads in two graves that also contain Quoit Brooch Style items that probably also derive from a mixed British and Anglo-Saxon context.[9]

Interestingly, there is also what seems to be a stylistically linked but later group of spearheads with British connections; these are found across the same

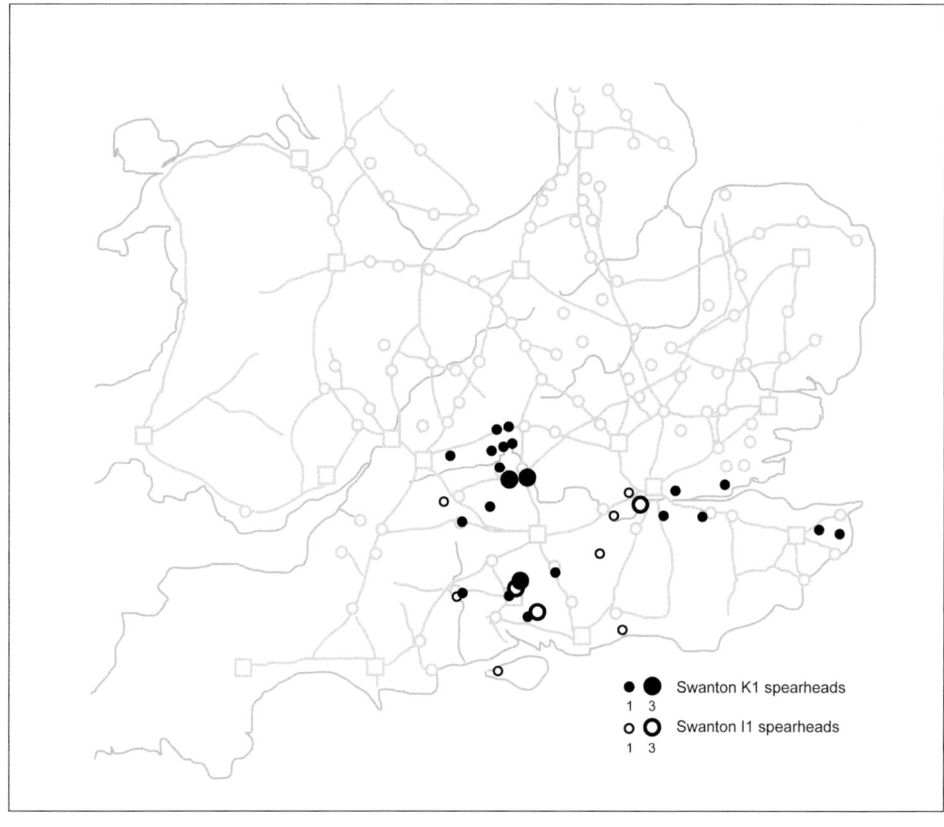


*73* Distribution of spearheads, showing the northwards advance from I1 to K1 types. *(After Swanton, 1973)*

areas of Hampshire as the group mentioned in Chapter 6 (*72*). However, this style of spearhead also extends further north towards the Thames. The group dates up until the middle of the sixth century or possibly later, and could conceivably echo an expansion of Atrebatic/Wessex power northwards under Cerdic and his successors (*73*).[10]

This idea of continuity between an Atrebatic political entity and the kingdom of the West Saxons also seems to be confirmed by the history of Wessex in the late sixth and early seventh centuries. In addition to attacking the Dobunni, Wessex also expanded in two directions perfectly consistently with an Atrebatic heritage. We have already touched upon the expansion of Wessex northwards towards the Thames. Atrebatic territory had extended almost as far as this in pre-Roman times, and it was probably an area that witnessed some of the conflict between the Atrebates and the Catuvellauni in that period. Certainly there is an unusual concentration here of defensive earthworks from the pre-Roman period.[11] The other direction in which Wessex expanded was eastwards towards Kent. In 568 the Chronicle records Ceawlin and his brother beating Ethelbert, the king of Kent, at Wibbandun and pursuing him into Kent. The location of Wibbandun is unclear, but the expansion of West Saxon power into (presumably) east Kent is a repeat of the Atrebatic expansion into Kent in pre-Roman times.

One interesting feature of the battle of Wibbandun and the subsequent pursuit into Kent was that this action must almost inevitably have involved Ceawlin and his forces moving through the Atrebatic area around Silchester. The fact that there is no mention of fighting between the West Saxons and another power in this area at around this time again seems to confirm the essential unity of Atrebatic territory (apart from Sussex) in the transition to the Anglo-Saxon kingdom of Wessex.

Another factor supporting the picture of overall continuity is the development of Salisbury (or at least nearby Wilton, now almost a suburb of Salisbury) and Winchester, both significant Roman-period centres in the *civitas* of the Belgae, as two of the major centres of the kingdom of Wessex, not to mention the fact that the Atrebatic heartlands remained for a long time also the heartlands of Wessex.

There is one final aspect of continuity between the Atrebates and Wessex which is worth considering, as it had a far wider geographical impact. As mentioned previously, the Atrebates were (along with the Catuvellauni, Trinovantes and Cantii) one of the tribes that most quickly adopted Roman culture in the pre-Roman period, and they were probably instrumental in bringing about the Roman occupation of Britain, with their king Verica inviting the Romans into Britain to aid him in his battle with the Catuvellaunian/Trinovantian confederation. The Atrebates therefore represented, perhaps because of their central location in southern Britain, the key swing-state both culturally and politically in the creation of Roman Britain.

In the post-Roman period they may well also have been the key swing-state in aiding the creation of an Anglo-Saxon England. Again, they do not seem to have been the only British tribe to adopt Anglo-Saxon culture and invite Anglo-Saxons in to help them in their battles with other Britons. However, the Briton Cerdic's apparent decision to recreate himself as an Anglo-Saxon and to recreate the Atrebates as the West Saxons may ultimately have played a deciding role in ensuring that central, southern and eastern Britain became firmly Anglo-Saxon. Anglo-Saxon culture expanded hand in hand with West Saxon political power. Within decades of Cerdic's activities, West Saxon expansion led to the battle of Bedcanford in 571 which probably shattered forever the Catuvellaunian/Trinovantian confederation (the last explicitly British power base in the centre and east of Britain) and paved the way for its adoption of Anglo-Saxon culture. It also led to the smashing of Dobunnic might at Deorham just a few years later, leaving the way free for the expansion of Anglo-Saxon culture westwards to the Bristol Channel to separate still culturally British Cornwall and Devon from Wales. If the Atrebates had suffered at the hands of the Catuvellauni in pre-Roman times, and at the hands of the Dobunni in post-Roman times, they had now finally got their revenge and because of it, Britain was changed forever.

# CHAPTER 10

# EDWIN, CADWALLON AND PENDA

Cerdic, Cynric and Ceawlin were not by any means the last warlords Britain produced in the years following the end of Roman Britain. Far from it. The seventh century was to produce a bumper crop of ruthless, ambitious men not too bothered by conscience and moral qualms and very ready to use violence to impose their will both on their own people and on their neighbours.

As time went on, so the causes and conduct of conflict remained pretty much the same. A closer look at the intertwined careers of three major warlords in what is usually regarded as a key period of Anglo-Saxon expansion reveals once again a much more complex reality than the old view of a straightforward confrontation between Britons and Anglo-Saxons. This is a world in which it is clear that what was still paramount in the minds of the warlords were not questions of Anglo-Saxon or British identity but matters of sheer political power – power for themselves and power for their tribe or kingdom.

In 604 Æthelfrith of Bernicia invaded the kingdom of Deira to the south, killing the king and forcing the young prince Edwin to flee. After a period in exile at the court of King Rædwald in East Anglia, where he narrowly escaped assassination, Edwin returned north with Rædwald and his army. In 616 the forces of Rædwald and Edwin defeated and killed Æthelfrith at the battle of the River Idle and placed Edwin on the throne of the united and ostensibly Anglo-Saxon kingdom of Northumbria.

It is worth pausing for a moment at this point to take a look at this kingdom of Edwin's, because though it is commonly referred to as an Anglo-Saxon kingdom, there was quite a lot about it that was actually British as well. In fact, in many ways it was arguably rather more British than Anglo-Saxon. Bearing in mind the closeness of the kingdom (particularly of Bernicia, its northern part) to the continuing British culture in what is now Scotland, and the distance of this kingdom away from the short southern sea crossings that would have brought most Anglo-Saxon immigrants across from the continent, this should be no surprise.

74 A seventh-century Anglo-Saxon warrior. *(Courtesy of John Conyard and www.comitatus.net)*

Let us then start with Edwin's own kingdom of origin, Deira. The name Deira, for a start, is British, deriving almost certainly from the same root as the name of the main Roman-period town in the area, Derventio (Malton). This name of course survives today in the name of the local river, the Derwent. The kingdom of Deira seems to have been based on the territory of the Roman-period *civitas* of the Parisi, which in turn took over the territory of the so-called Arras culture, which occupied the area from the fourth century BC onwards. The first Anglo-Saxon king of Deira who can be definitely be identified is Ælle (not the same man as the Sussex Ælle), who ruled in the late sixth century. This, of course, suggests that just as British political power survived in Catuvellaunian territory as late as 571, the same could easily have been true of Deira as well. In fact events in the area in the pre-Roman period may have been remarkably similar to events there in the post-Roman period.

The so-called Arras culture seems to represent the adoption by Britons in east Yorkshire of both a foreign name and a foreign culture, promoted no doubt by the arrival of some actual foreigners as well. In the fourth century BC a number of cemeteries appear there which feature burials where the body is accompanied by a cart (either simply placed upright in the grave or with its wheels removed and laid by the side of the cart). In Britain this burial rite is restricted to this area of Yorkshire. However, it has close parallels in mainland Europe, particularly in Burgundy and in the area occupied by a continental tribe called the Parisi. British artefacts from the so-called Arras Culture are, however, generally not exact matches for their continental counterparts and only some aspects of the continental culture are copied. This suggests a process in which the local British population adopted key aspects of the culture and eventually the political identity of a number of (presumably influential) immigrants, a process that could therefore be seen as a precursor to events in the same area in the post-Roman period.[1]

The other constituent part of the kingdom of Northumbria, Bernicia, probably had even less about it than Deira to mark it out as Anglo-Saxon. The Anglo-Saxon Chronicle mentions Ida establishing himself as the first king of Bernicia and making a base at Bamburgh in 547 (though there are two shadowy potential king figures earlier in the Bernician royal genealogy, Esa and Eoppa). However, that date still leaves plenty of time for the survival of post-Roman British power in the area.

In fact, what we seem to have in Bernicia is essentially the southern half of the tribal territory of the Votadini.[2] This appears to have broken in two at some stage in the post-Roman period (just as a number of other tribal areas broke in two at the same time). In the instance of Bernicia, this part of Votadinian territory seems already to have been distinct in terms of burial practices from the northern half of Votadinian territory. Extended inhumations in cists and in dug graves are common in Votadinian territory north of the Tweed. However, in the Votadinian territory between the Tweed and the Tyne (which was to form the core of the kingdom of Bernicia) the lack of evidence of burials or cremations suggests a continuation with the archaeologically invisible and little understood practices widespread in Britain to the south in pre-Roman times.[3] Thus it would appear that pre-existing cultural variations between different parts of the Votadini subsequently became political variations as well.

As with the kingdom of Deira, the name of Bernicia seems to be essentially British. It is quoted in the form of Bryneich in Welsh texts and this may well be close to its original form.

In archaeological terms there are relatively few cemeteries in Bernicia that are culturally recognisable as Anglo-Saxon. Some of those cemeteries that were previously identified as Anglo-Saxon now have question marks over them, and even where a cemetery is still firmly accepted as Anglo-Saxon (such as the one at Norton on Tees) there is likely to be evidence within it of British customs as well. In burial number 65 at Norton on Tees, for instance, a single penannular brooch was found, worn at the neck.[4]

When we are considering Bernicia's links to a British past, the Bernician royal centre at Yeavering is also extremely interesting. Firm connections to British tradition are shown by, for instance, its positioning next to the largest hillfort in Northumberland (Yeavering Bell) and also by the inclusion within the site of the so-called Great Enclosure, dating from the fourth or fifth century. In addition to this, Yeavering also features a unique construction that was probably built for royal audiences and most closely resembles a Roman auditorium in terms of its layout.

With suggestions of a strong connection to the British past in both Deira and Bernicia, it is hardly surprising that the kingdom of Northumbria under Edwin and his successors looked in many ways almost as much British as Anglo-Saxon and acted in many ways in a fashion that was also as much British as Anglo-Saxon.

Having united Deira and Bernicia to form Northumbria, Edwin then established an alliance with Kent, marrying Æthelburh, the sister of King Eadbald and he also converted to Christianity. Northumbria's main direction of expansion was into other British kingdoms. Edwin went on to absorb the small British kingdom of Elmet (located in the area around Leeds), the outwardly Anglo-Saxon kingdom of Lindsey (the northern half of Corieltauvian territory, and as we have already considered, an area showing distinct signs of continuity from its British past), and strongly culturally British territories such as Anglesey and the Isle of Man. According to Bede, Oswald, king of Northumbria later in the seventh century, was overlord not only of all the English (i.e. Anglo-Saxon) kingdoms in Britain, but also of all the British, Irish and Pictish kingdoms in the island as well.

The supposedly Anglo-Saxon royal house of Northumbria almost certainly had British blood in it from the start (just as the royal houses of Wessex and possibly Sussex did) and it continued to have close contacts with the royal families of other British kingdoms. For instance, after Æthelfrith's death in battle, his sons fled for refuge to Ireland and the kingdoms of Scotland. Similarly, the king of the Picts between 653 and 657 was one Talorcan, the son of a Pictish mother but also the nephew of Oswiu of Bernicia. Oswiu himself may have married Rhiainfellt, a princess of the British kingdom of Rheged.[5]

Culturally and artistically, early Northumbria also shows signs of distinctly British influence. Oswald, having been converted in Dalriada, introduced Celtic Christianity into Bernicia with the help of missionaries from the Dalriadic centre of Iona, and a mixture of British and Anglo-Saxon artistic traditions in Northumbria produced masterpieces like the Lindisfarne Gospels, and possibly the Book of Durrow as well.

Similarly the great Anglo-Saxon poet Cædmon was writing at Whitby Abbey in the seventh century. He was originally a herdsman looking after the cattle and may have been born somewhere local, in the area of Whitby. It is interesting to note, therefore, that Cædmon is, in fact, a British name.

Edwin was regarded as the leading Anglo-Saxon warlord of his day (even though his power base was in a kingdom that was probably as much British as Anglo-Saxon) and on that basis is accorded by both Bede and the Anglo-Saxon Chronicle the distinction of being a *Bretwalda*. As touched upon before, the exact meaning of this term and the date at which it came into use are matters of some dispute, but it seems to be applied to an Anglo-Saxon leader who had wider political influence than any other in his period.

Edwin's position as supreme warlord in Britain was not, however, to last long. It is fascinating to note that his end came at the hands of a British warlord based in Wales and of another ostensibly Anglo-Saxon warlord who was based in another nominally Anglo-Saxon kingdom that in fact shows significant British influence. This is about as far as you can get from the old simplistic ideas of Britons versus Anglo-Saxons, and is further confirmation of the essential idea that what largely mattered in the post-Roman period was not whether a person was an Anglo-Saxon or a Briton, but to which tribe/*civitas*/kingdom they belonged, and with which tribe/*civitas*/kingdom they were in conflict.

In 633 the British warlord Cadwallon of Gwynedd and the ostensibly Anglo-Saxon warlord Penda of Mercia defeated and killed Edwin at the battle of Hatfield Chase.

We have already noted the growing power and expansionist policies of Gwynedd in the post-Roman period. Gildas, referring to Maglocunus of Gwynedd, says:

> And you also, dragon of the island, have robbed many tyrants of their kingdoms and of their lives as well.
>
> (Gildas, *On the Ruin of Britain*, 33)

Cadwallon, who seems to have been very much a man in the tradition of his predecessor on the throne of Gwynedd, briefly managed to extend the power of

Gwynedd across northern England. The kingdom of Northumbria fragmented into its two constituent parts after Edwin's death and Cadwallon managed to kill both Edwin's successors, Osric of Deira and Eanfrith of Bernicia. Bede was clearly not a fan of Cadwallon, and the Christian leader's alliance with the pagan Penda against the Christian Edwin is likely to have been one factor in Bede's disapproval. However, his description of the excesses of Cadwallon's rule in Northumbria is not a million miles from the descriptions by Gildas of his five tyrants, so while Bede may be exaggerating for effect we should not discount his descriptions entirely. Cadwallon is said to have ruled over the provinces of the Northumbrians for a year, 'not like a victorious king, but like a rapacious, bloodthirsty tyrant' (Bede, *Ecclesiastical History* 3, 1). Bede also says of Cadwallon that:

> though he was called a Christian and claimed to be one, he was so barbaric in the way he acted that he did not spare either women or innocent young children, but cruelly killed them in terrible deaths, ravaging the whole of their country for a long time.
>
> (Bede, *Ecclesiastical History* 2, 20)

Ultimately, however, Cadwallon's moment of triumph was to be short-lived. He was killed by Eanfrith's brother Oswald at the battle of Heavenfield, just a year after Hatfield Chase.

Cadwallon's ally at the scene of his major triumph was Penda of Mercia. Like Northumbria, Mercia was an ostensibly Anglo-Saxon kingdom that in fact probably had deep British roots. Its origins are obscure, but it seems most likely that if Lindsey represented the northern half of the *civitas* of the Corieltauvi broken in two in the post-Roman period, then Mercia represented the southern half.[6]

As with a number of Anglo-Saxon kingdoms, there is again evidence of a British element within the Anglo-Saxon royal house of Mercia. The *walh* element, thought to refer to people of British descent, occurs repeatedly among the names of early Mercian royals. Penda himself seems to have had a brother called Cenwalh, a nephew called Cundwalh and a son called Merewalh.[7]

This combination of British and Anglo-Saxon elements within Mercia also seems to be confirmed by the archaeology of the area. In what is likely to have been the core territory of early Mercia a large proportion of early Anglo-Saxon cemeteries are located next to Roman-period British settlements suggesting that the Anglo-Saxons arrived here with some kind of British involvement. Cemeteries like these are found at Leicester, Medbourne, Barrow/Quorn, Kirby Bellars, Wymeswold/Willoughby, Mancetter and Ancaster. There are no cemeteries immediately adjoining the sites at Caves Inn and Thistleton, but there are cemeteries less than a mile from both.[8]

75 The Anglo-Saxon church at Brixworth in Mercia.

This sense of a combination of traditions is continued within the cemeteries of the area. It has been suggested, for instance, that in the fifth/sixth-century cemetery at Sleaford a group of west–east aligned burials without grave goods, in which the dead were found lying on their sides with their knees bent and hands by the face, may actually be British burials, while the mixed inhumation and cremation cemetery at Quarrington could also represent continuity from the Roman into the Anglo-Saxon period. It is also thought that a combination of British and Anglo-Saxon customs can be seen at Loveden Hill.[9] What's more, this evidence of the survival of some British customs within Anglo-Saxon cemeteries becomes even more marked as we move further west within Mercian territory. For example, at Stretton-on-Fosse radiocarbon dates suggest the cemetery was in continuous use from the third to the seventh century. Of the 200 inhumations at Wasperton, 117 seem to show a specifically Anglo-Saxon cultural identity. However, evidence from varying combinations of types of metalwork, hobnails, mutilation and orientation suggests that a further 36 should probably be regarded as culturally British burials.[10]

The history of Mercia prior to Penda's reign is hazy to say the least. Some medieval annalists claim that Penda's grandfather Creoda founded Mercia in 585. A similar name, Cretta, also appears in the king list of Lindsey. It is conceivable that they are the same person and that it was Creoda/Cretta or his son Pybba who separated Mercia from Lindsey, breaking the Corieltauvian *civitas* (or a successor kingdom) in two.

Little is known of Penda's early career but an entry in the Anglo-Saxon Chronicle for 628 says: 'This year Cynegils and Cwichelm fought Penda at Cirencester, and afterwards they agreed a treaty there.' It is assumed that Penda won the battle, because in the ensuing period there is an expansion of Mercian power into the northern part of previously Dobunnic territory.

The alliance between the Mercian warlord Penda and Cadwallon which resulted in the death of the ostensibly Anglo-Saxon warlord Edwin at the battle of Hatfield Chase in 633 is completely in keeping with the Mercian mixing of Anglo-Saxon and British culture. And this pattern of alliances with Britons against other Anglo-Saxons did not stop with the deaths of Cadwallon and Edwin, as we shall see.

As well as westwards, Penda was also seeking to expand Mercian power eastwards. Sometime probably in the later 630s or early 640s he clashed with the East Angles, killing their king Ecgric and their former king Sigebert (brought out of retirement in a monastery specially for the battle). Penda is described by Bede as a 'very warlike man', and since Bede was presumably judging him by the notably bellicose standards of his day that's really saying something.

In the period after Cadwallon's death, Penda clashed with Cadwallon's conqueror Oswald of Bernicia (Northumbria having temporarily split into its constituent parts after the death of Edwin) and killed him at the battle of Maserfield in 642.

At some stage Penda's sister was married to Cenwalh of Wessex. When Cenwalh repudiated her, Penda invaded Wessex and in 645 drove Cenwalh into exile for three years. In 654 Penda also killed Anna, the king of the East Angles, who had given Cenwalh shelter during his exile.

Intermittent conflict seems to have continued between Penda and Northumbria and this finally led to Penda's downfall. In 655, continuing his pattern of alliances with Britons, Penda attacked Bernicia with an army that included Cadafael of Gwynedd (who seized the throne of Gwynedd after the death of Cadwallon). However, this time the tables were turned and Penda was defeated and killed by the forces of Oswiu, brother of Oswald, at the battle of the Winwæd.

# AFTER POST-ROMAN BRITAIN

Edwin, Cadwallon and Penda were some of the last of the major post-Roman warlords from the phase in which Britons and Anglo-Saxons mingled and fought in a variety of combinations, alongside as well as against each other, based essentially on tribe, *civitas* and kingdom and with much less regard to whether these were supposed to be British or Anglo-Saxon. However, one last character does emerge in the late seventh century, combining in some way a British and an Anglo-Saxon heritage and therefore representing perhaps the last figure who can claim the dubious distinction of the title of post-Roman warlord.

Cædwalla, a West Saxon warlord with a British name (just like his predecessor Cerdic), came to prominence by attacking Sussex, but then was driven out again. However, after taking control of Wessex, he returned to Sussex and duly took control of it, and followed this up by taking the Isle of Wight and Surrey as well. An Anglo-Saxon warlord, probably with Atrebatic blood in his veins, thus ended up pretty much recreating the pre-Roman Atrebatic Empire. Just as the Atrebates had done so many years before, Cædwalla also subsequently expanded his power into Kent and then lost control of it again shortly afterwards. There were some changes, though, from the pre-Roman past. Cædwalla ended his violent career not dead on a British battlefield or seeking Roman aid to reclaim his kingdom, or even as emperor in Rome after a triumphant grab for power. He did die in Rome, but in his case it was after abdicating and travelling there to be baptised. He died ten days after he achieved this goal, in 689.

And change was coming elsewhere as well. A few decades after Cædwalla's death Bede composed his *Ecclesiastical History of the English People*, and perhaps for the first time presented the idea of England as a separate united entity. That entity was not at this point defined in political terms (there were still far too many competing kingdoms and competing warlords for that) but in religious terms. Just as Gildas seems to have particularly disliked the early Anglo-Saxons because they were pagans, so Bede disliked those Britons of his day who had not accepted Anglo-Saxon culture, because their priests refused to accept his view on the date when Easter should be celebrated, as well as some other theological controversies. He made this explicitly clear at the end of his huge work when he summed up the 'state of the nation' in his time:

> Though, for the most part, the Britons, through deep hatred, detest the English people, and mistakenly, and in a wicked way, object to the Easter agreed upon by the entire Catholic Church, nevertheless they cannot achieve their goals because of both the Divine and human power that opposes them …
>
> (Bede, *Ecclesiastical History of the English People* 5, 23)

To many modern readers the question of the exact date on which Easter should be celebrated might seem like a comparatively minor one, but to Bede and the Roman Catholic Church of his day it was a huge issue. Bede, in fact, saw the conflict between culturally Anglo-Saxon kingdoms and culturally British kingdoms as something of a crusade in which he thought God was on the side of the English spreading the true date of Easter.

Bede went into great detail about how, when St Augustine came to Britain to convert the English, the British churchmen disagreed with him theologically.

Bede has Augustine say to the British churchmen:

> What you do is in many ways against our custom or rather against the custom of the whole church. Nevertheless, if you agree with me on these three issues, that is firstly celebrating Easter at the proper time, secondly administering baptism, by which we are born again to God, in the manner of the Holy Roman Apostolic Church, and thirdly preaching with us the Word of God to the English people, then we will certainly accept all your other customs, even though they are contrary to ours.
>
> (Bede, *Ecclesiastical History of the English People* 2, 2)

But the British churchmen refused Augustine on all points, and Bede was evidently still furious about this over a hundred years later, so much so that he appears to have no problem with King Æthelfrith massacring the British monks and priests who had come to pray for the forces opposing him at the battle of Chester. As Bede himself wrote:

> It is said that some twelve hundred of those who had come to pray were killed, while only fifty escaped in flight. Brocmail turned his back at the first sign of the enemy and abandoned those he was duty-bound to protect, defenceless before the swords of their enemies. In this way the prediction of the holy Bishop Augustine came true, even though he had been taken to the heavenly kingdom long before, since he

said that because they had despised the offer of eternal life, they would also suffer the punishment of death in this world.

(Bede, *Ecclesiastical History of the English People* 2, 2)

Bede was perhaps sensitive to the charge that the Britons had kept to their Christian faith even while the Anglo-Saxons were still pagan, but he is reluctant even to allow them much credit for this. Instead he almost attributes the Anglo-Saxons' period of paganism in Britain to the Britons by blaming them for not converting the Anglo-Saxons. He introduces his account of the dispatch of St Augustine to convert the English with this comment on the British:

Among other unspeakable crimes is, as noted by their own historian Gildas, that they never preached the word to the Saxons, or English, who lived among them. Nevertheless, God, in his goodness, did not abandon his people, whom he knew already, and sent to them much more holy preachers to bring them to the faith.

(Bede, *Ecclesiastical History of the English People* 1, 22)

It is probably in this context that he also effectively wrote the Britons out of the post-Roman history of central and eastern England. In one famous passage he wrote:

Those who came over originated from the three mightiest German peoples, that is the Saxons, the Angles and the Jutes. From the Jutes come the people of Kent and of the Isle of Wight, and also those who are even today called Jutes and live in the province of the West Saxons across from the Isle of Wight. From the Saxons, that is the area which is today called Old Saxony, come the East Saxons, the South Saxons and the West Saxons. From the Angles, that is from the area now called Anglia which lies between the provinces of the Jutes and Saxons and which, so they say, still remains deserted today, are descended the East Angles, the Middle Angles, the Mercians, all the Northumbrian people, that is those nations that live north of the Humber, and all the other English nations.

(Bede, *Ecclesiastical History of the English People* 1, 15)

There is no mention of the large numbers of Britons who doubtless survived in the Anglo-Saxon kingdoms and were an integral part of their development. Bede wanted to show the English as entirely separate from the Britons, with their, to him, dubious ideas about Easter.

Yet we have already seen that there is a large body of evidence indicating that Britons remained the majority in central and eastern England and that the Anglo-Saxon kingdoms were effectively the old British tribes with a new Anglo-Saxon cultural face, plus new Anglo-Saxon additions to their aristocracies and (to a limited extent) to their people.

A comparatively new science that Bede could only have imagined in his wildest dreams is now confirming this picture. Genetic research shows the apparent survival of large numbers of Britons in the supposedly Anglo-Saxon centre and east of England (as well as, less surprisingly, in the west of England and Wales). The results are still controversial, but some estimates suggest Anglo-Saxon immigrants into England in the post-Roman period to have constituted well below 10 per cent of the population. The answer, as so often in these situations, probably lies somewhere in the middle of the assorted estimates, perhaps in around the 10–20 per cent bracket (with the higher levels concentrated in the east of England), a figure that is also consistent with recent estimates based on the analysis of burials.[1]

Bede may have been the first person to stress a united English identity (even if at this stage it was mainly a religious ideal) but in the centuries after him today's national identities did emerge, with the cultural, political and ethnic complexities of the past being blurred to create specifically separate English, Welsh and Scottish identities. Bede's was the first attempt at rewriting the past in order to support and develop these national identities. He would, however, be followed by many others.

Some of the old tribal territories and early post-Roman kingdoms did, of course, survive as regions and counties within the new kingdoms, even in England, where there were attempts to erase memories of a British heritage. Kent, for instance, survives with the same name and much the same boundaries. Norfolk and Suffolk essentially represent the old Icenian *civitas* and the kingdom of the East Angles. Some of the most powerful tribal units are, however, gone forever. The Catuvellauni, for instance, their unity smashed by the growing power of Wessex in 571, disappear from history as a single entity, although their allies the Trinovantes have survived in some sense in first the kingdom of the East Saxons and subsequently in the modern county of Essex.

Some of the old tribal identities may have disappeared, but warlords, of course, have not. There will always be warlords; wherever there is instability and a weakening of the rule of law, ambitious men (and occasionally women) will take the opportunity to seize by force the power and possessions they long for. Across the world today there are still figures who would feel entirely at home with the politics and violence of post-Roman Britain.

A hard-bitten war reporter talking to camera on 24 hour news could take his script straight from Gildas:

> They fight but when they fight it's for the wrong reasons and against their own people. They clamp down on some crime but their social set is full of gangsters. They may give generously to worthy causes but that's against the background of an appalling, and fast growing, list of crimes. They turn up to court but rarely bother with handing out justice. They despise ordinary, decent people but if you're an arrogant, sadistic psychopath with contempt for conventional morality, they're going to love you.

# NOTES

## INTRODUCTION

1 Gidlow, 2004, 132.
2 Laycock, 2008.
3 Though some coins marked Commius could belong to a younger successor also called Commius; see Cunliffe, 2005, 142, 169.
4 See Cunliffe, 2005 fig. 7.9 for a comparative distribution of the coins of Tasciovanus and Cunobelin.
5 See Cunliffe, 2005, 147 for these developments.
6 Laycock, 2008, 63–84.
7 Crummy, 1997, 86, 90.

## CHAPTER 1: GERONTIUS

1 RIB 192, RIB 1065, AE 1956.249.
2 Malim *et al.*, 1996, 117.
3 Woodfield, 1995; Laycock, 2008, 93–108.
4 Theodosian Codex VII, 13, 16 and 17.
5 See Laycock, 2008, 129–30.
6 Laycock, 2008, 135–48.
7 Orosius, *History against the Pagans*, 7, 40.
8 Laycock, 2008, 131, 158.
9 Sozomen, *Ecclesiastical History*, 9, 11.
10 See Aurrecoechea Fernandez, 1999 and 2001 for Spanish buckles of the fourth century. See Laycock, 2008 116–17 for discussion of Spanish buckles and what they suggest about British buckles.
11 Pearson, 2002, 163, fig. 77.
12 Sozomen, *Ecclesiastical History*, 7,13.
13 Gil, Filloy, Iriarte, 2000, 26.
14 Compare Aurrecoechea Fernandez, 1999, fig 2.1 with Portable Antiquities Scheme SF-9EFED0, Hawkes & Dunning, 1961, fig. 18a and Mills, 2000, fig. R199.
15 Compare, for instance, Appels & Laycock, 2007, fig. SL5.10 with Aurrecoechea

Fernandez, 1999, figs 2.4, 2.5 and 7.8.

16 Branigan, 1985, 57.

17 See Knight, 2007, 54–6 for a general discussion of the *bagaudae*. See Halsall, 2007, 341 for the Senate of Cantabria.

## CHAPTER 2: VORTIGERN

1 See Dark, 1994 and 2000 for an examination of this phenomenon in the west of Britain, and see Laycock, 2008 for an examination of the phenomenon in central and eastern Britain.

2 Dark, 2000, 150–92.

3 See, for instance, Laycock, 2008, 169–236; Henson, 2006, 82.

4 Dark, 2000, 48–9.

5 See Yorke, 1993 for a discussion.

6 Martindale, 1980, 1171–7.

7 Cunliffe, 2003, 182.

8 See http://www.vortigernstudies.org.uk/artcit/wirtgern.htm.

9 Cunliffe, 2005, 189–90.

10 Cunliffe, 2005, fig. 7.9.

11 See Laycock, 2008, 99–101.

12 Millett, 2005, fig. 72.

13 Dark, 2000, 146–9.

14 For the cluster of Dobunnic buckles and belt fittings in Atrebatic territory, see Portable Antiquities Scheme HAMP-722FA3; Henig, 2000, fig. 56; Hawkes & Dunning, 1961, figs 15p and 15q.

15 See White, 2005 for Wroxeter, Bayley & Butcher, 2004, fig. 172 for Polden Hill brooches and http://www.potsherd.uklinux.net/atlas/Source/BRIT.php for pottery distribution. See White, 2007, 40 generally for evidence of significant links between Dobunni and Cornovii.

16 Dark, 1994, 79.

17 Knight, 1996, 43–5, Vermaat personal comment.

18 Reece, 1997, 10.

19 Dark, 1994, 83–6.

20 For instance, Cunliffe, 2005, fig. 7.17.

21 Creighton, 2000, 77.

22 Creighton, 2000, 78.

23 For Mildenhall see Corney, 2001, 16–18. For Silchester linear earthworks see Wacher, 1995, fig. 186.

24 Fulford, 2000, 356–8.

25 Dark, 1994, 225.

26 Laycock, 2008, 119–23.

27 Suzuki, 2000.

28 Suzuki, 2000, 80–4, 108–9.

29 See Laycock, 2008, 109–34.

30 For West Stow see Arnold, 1984, 66–7. For St John's College cricket field see

O'Brien, 1999, 101. For Frilford see O'Brien, 1999, 161. For Barton Court Farm see Arnold, 1984, 64–5.

31 Bassett, 1989, 10–16; Henson, 2006, 82; Dark, 1994, 107–8.

32 Dark, 1994, 78–9.

## CHAPTER 3: HENGEST

1 Hawkes & Dunning, 1961, 5–6; Knight, 2007, 38, 43–43, 50–3; Sommer, 1984, 43–44 *Tafel* 71, 74, 81 etc.

2 Knight, 2007, 43.

3 See Halsall, 2007, 153–9.

4 See Laycock, 2008, 169–79 for a full discussion.

5 See Hawkes & Dunning, 1961, fig. 20g and 20h; Appels & Laycock, 2007, 242 for dragon buckles with fixed plates. See Laycock, 2008, fig. 84 for distribution in Britain of dragon buckles with fixed plates plus associated belt fittings.

6 Wade-Martins, 1974, 31.

7 Fincham, 2000, 72–3.

8 O'Brien, 1999, 112, 117.

9 Liddle, 2000, 1.

10 Laycock, 2008, fig.74.

11 Laycock, 2008, fig. 84.

12 See Schulze-Dörrlamm, 2002.

13 For instance, see Halsall, 2007, 105.

14 See Suzuki, 2000, 122–3 for Alfriston belt set. Compare ribbed kidney-shaped buckle with Sommer, 1984, Tafel 80, Tafel 82. For dating of such buckles see Schulze-Dörrlamm, 2002, 238, 240.

15 Suzuki, 2000, 128–9 and 150–1.

16 Swanton, 1973, 154–5; Böhme, 1986, fig. 40.

17 Suzuki, 2000, 96–102.

18 For cruciform brooches see Suzuki, 2000, 94–5. For supporting arm brooch see Ager, 1989. For later examples of Quoit Brooch Style items, see Suzuki, 2000, 120 for a discussion.

19 Suzuki, 2000, 94.

20 See Suzuki, 2000 generally and figs 78 and 79 in particular.

21 Suzuki, 2000, 111–21.

22 Dark, 2000, 101–2.

23 Yorke, 1990, 27.

24 Härke, 2007, 61–2.

25 Coates, 2007, 187; Lambert, 1997, 186–203.

26 Schrijver, 2007.

27 Gildas, *On the Ruin of Britain*, 25. Gildas is characteristically pessimistic about the treatment of Britons staying on under the Anglo-Saxons, but he does admit they exist.

28 See Halsall, 2007, 101–10 for a discussion.

29 Halsall, 2007, 334–5.

## CHAPTER 4: AMBROSIUS

1 Gidlow, 2004, 80.
2 See Laycock, 2008, 137–48 for a full discussion.
3 Dark, 2000, 146–8.
4 Swift, 2000, 69–77.
5 Zosimus, *New History*, 1, 68
6 Laycock, 2008, fig. 74.
7 Dark, 1994, 258–66.
8 Cunliffe, 2005, 147.
9 Salvian, *On God's Government* 5, 23.

## CHAPTER 5: RIOTHAMUS

1 See Fleuriot, 1999, 170–6 for the idea that Riothamus should be seen as Ambrosius Aurelianus. See Ashe, 2003 for the idea of a connection between Riothamus and Arthur.
2 See Thomas, 1994 for post-Roman names and inscriptions in western Britain.
3 Dark, 2000, 119–20.
4 Cunliffe, 2005, 205–6.
5 Cunliffe, 2005, 201–3.
6 Cunliffe, 2005, 182.
7 *Cornwall's Archaeological Heritage* 12–13.
8 Harris, 2003, 152.
9 Dark, 1994, 211.
10 Dark, 2000, 125; Morris, 1999, 211.
11 Harris, 2004, 43–60 and see fig. 11.
12 Halsall, 2007, 272.
13 Ewan Campbell, pers comm.
14 Harris, 2003, 145.
15 See, for instance, Giot, Guigon, Merdrignac, 2003, 103.
16 Morris, 1995, 256; Fleuriot, 1999, 172.

## CHAPTER 6: ÆLLE

1 Welch, 1989, 81.
2 Welch, 1989, 78–9.
3 For Beddingham see Dark, 2000, 102. For Thundersbarrow and Rookery Hill see O'Brien, 1999, 145.
4 See Bassett, 1989, 175.
5 See Yorke, 1990, 144.
6 O'Brien, 1999, 145, 161.
7 Dark, 2000, 100–1.
8 Swanton, 1973, 115–23.

## CHAPTER 7: THE FIVE WARLORDS OF GILDAS

1 *Historia Brittonum*, 62.
2 Snyder, 2003, 188.
3 Thomas, 1994, 192–3.
4 Dark, 2000, 154–8.
5 For Brawdy and Gateholm see Dark, 2000, 185. For pottery in Dyfed, see Dark, 2000, fig. 33.
6 Harris, 2003, 176 discusses the possibility of Gildas' reference to luxuries having been brought up the Severn also referring to imports from the Mediterranean at this time.
7 Thomas, 1994, 53–6.
8 See Dark, 2000, 188–90 for a discussion.
9 Rance, 2001, 247–9.
10 Dark, 2000, 170–3.
11 See Harris, 2003, fig. 43.
12 See Dark, 2000, 180–1 for a discussion.
13 Dark, 1994, 76.
14 Dark, 2000, 181–2.
15 See Gidlow, 2004, 95 for instance.
16 Dark, 2000, 182–3.
17 Dark, 1994, 225.
18 Gildas, *On the Ruin of Britain*, 30.
19 Gildas, *On the Ruin of Britain*, 31.

## CHAPTER 8: ARTHUR

1 Halsall, 2007, 408.
2 See Higham, 2002, 144–50 for a discussion.
3 Higham, 2002, 7.
4 Higham, 2002, 76–7.
5 See Higham, 2002, 75–6 for a discussion of this idea.
6 Higham, 2002, 77.
7 Higham, 2002, 77.
8 Room, 2003, 21.
9 See Bosworth & Toller, 1972.
10 See Bosworth & Toller, 1972.
11 Thornton, 2007, 149.
12 See, for instance, Leahy, 2007, 107–11 and a number of works by Thomas Green on the subject, including Green, 2008.
13 Leahy, 2008, 82–86.
14 Dark, 2000, 52.
15 See Niblett, 2001, 131–46 for full discussion of post-Roman Verulamium and St Albans.
16 Rivet & Smith, 1981, 406.

## CHAPTER 9: CERDIC

1 Dumville, 1985 and 1986.
2 See Henson, 2006, 238–239 for a discussion.
3 See Thomas, 1994.
4 Yorke, 1990, 142–3.
5 See Draper, 2006, 38–9, 46–8 for evidence of continuity.
6 Van Arsdell, 1994, 8.
7 Yorke, 1989.
8 Swanton, 1973, 115–23.
9 Swanton, 1973, 207, fig. 83. One or two graves depending on how Quoit Brooch Style is defined.
10 Swanton, 1973, 128–31.
11 Limbrick, 1998.

## CHAPTER 10: EDWIN, CADWALLON AND PENDA

1 See Cunliffe, 2005, 85 and Stead, 1979, 7–39 for Arras culture. See Pryor, 2004, 232–4 for parallels between the adoption of the Arras culture and the adoption of Anglo-Saxon culture in the area.
2 See Laycock, 2008, 234–6 for a full discussion.
3 O'Brien, 1999, 62.
4 O'Brien, 1999, 69.
5 Yorke, 1990, 83–6.
6 See Laycock, 2008, 228–32 for a full discussion.
7 For *walh* elements in personal names, see Pretty, 1989, 175.
8 Liddle, 2000, 1.
9 O'Brien, 1999, 82.
10 O'Brien, 1999, 93–4.

## AFTER POST-ROMAN BRITAIN

1 See Sykes, 2006, 286 and Oppenheimer, 2006, 356–76 for the debate on genetic research. See Jones, 1996, 26–8 for estimates based on the archaeology.

# BIBLIOGRAPHY

The following abbreviations have been used:
AE: *Année Epigraphique*
CIL: *Corpus Inscriptionum Latinarum*
RIB: *The Roman Inscriptions of Britain*, vol. 1, ed. Collingwood & Wright (Oxford, 1965)


Abdy, R.A. (2002) *Roman-British Coin Hoards*, Shire

Ager, B. (1989) 'An Anglo-Saxon Supporting-Arm Brooch from Eastry, Kent', in *Medieval Archaeology* 33, 148–51

Appels, A. & Laycock, S. (2007) *Roman Buckles & Military Fittings*, Greenlight

Arnold, C.J. (1984) *Roman Britain to Saxon England*, Routledge

Ashe, G. (2003) *The Discovery of King Arthur*, The History Press

Aurrecoechea Fernandez, J. (1999) 'Late Roman Belts in Hispania', in *Journal of Roman Military Equipment Studies* 10, 55–62

Aurrecoechea Fernandez, J. (2001) *Los cinturones romanos en la Hispania del Bajo Imperio*, Monographies Instrumentum 19

Bassett, S. (1989) *The Origins of Anglo-Saxon Kingdoms*, Leicester University Press

Bayley, J. & Butcher, S. (2004) *Roman Brooches in Britain*, Society of Antiquaries

Böhme, H.W. (1986) 'Das Ende der Römerherrschaft in Britannien und die Angelsachsische Besiedlung Englands im 5. Jahrhundert', in *Jahrbuch des Römisch-Germanischen Zentralmuseum Mainz* 33, 469–574

Bosworth, J. & Toller, T. (1972) *An Anglo-Saxon Dictionary*, Oxford

Branigan, K. (1977) *The Roman Villa in South-West England*, Moonraker Press

Branigan, K. (1985) *The Catuvellauni*, Sutton

Campbell, J. (1991) *The Anglo-Saxons*, Penguin

Charles-Edwards, T.M. (2006) *The Chronicle of Ireland*, Liverpool University Press

Clarke, G. (1979) *The Roman Cemetery at Lankhills*, Winchester Studies 3, Oxford

Coates, R. (2007) 'Invisible Britons: Linguistics', in *Britons in Anglo-Saxon England*, ed. N.J. Higham, The Boydell Press

Corney, M. (2001) 'The Romano-British nucleated settlements of Wiltshire', in *Roman Wiltshire and After*, Papers in Honour of Ken Annable, ed. P. Ellis, Wiltshire Archaeological and Natural History Society, 5–38

Creighton, J. (2000) *Coins and Power in Late Iron Age Britain*, Cambridge University Press

Crummy, P. (1997) *City of Victory*, Colchester Archaeological Trust
Cunliffe, B. (2003) *Danebury Hillfort*, Tempus
Cunliffe, B. (2004) *Iron Age Britain*, English Heritage
Cunliffe, B. (2005) *Iron Age Communities in Britain*, Routledge
Dark, K. (1994) *Civitas to Kingdom, British Political Continuity 300–800*, Studies in the Early History of Britain, Leicester
Dark, K. (2000) *Britain and the End of the Roman Empire*, Tempus
Dixon, P.H. (1993) 'The Anglo-Saxon Settlement at Mucking', in *Anglo-Saxon Studies in Archaeology and History 6*, Oxford University Committee for Archaeology, 125–47
Draper, S. (2006) *Landscape, Settlement and Society in Roman and Early Medieval Wiltshire*, British Archaeological Reports, British Series 419
Dumville, D.N. (1985) 'The West Saxon Genealogical Regnal List and the chronology of Wessex', in *Peritia* 4, 21–66
Dumville, D.N. (1986) 'The West Saxon Genealogical Regnal List: manuscripts and texts', in *Anglia* 104, 1–32
Eagles, B. (2001) 'Anglo-Saxon Presence and Culture in Wiltshire c. AD 450 – c. 675', in *Roman Wiltshire and After*, Papers in Honour of Ken Annable, ed. P. Ellis, Wiltshire Archaeological and Natural History Society, 199–233
Eagles, B. (2004) 'Britons and Saxons on the Eastern Boundary of the Civitas Durotrigum', in *Britannia* 34, 234–40
Esmonde Cleary, A.S. (1989) *The Ending of Roman Britain*, Routledge
Faulkner, N. (2000) *The Decline & Fall of Roman Britain*, Tempus
Fincham, G. (2002) *Landscapes of Imperialism: Roman and native interaction in the East Anglian Fenland*, British Archaeological Reports, British Series 338
Flueriot, L. (1999) *Les origines de la Bretagne*, Payot
Frere, S. (1967) *Britannia – A History of Roman Britain*, Routledge
Fulford, M. (2000) 'Human Remains from the North Gate, Silchester', in *Britannia* 31, 356–8
Gidlow, C. (2004) *The Reign of Arthur, From History to Legend*, Sutton
Gil, E., Filloy, I., Iriarte A. (2000) 'Late Roman Military Equipment from the City of Iruña/Veleia (Alava/Spain)', in *Journal of Roman Military Equipment Studies* 11, 25–35
Giot, P., Guigon, P., Merdrignac, B. (2003) *The British Settlement of Brittany*, Tempus
Green, T. (2008) *Concepts of Arthur*, Tempus
Halsall, G. (2007) *Barbarian Migrations and the Roman West*, Cambridge, 376–568
Härke, H. (2007) 'Invisible Britons: Culture Change', in *Britons in Anglo-Saxon England*, ed. N.J. Higham, The Boydell Press
Harris, A. (2003) *Byzantium, Britain and the West*, Tempus
Hawkes, S.C. (1974) 'Some recent finds of Late Roman Buckles', in *Britannia* 5, 386–93
Hawkes, S.C. & Dunning, G.C. (1961) 'Soldiers and settlers in Britain, fourth to fifth century', in *Medieval Archaeology* 5, 1–70
Henig, M. (2002) *The Heirs of King Verica*, Tempus
Henson, D. (2006) *The Origins of the Anglo-Saxons*, Anglo-Saxon Books
Higham, N. (1992) *Rome, Britain and the Anglo-Saxons*, Routledge
Higham, N.J. (2002) *King Arthur, Myth-Making and History*, Routledge
Higham, N.J. (ed.) (2007) *Britons in Anglo-Saxon England*, The Boydell Press
Jones, B. & Mattingly, D. (1990) *An Atlas of Roman Britain*, Blackwell
Jones, M. (1996) *The End of Roman Britain*, Cornell University Press
Kilbride-Jones, H.E. (1980) *Celtic Craftsmanship in Bronze*, St Martin's Press

Knight, J. (1996) 'Late Roman and Post-Roman Caerwent, some evidence from metalwork', in *Archaeologia Cambrensis*, vol. 145, 35–65
Knight, J. (2007) *The End of Antiquity*, Tempus
Lambert, P. (1997) *La Langue Gauloise*, Paris
Laycock, S. (2006) 'The Threat Within', in *British Archaeology*, Vol 87 March/April, 11–15
Laycock, S. (2008) *Britannia: the Failed State*, The History Press
Leahy, K. (2007) *The Anglo-Saxon Kingdom of Lindsey*, Tempus
Liddle, P. (2000) *An Archaeological Resource Assessment of Anglo-Saxon Leicestershire and Rutland*, Leicestershire Museums.
Limbrick, G. (1998) 'Frontier Territory Along the Thames', in *British Archaeology* 33
MacDowall, S. (1995) *Late Roman Cavalryman*, Osprey
Malim, T. with Penn, Robinson, Wait & Walsh, (1996) 'New Evidence on the Cambridgeshire Dykes and Worsted Street Roman Road', in *Proceedings of the Cambridge Antiquarian Society* 85, 27–122
Martindale, J.R. (1980) *The Prosopography of the Later Roman Empire: Volume 2, A.D. 395-452*, Cambridge University Press
Mattingly, D. (2006) *An Imperial Possession, Britain in the Roman Empire*, Penguin
Millett, M. (1990) *The Romanization of Britain*, Cambridge University Press
Mills, N. (2000) *Celtic and Roman Artefacts*, Greenlight Publishing
Morris, C. with Batey, Brady, Harry, Johnson & Thomas (1990) 'Recent Work at Tintagel', in *Medieval Archaeology* 43, 206–15
Moorhead, T.S.N. (2001) 'Roman Coin Finds from Wiltshire', in *Roman Wiltshire and After*, Papers in Honour of Ken Annable, ed. P. Ellis, Wiltshire Archaeological and Natural History Society, 85–106
Morris, J. (1995) *The Age of Arthur*, Phoenix
Myres, J.N.L. (1986) *The English Settlements*, Oxford University Press
Niblett, R. (2001) *Verulamium, the Roman City of St. Albans*, Tempus
O'Brien, E. (1999) *Post-Roman Britain to Anglo-Saxon England: Burial Practices Reviewed*, British Archaeological Reports, British Series 289
Oppenheimer, S. (2006) *The Origins of the British, a Genetic Detective Story*, Constable
Ordnance Survey (1966) *Map of Britain in the Dark Ages*
Pearson, A. (2002) *The Roman Shore Forts*, Tempus
Pretty, K. (1989) 'Defining the Magonsæte', in *The Origins of Anglo-Saxon Kingdoms*, ed. S. Bassett, Leicester University Press
Pryor, F. (2004) *AD*, Harper Collins
Puttnam, B. (2000) *Discover Dorset: The Romans*, Dovecote Press
Rance, P. (2001) 'Attacotti, Déisi and Magnus Maximus: The Case for Irish Federates in Late Roman Britain', in *Britannia* 32, 243–70
Reece, R. (1997) *The Future of Roman Military Archaeology*, National Museums and Galleries of Wales
Rivet, A. & Smith, C. (1981) *The Place-Names of Roman Britain*, Book Club Associates
Robertson, A.S. (2000) *An Inventory of British Coin Hoards*, Royal Numismatic Society Special Publication 20
Room, A. (2003) *The Penguin Dictionary of British Place Names*, Penguin
Russell, M. (2006) *Roman Sussex*, Tempus
Salway, P. (1993) *The Oxford Illustrated History of Roman Britain*, Oxford University Press

Salway, P. (2002) *The Roman Era, Short Oxford History of the British Isles*, Oxford University Press
Schrijver, P. (2007) 'What Britons Spoke around 400 AD', in *Britons in Anglo-Saxon England*, ed. N.J. Higham, The Boydell Press
Schulze-Dörrlamm, M. (2002) *Byzantinische Gürtelschnallen und Gürtelbeschläge im Römisch-Germanischen Zentralmuseum*, Mainz
Sims-Williams, P. (1983) 'The settlement of England in Bede and the Chronicle', in *Anglo-Saxon England* 12, 1–41
Snyder, C. (2003) *The Britons*, Blackwell
Sommer, M. (1984) *Die Gürtel und Gürtelbeschläge des 4. und 5. Jahrhunderts im Römischen Reich*, Bonner, Hefte zur Vorgeschichte 22, Bonn
Stead, I.M. (1979) *The Arras Culture*, York
Suzuki, S. (2000) *The Quoit Brooch Style and Anglo-Saxon Settlement*, The Boydell Press
Swanton, M.J. (1973) *The Spearheads of the Anglo-Saxon Settlements*, The Royal Archaeological Institute
Swift, E. (2000) *The End of the Western Roman Empire, An Archaeological Investigation*, Tempus
Sykes, B. (2006) *Blood of the Isles*, Bantam Press
Taylor, A. (1998) *Archaeology of Cambridgeshire, South-East Cambridgeshire and the Fen Edge*, Cambridgeshire County Council
Thomas, C. (1994) *And Shall These Mute Stones Speak?*, University of Wales Press
Thornton, D.E. (2007) 'Some Welshmen in Domesday Book', in *Britons in Anglo-Saxon England*, ed. N.J. Higham, The Boydell Press
Van Arsdell, R.D. (1989) *Celtic Coinage of Britain*, London
Van Arsdell, R.D. (1994) *The Coinage of the Dobunni: Money Supply and Coin Circulation in Dobunnic Territory*, Oxford University School of Archaeology
Vermaat, R., www.vortigernstudies.org.uk
Wacher, J. (1995) *The Towns of Roman Britain*, Batsford
Wade-Martins, P. (1974) 'The Linear Earthworks of West Norfolk', in *Norfolk Archaeology* 36, 23–38
White, R. (2005) 'The Romans in the West Midlands', in *Newsletter 40*, Study Group for Roman Pottery
White, R. (2007) *Britannia Prima*, Tempus
Woodfield, C. (1995) 'New thoughts on town defences in the western territory of Catuvellauni', in *Roman Small Towns in Eastern England and Beyond*, ed. A. E. Brown, Oxbow
Yorke, B. (1989) 'The Jutes of Hampshire and Wight and the origins of Wessex', in *The Origins of Anglo-Saxon Kingdoms*, ed. S. Bassett, Leicester University Press
Yorke, B. (1990) *Kings and Kingdoms of Early Anglo-Saxon England*, Routledge
Yorke, B. (1993) 'Fact or Fiction? The written evidence for the fifth and sixth centuries AD', in *Anglo-Saxon Studies in Archaeology and History* 6, Oxford University Committee for Archaeology

# INDEX

*Figure references in italics*